MW00803237

Inventory Management

Fourth Edition

Steven M. Bragg

For more information about AccountingTools® products, visit our Web site at www.ac-countingtools.com.

ISBN-13: 978-1-64221-064-4

Printed in the United States of America

Table of Contents

Preface

Inventory is one of the largest investments that a company may have, and so is worthy of continual examination to maximize the return from this asset. It is of critical importance to ensure that funds are only used for the exact inventory items needed to further an organization's goals. All other inventory is a liability, since it soaks up excess cash and is in danger of becoming obsolete. In *Inventory Management*, we explore a broad range of alternatives that can be used to precisely target the use of inventory, while minimizing the inventory investment. The topics covered include inventory strategy, materials forecasting, production processes, warehouse management, product design, the supply chain, and more – essentially all areas of a business that touch upon the inventory asset. As examples of the topics covered, *Inventory Management* provides answers to the following questions:

- How can I incorporate inventory into a competitive strategy?
- How can I improve the accuracy of my sales forecasts?
- Are there supplier delivery arrangements that can reduce the level of on-hand inventory?
- What types of equipment are available to assist in the putaway and picking tasks?
- How do the push and pull flow systems impact the amount of inventory in production?
- What options are available for maximizing the return from the disposition of obsolete inventory?
- How can products be designed to minimize the inventory investment?
- What methods are available for improving the accuracy of inventory records?
- How can I set up an effective cycle counting program?
- Under what circumstances is a flow-through warehouse system used?
- Which storage systems should be installed to maximize the use of warehouse space?
- What measurements should be tracked to monitor inventory?

Inventory Management is intended for managers, inventory planners, and students, who can benefit from its broad range of inventory management topics. The book also provides references to the author's popular Accounting Best Practices podcast, which provides additional coverage of several inventory topics. As such, it may earn a place on your book shelf as a reference tool for years to come.

Centennial, Colorado
March 2021

About the Author

Steven Bragg, CPA, has been the chief financial officer or controller of four companies, as well as a consulting manager at Ernst & Young. He received a master's degree in finance from Bentley College, an MBA from Babson College, and a Bachelor's degree in Economics from the University of Maine. He has been a two-time president of the Colorado Mountain Club, and is an avid alpine skier, mountain biker, and certified master diver. Mr. Bragg resides in Centennial, Colorado. He has written more than 250 books and courses, including *New Controller Guidebook*, *GAAP Guidebook*, and *Payroll Management*.

Steven maintains the accountingtools.com web site, which contains continuing professional education courses, the Accounting Best Practices podcast, and thousands of articles on accounting subjects.

Buy Additional AccountingTools Courses

AccountingTools offers more than 1,200 hours of CPE courses, with concentrations in accounting, auditing, finance, taxation, and ethics. Related courses that you might like include:

- Accounting for Inventory
- Operations Management
- Purchasing Guidebook

Go to accountingtools.com/cpe to view these additional courses.

Chapter 1
The Nature of Inventory

Introduction

This book is about the management of inventory, but we must first begin with an examination of why inventory is present in a business at all, and how it enters the organization. Accordingly, this chapter starts us off with a review of the types of inventory, the types of demand for that inventory, and the systems used to order it. The coverage is at a high level – we will delve into all aspects of inventory management in much greater detail in the following chapters.

Types of Inventory

At the most general level, inventory can be defined as those assets that a business has or will have available for sale. Inventory is usually classified in more detail as raw materials, work-in-process, or finished goods, to reflect its state of completion. This classification is commonly used in the accounting records, and so has become the standard form of identification. However, these terms do not reveal the functional reasons *why* inventory is being held. The following classifications do a better job of revealing why an organization needs inventory:

- *Batch replenishment inventory.* Some inventory is created simply because the production system is designed to create inventory in batches, rather than one at a time. For example, if the setup interval for a machine is quite lengthy, the production manager may elect to process 1,000 units of inventory through it in order to justify the long setup, rather than the 100 units that are actually needed at the moment. The remaining 900 units are batch replenishment inventory, and will sit in the warehouse until needed at some later date. The same logic applies to volume discounts that can be obtained from a supplier. The purchasing manager buys 500 units at a discounted price, instead of the 50 units that are actually needed. The 450 unused units are all batch replenishment inventory.
- *Safety stock.* Some inventory is kept on hand as a buffer to guard against shortages. For example, the high variability of customer demand dictates that 80 units of a green widget be maintained to avoid imposing backorders on customers. Similarly, if there is a risk of having a shortfall of raw materials before a supplier can replenish them, a certain amount of safety stock is maintained. The need for safety stock is eliminated if a company has perfect information about future customer orders, and knows exactly how long it will take for a supplier to fulfill an order. Since the reduction of lead times reduces forecasting uncertainty, such a reduction also reduces the need for safety stock.

- *Seasonal inventory*. When sales are seasonal, production continues through low-sale months, so that inventory levels will be high enough to sustain customer orders during high-demand months. A company may elect to avoid some of this inventory by instead incurring overtime costs to produce for longer periods of time during high-demand months.
- *Work-in-process inventory*. This is the only case where the accounting designation for inventory matches its actual function. This inventory type refers to the inventory passing through the production system. Large amounts of work-in-process inventory tend to build up between work stations in a production process. This buildup can be caused by the distance between work stations, and can be mitigated by compressing the distance.
- *Investment inventory*. Some types of inventory can increase in value over time, such as wines, precious metals, and precious stones. Oil and gas and other commodities may also be held over the short term in order to take advantage of spikes in spot rates. If management wants to engage in this type of speculation, it may hold substantial amounts of inventory for prolonged periods.

The preceding classifications can be used as a tool to more clearly identify the reasons for the existence of inventory. Once identified in this manner, one can more easily make decisions about whether inventory levels should be maintained, or whether changes can be enacted to alter the investment.

Types of Inventory Demand

The demand for inventory can fall into two categories. One is called *independent demand*, and means that the demand for goods comes directly from customers. The other type of demand is called (predictably enough) *dependent demand*, and refers to demand that is related to stock levels of a different, related inventory item. For example, if a company sells a blue widget directly to customers, then this widget experiences independent demand. However, the raw materials that are used to produce the blue widget have dependent demand, since the quantities required depend upon the number of blue widgets sold. Thus, items experiencing dependent demand are the raw materials, components, and sub-assemblies used in the manufacture of finished goods.

The concepts of dependent and independent demand lead to the conclusion that each type requires an entirely different method of inventory planning, as noted in the following bullet points:

- *Independent demand planning*. Customer orders are examined to see if there is a historical pattern that can be carried forward into a production forecast. A buffer stock is usually incorporated into this forecast, to ensure that customer orders can always be filled within a short period of time. There can be considerable uncertainty in independent demand planning.
- *Dependent demand planning*. In-house production plans are examined and compared to on-hand raw material inventory balances to determine which raw

materials must be ordered. Planning for these types of items can be made with precision, as long as the production plans upon which they are based are not continually changed.

It is of some importance not to confuse the type of demand for an inventory item. Doing so could mean that inventory levels are wildly incorrect when compared to actual usage levels. For example, if a raw material item is tagged as having independent demand, it will not be included in the planning for a production run, and so the amount on hand could be much too low, thereby terminating the production run.

The Reorder Point

A reorder point is the inventory unit quantity on hand that triggers the purchase of a predetermined amount of replenishment inventory. If the purchasing process and supplier fulfillment work as planned, the reorder point should result in the replenishment inventory arriving just as the last of the on-hand inventory is used up. The reorder point is designed for goods that experience independent demand.

The reorder point can be different for every item of inventory, since every item may have a different usage rate, and require differing amounts of time to receive a replenishment delivery from a supplier. For example, a company can elect to buy the same part from two different suppliers; if one supplier requires one day to deliver an order and the other supplier requires three days, the company's reorder point for the first supplier would be when there is one day's supply left on hand, or three days' supply for the second supplier.

The basic formula for the reorder point is to multiply the average daily usage rate for an inventory item by the lead time in days to replenish it.

EXAMPLE

ABC International uses an average of 25 units of its green widget every day, and the number of days it takes for the supplier to replenish inventory is four days. Therefore, ABC should set the reorder point for the green widget at 100 units. When the inventory balance declines to 100 units, ABC places an order, and the new units should arrive four days later, just as the last of the on-hand widgets are being used up.

However, this formula for the reorder point is only based on *average* usage; in reality, demand may spike above or decline below the average level, so there may still be some inventory on hand when the replenishment order arrives, or there may have been a stockout condition for several days.

To guard against the latter situation, a company may alter the reorder formula to add a safety stock (see the next section), so that the formula becomes:

(Average daily usage rate × Lead time) + Safety stock = Reorder quantity

This formula alteration means that replenishment stock will be ordered sooner, which greatly reduces the risk that there will be a stockout condition. However, it also means that a company will have a larger investment in its on-hand inventory, so there is a trade-off between always having available inventory and funding a larger inventory asset.

Safety Stock

Some inventory is kept on hand as a buffer to guard against shortages, which is known as safety stock. For example, a company may usually receive an average order total of 100 units of a widget per week. However, actual customer demand can vary around this 100 unit level by as much as 25 units. Thus, orders may be received for 75 units in one week and for 125 in the next week. To guard against a stockout condition, a company could incorporate into its required on-hand balance an additional 25 widgets, so that the company will be able to meet the maximum possible level of customer demand.

The amount of safety stock to be maintained is usually loaded into a company's materials planning system, after which this information is promptly forgotten – unless there is still a stockout, despite the amount of safety stock listed in the system. Safety stock is a laudable idea, since it ensures a higher level of customer service. However, it comes at the cost of an increased investment in working capital. To mitigate this cost, it can be worthwhile to examine demand levels for each product over a full year, to see if the variability of demand changes over time. It is quite possible that there are demand spikes only during limited time periods, with much reducing ordering variability in other periods. If this is the case, consider altering the safety stock level to coincide with expected changes in demand variability.

If the materials planning system does not automate an ongoing reset of safety stock levels, it will be necessary to do so manually. If so, conduct the safety stock investigation and reset only those inventory items for which the company has a significant investment. It is not worthwhile to periodically reset safety stock levels for low-investment goods, since the impact on working capital will be immaterial.

Another way to deal with safety stock is to segment the reasons for its use among different customers. It is possible that the ordering histories of only a small number of customers are highly variable. If so, the company is essentially maintaining extra safety stock just for these customers. In this case, there are several possible courses of action:

- Calculate the cost of holding the extra safety stock for these customers, and include the cost in an analysis of customer profitability. If the extra cost makes a customer unprofitable, drop the customer.
- Approach the customer about paying the company a fee in exchange for maintaining a reserve of inventory for their specific use.
- If the company earns a large profit percentage on the sale of a product, it makes more sense to maintain a large safety stock than if the profit is inconsequential.

- There may be a contractual obligation to provide a certain speed of fulfillment to a customer. If the company cannot deliver goods on a timely basis, it may be under default, and is contractually penalized. If so, there is no way to avoid retaining a large amount of safety stock.
- If there is strong competition for a customer, the company may be forced to maintain a large safety stock for that customer; otherwise, someone else with a better fulfillment speed may obtain the business.

> **Tip:** If management wants to maintain a certain average fulfillment rate, it can address the issue in aggregate, by always maintaining sufficient safety stocks for high-volume items, and never maintaining stock for a certain proportion of low-volume items. The result is that some items will always be backordered, while the overall fulfillment rate remains high.

Safety Time

Safety time is a variation on safety stock. Rather than focusing on a certain amount of buffer stock, we focus on having a buffer for a certain period of time. Safety time is an important concept when demand varies by a significant amount over time. For example, a company sets a safety stock level of 500 units, based on variability of approximately 500 units around an average monthly order volume by customers of 2,000 units. However, this safety stock level was originally calculated during the summer months, when the average monthly demand was peaking. During those months, a 500 unit safety stock equaled one quarter of a month of total demand. In the winter, average monthly demand plummets to 600 units. If the company continues to maintain the fixed safety stock level of 500 units, the amount now equates to 5/6ths of a month. If the company were to instead focus on having safety stock of one-quarter of a month throughout the year, this means the amount of safety stock kept on hand during the winter months would be only one-quarter of 600 units, or 150 units.

Economic Order Quantity

The economic order quantity is a formula used to derive that number of units of inventory to order that represents the lowest possible total cost to the buyer. It essentially creates a least-cost balance between the cost of ordering inventory and the cost of holding inventory. The formula is designed for situations in which there is a recurring and consistent rate of demand for goods, and the lead time is known. The economic order quantity is derived from the following formula:

$$EOQ = \sqrt{\frac{2(\text{Annual usage in units})(\text{Order cost})}{(\text{Annual carrying cost per unit})}}$$

The inputs to the model are noted within the formula.

EXAMPLE

Smithy Smelter uses 100,000 pounds of aluminum ingots per year, and the cost to place each order is $15. The carrying cost for one pound of aluminum ingots is $5 per year. The economic order quantity, based on this information, is the square root of:

$$(2 \times 100,000 \text{ Pounds of ingots} \times \$15 \text{ Order cost}) \div \$5 \text{ Carrying cost}$$

$$= 775 \text{ Units economic order quantity}$$

It is useful to test variations on the ordering cost and annual carrying cost to see how they impact the economic order quantity. It is possible that driving down the annual carrying cost of inventory can significantly alter the economic order quantity. A key factor in this analysis is determining which carrying costs actually vary with inventory volumes, and which are unrelated fixed costs. If they are unrelated, do not include them in the denominator of the calculation.

The EOQ model is subject to alteration in certain circumstances. Any of the following situations may limit its applicability:

- *Long-term supply.* A large recommended purchase volume may not be practicable if doing so results in such a long-term supply that there is a risk of obsolescence, or there is a risk that demand levels will become more uncertain. In this case, a smaller purchasing quantity is indicated.
- *Shelf life.* There may be a short shelf life on goods that constrain the maximum amount of units that can be ordered. In this case, the actual amount ordered may be much less than the optimum amount indicated by the model.
- *Storage constraints.* There may be an upper limit on the amount of storage space available for a particular item. This situation most commonly arises for a rarely-used item for which the warehouse manager does not want to reserve extra space. If so, a smaller purchase quantity is needed.

The economic order quantity is not used in a "pull" manufacturing system, where components are ordered from suppliers only as needed and in the quantities needed; thus, a pull system tends to order fewer components than would be indicated by the economic order quantity formula.

Dependent Demand Reordering Systems

When goods have dependent demand, the need for them is dependent on the stock levels of a different, related inventory item. Thus, if a company sells a widget to a customer, all of the components used to manufacture that widget have dependent demand that is based on the sales of the widget. The demand for these items can be planned with great precision through a computer system called material requirements planning (MRP).

The goal of an MRP system is to always have sufficient components on hand to support the requirements of a company's production schedule. To do so, an MRP system follows these steps:

1. Create a production schedule that states the quantities of goods to be produced, and the dates on which production is scheduled.
2. Using a bill of materials (i.e., a list of the parts used to manufacture a product), break down the scheduled goods into their component parts, which creates a listing of all the parts needed to support the production schedule.
3. Compare this list of required parts to the on-hand inventory of parts that are not already allocated for other needs.
4. If there are any shortages that must be filled by suppliers, calculate the amount of lead time required to obtain the goods and place orders with the relevant suppliers.

The MRP system is extremely computer-intensive, which means that the information used to construct orders to be placed with suppliers must be accurate. For the system to operate properly, the production department must commit to produce exactly in accordance with the production schedule, while both the bill of material and inventory records must have extraordinarily high accuracy levels. Otherwise, the system will generate nonsensical orders to suppliers (or no orders at all), possibly resulting in the inability to produce goods and/or excessive raw material inventory quantities.

Conversely, if the information used as input to an MRP system is accurate, the result can be quite low raw material inventory balances on hand, since only enough is kept on-site to deal with planned production. Also, the ability of a business to manufacture on a timely basis is heightened, since all component parts are available on time.

A different type of dependent demand reordering system is provided by a just-in-time (JIT) system. A JIT system is designed around the concept of only producing goods if there is a customer order. If there is no order, there is no production. This is a general target that is not always achieved; in reality, estimates of expected customer orders may also be used.

A JIT system uses very short production runs. Since the goal is to immediately produce to the requirements of a single order, it may be necessary to manufacture just a single product in a production run. From an inventory perspective, this means that a small amount of component parts may be needed at any time for immediate production purposes. Accordingly, a notification is sent to suppliers whenever a product is to be manufactured, which calls for an immediate delivery from a supplier, preferably straight to the production area, and only for the amount immediately needed. The notification sent to a supplier is usually an electronic one, to eliminate transit times.

A JIT system is not a specific type of computer package, but rather a philosophy intended to strip excess inventory out of the production process (among other goals) by compressing the time required to produce goods, as well as to produce only in accordance with actual customer orders.

The MRP and JIT concepts are discussed again in the Impact of Production on Inventory chapter.

Visual Reordering Systems

The reorder point described in an earlier section is designed for goods having independent demand, and for which quantities are tracked in real time through a computer system. If there is no up-to-date tracking system in place, a visual reordering system should be installed instead. There are two variations on the same concept that work well:

- *Two bin system.* Goods are stored in two bins, one of which contains working stock and the other containing reserve stock. The amount of inventory kept in the reserve stock bin equals the amount the company expects to use during the ordering lead time associated with that item. To use this system, reorder goods as soon as the working stock bin is empty, and replacement parts should arrive before the reserve stock bin is empty. It is possible to fine-tune the inventory investment by altering the amount of goods kept in the reserve stock bin. The calculation for the amount of inventory to keep in the reserve stock bin is:

    (Daily usage rate × Lead time) + Safety stock = Reserve bin quantity

- *Order line system.* This is the same as the two bin system, except that only a single bin is used. A line is drawn across the back of the bin. When the stock level in the bin declines to the point where the line is visible, additional inventory is ordered.

Which of these two versions is selected may depend upon the storage configuration; if there is not enough room for a two bin system, the single bin version is used. However, the single bin version requires larger bins, so the space savings is not that large.

EXAMPLE

Entwhistle Electric experiences weekly usage of 500 units of a purple cell battery, so the daily usage rate is 100 units. The lead time for the battery is three days. The reserve storage bin should contain at least 300 batteries, to cover expected usage during the three-day lead time.

In addition, the company assumes that usage levels can vary by as much as 25% from the average usage rate. Consequently, 75 additional batteries are kept in the reserve storage bin. This is calculated as 300 reserve units × 25% safety stock allowance. Thus, the total reserve stock is 375 units.

Tip: A visual re-ordering system may also be used for dependent demand items whose on-hand balances are not tracked through the inventory computer system. This approach is commonly used for incidental items, such as fittings and fasteners.

A visual reordering system suffers from a major flaw, which is the assumption that someone will periodically conduct a visual review of on-hand balances. If this does not happen, or there is confusion about who is responsible for re-ordering, there can be an unanticipated stockout condition. This issue can be addressed in two ways:

- *Responsibility.* Assign reordering responsibility for every bin using a visual reordering system. With just one person responsible, there can be no confusion about who places replenishment orders.
- *Card trigger.* Include a reorder notification card in the reserve stock bin. The card is removed when an order is placed, and is returned when the bin is refilled. Therefore, if there is no card in the bin, an order has been placed.

Summary

The Types of Inventory section should make it clear that there are a number of valid needs for inventory within a business. These needs may justify a hefty investment in inventory, as well as comprehensive systems for ensuring that more inventory is acquired at regular intervals. The trick to monitoring this investment is to ensure that management understands the specific reasons for maintaining inventory, and that there are adequate policies and procedures in place to ensure that the inventory investment is a prudent one. In the following chapters, we examine several corporate strategies that employ inventory as a competitive weapon, and explore the systems used to manage inventory levels. Throughout the discussion, we insert recommendations for fine-tuning how inventory is designed, ordered, stored, produced, and shipped. By implementing the suggestions in the following chapters, it should be possible to maximize the use of inventory within an organization while minimizing the investment in inventory.

Chapter 2
Inventory Strategy

Introduction

The management of inventory is usually considered to relate solely to immediate tactical issues, such as reducing inventory holding costs or reducing the overall working capital investment in inventory. However, there is more to inventory management than these goals. In this chapter, we address several key strategies that center on the use (or non-use) of inventory, and how they can help a company compete.

Replenishment Strategy

A company can pursue a strategy of replenishing its inventory at a rate much faster than its competitors. This means that the total stock of inventory is being replaced by new inventory during a period when competitors are still offering older goods for sale. By doing so, a business can achieve the following advantages:

- *Investable cash.* The company can maintain the same order fulfillment rate as competitors, while investing far less money in inventory. The difference can be used elsewhere to gain a competitive advantage, such as by increasing spending on new product development, loosening credit to expand sales, or by investing in more efficient production equipment.
- *Broader product line.* The company can choose to match the total inventory investment of competitors, but because it is replenishing inventory much more quickly, the result is a broader product line from which customers can choose.
- *Faster product replacement.* Since inventory is being flushed out of the company much faster than for competitors, the company can choose to replace its product line at more frequent intervals. This is a particular advantage in fashion or trend-oriented businesses, where sales can spike and suddenly decline within very short periods of time. A fashion business can use fast replenishment to test designs without having to build up unwanted stock that it might otherwise need to sell off at a steep discount. Also, faster product replacement allows the seller to lock up the best distributors, since distributors want to differentiate themselves by offering the latest product innovations.

EXAMPLE

Quest Adventure Gear has achieved an inventory turnover rate that is double the rate attained by its competitors. By doing so, Quest has reduced its investment in inventory by $5,000,000. The management team decides to use this advantage by creating a new product line, which will require $2,000,000 of development costs to create and $3,000,000 of an investment in inventory to support. Competitors cannot match this action, unless they raise $5,000,000 through an equity offering or obtain $5,000,000 of debt (for which interest payments must be made).

In addition to the advantages already noted, it is possible that the following ancillary benefits may also be gained from a fast replenishment strategy:

- *Reduced obsolescence cost*. If inventory is being flushed out of a company at an accelerated rate, it is possible that there will be a reduced amount of loss from product obsolescence. However, obsolescence can still occur, since a few products may only sell poorly, irrespective of the overall inventory turnover rate. Also, some raw materials may still become obsolete if they are not used up prior to the official termination of a product.
- *Increased prices*. If a company markets its accelerated replenishment strategy properly, customers will come to appreciate their ability to buy the freshest product concepts from the company. This can be a powerful branding tool that may allow the company to charge higher prices than competitors.
- *Reduced forecasting uncertainty*. If inventory is being replaced with great rapidity, this means that product demand only needs to be forecasted for a relatively short period of time. Since forecasting tends to be more accurate over the short-term, this means that a company is at much less risk of adopting a production schedule that mandates the manufacture of goods that will not be sold.
- *Better reseller penetration*. When the supplier can replenish the stocks of a retailer or distributor within a few days, this means that the retailer or distributor can keep less inventory on hand to guard against stockout conditions. The retailer or distributor therefore invests less cash in inventory, and so will be more likely to buy goods from the fast-replenishment supplier. Further, retailers and distributors can use the savings from reduced funding to grant easier credit to *their* customers, which in turn increases the orders they place with the supplier.

EXAMPLE

Quest Clothiers produces clothes designed for the adventure market, specifically focusing on women's products. Changes in this market are more rapid than for men's adventure clothes, with styling changes occurring in as little as three months. Quest has concentrated on increasing the replenishment speed of its inventory by forcing a key supplier to locate a facility a short distance away from Quest's headquarters. The result is an ability to issue new fashions in just six weeks, which is twice the speed of every other competitor. This triggers an immediate increase in market share, as competitors struggle to keep up with Quest's continuing product line changes.

> **Tip:** Reduced forecasting uncertainty is particularly important when a company forecasts demand too low, since this equates to lost sales. Consequently, in industries where forecasted demand is especially prone to error, it can be especially important to pursue a rapid replenishment strategy with the specific target of shortening the forecasting period.

Fulfillment Strategy

A company may elect to be a full-service provider of goods to its customers. This means being the monolithic supplier of as many goods as possible. This approach can be comprehensive, such as being the sole supplier of maintenance, repair and operations (MRO) supplies. Alternatively, it can mean being the sole supplier of a particular category of goods, such as the supplier of all air filters to large industrial suppliers, no matter what type of filter is required.

The fulfillment strategy may call for a large investment in inventory, in order to ship most customer order line items on the same day of receipt. Alternatively, it may mean that the seller can improve upon the promised ship dates of its competitors, as may be the case when products are configured for a specific customer. This strategy also involves building relations with a financially sound and reliable group of suppliers, so that they can forward materials and goods to the company in an extremely reliable manner. The outcome of these actions is to present to customers a business that can comprehensively meet their needs on the shortest possible delivery terms, as reliably as possible. In exchange for pursuing this strategy, a company can expect the following outcomes:

- *Increased market share.* As customers realize the reliability of the company, they will allocate a greater percentage of their spend to the company, resulting in an ongoing increase in market share.
- *Reduced unit costs.* As market share expands, the company can increase its production volumes, which means that fixed costs are spread over more units, resulting in a decline in average costs and therefore increased profits.

However, this strategy is not without its risks. The company must carefully monitor its inventory levels, since it may be committing to maintain much larger stocks of inventory than might normally have been the case. Also, customers may ask the company to act as primary supplier for a whole range of products, which means that the company must have the managerial skill to coordinate the actions of a number of secondary suppliers.

> **Tip:** To reduce the risk of obsolete inventory, a company following the fulfillment strategy should request access to the purchasing plans of its key customers, thereby reducing the uncertainty of its own production and procurement forecasts.

A variation on the fulfillment strategy concept for retail stores is to present customers with a broad range of product options, but to only have one of each product option in stock. Doing so gives customers the maximum possible choice, but also signals that these units may not be available for purchase later (after all, there is only one unit in stock). This approach tends to keep customers from shopping elsewhere, since they cannot assume that the items they want will still be in stock if they come back later to make a purchase.

Customization Strategy

Some customers want products that vary somewhat from the standard offerings that a seller provides. These customers may be more than willing to pay a premium for their non-standard demands, and will be especially willing to do so if the seller can provide customized goods within a short period of time. If a company can refine its order-handling and production systems to provide somewhat customized goods within a compressed time frame, this can be an excellent strategy. In addition to the pricing advantage, here are several other benefits of the inventory customization strategy:

- *Loyalty*. Few companies are willing to provide customized goods within a short time frame. Those that can do so garner high levels of customer loyalty, which translates into repeat business. Further, these customers may be so impressed with a company's service that they go out of their way to refer other potential customers – which reduces new customer acquisition costs for the organization.
- *Broader purchases*. A customer that has had a good experience with a customized product purchase is more likely to buy other, more standardized goods from the same seller. Thus, the use of customization can be used as a wedge to obtain all types of additional sales.

Further, customization does not have to be considered a niche strategy that only applies to small segments of a market. If a company can redefine its systems to handle modest amounts of customization for many orders, it can become the dominant player in an industry.

This strategy only applies to markets where customers value differentiated products. For example, a company could successfully pursue the customization of electric guitars or skis, but would be less successful in customizing cleaning products.

Showrooming Strategy

A business may choose to operate showrooms in which customers can view, touch, and try on its products, after which they are directed to a website to make actual purchases (possibly from a kiosk within the showroom). This approach has three advantages. First, the company can concentrate its inventory in a small number of warehouses, from which all sales are shipped. This is especially important when the customer base is spread across a large area, since stocking local stores to service them would otherwise require a massive inventory investment. Second, customers have a chance to examine the goods before placing on-line orders, which makes it more likely that they will select the right product options on the first order, requiring fewer product returns. And third, showrooms can be smaller than regular retail outlets and require fewer staff. Given their lower cost structures, it is possible to set up a large number of showrooms, possibly in lower-population areas that would not support a retail store.

The main downside of the showrooming strategy is that the purchasing process now has two steps – viewing the product and then placing an order, possibly at a later date. This more extended purchasing process could mean that fewer sales are realized. Another potential problem is that some customers may not be comfortable shopping online; a smaller number of more traditional retail outlets may be needed to service these customers.

Startup Outsourcing Strategy

The founders of a company may choose to invest their limited funds in only a small number of key areas, such as product design and marketing, and outsource all other activities. Since the production and warehousing of goods can require a large amount of funding, these activities are more likely to be outsourced. If so, the startup company trades off a higher per-unit cost to a third party contract manufacturer in exchange for reduced funding requirements. There is also a risk that the manufacturer will learn so much about the company's products that it can eventually become a direct competitor. However, if the company does an adequate job of branding its products, this can be a lesser concern.

The startup outsourcing strategy does not always work for the entire life cycle of a company. As the business grows, management may realize that a large part of the company's profits are being handed to suppliers. Also, customer concerns over the quality of goods and/or the speed of product delivery may lead the company to take over control of its production and warehousing. Nonetheless, avoiding all contact with inventory can be a smart strategy for a small startup operation.

Summary

In this chapter, we have noted several ways in which an organization can structure its strategy around a specific use of inventory. None of these strategies are easy to achieve, since they involve configuring many company processes to support the use (or non-use) of inventory in a particular way. Consequently, the management team should proceed with considerable deliberation when implementing one of these strategies, to ensure that the company can still operate effectively while not investing too much in its inventory asset.

In the following chapters, we address tactical issues relating to inventory. If you have selected one of the inventory strategies noted in this chapter, it is useful to peruse the following tactical issues and see which ones impact your chosen strategy. Doing so results in a cluster of actionable items as you plan for a winning business strategy.

Chapter 3
Inventory Policies

Introduction

Some of the techniques available for adjusting a company's investment in inventory do not relate to the physical use or storage of inventory at all – but rather to a set of corporate policies that can trigger inordinately high inventory levels or keep losses from occurring. It is useful to understand these policies and their impact on inventory, so that they can be fine-tuned to minimize a company's inventory investment while still achieving reasonable customer service targets. In this chapter, we describe the key policies related to inventory, and also note a number of sample policies that may be of use.

Receiving Policy

A company may find that its purchasing practices are so loose that it is receiving more goods than were formally ordered by the purchasing department. There may also be instances where suppliers are deliberately shipping more goods than were ordered, and yet other cases where goods are fraudulently shipped on the flimsiest of excuses, and then overbilled. If these issues arise regularly, a policy can be implemented that requires the receiving staff to reject all orders that are not accompanied by a valid purchase order number. For example:

> All deliveries to the company shall be rejected if they are not accompanied by an open purchase order. Also, any excess amounts delivered shall be rejected, at the discretion of the receiving department.

The receiving staff is not always happy about enforcing this policy, for it can make them unpopular figures within the company. For example, there may have been a rush order that was informally made by a department manager to deal with an emergency situation; a purchase order was not obtained for the order, so the receiving department rejects the delivery. Given this type of issue, the receiving staff is more likely to set such deliveries aside and investigate whether a valid purchase was made, rather than rejecting the deliveries at once.

Another issue with this policy is that it requires the issuance of an authorizing purchase order. Using purchase orders for every conceivable purchase is not an effective use of the purchasing department's time, and may be discouraged in favor of more streamlined techniques. If so, the receiving staff may find that this policy only functions for higher-cost deliveries.

Inventory Access Policy

The accuracy of the inventory records must be sacrosanct. In addition, the incidence of inventory theft must be kept to a minimum. Both goals can be achieved by instituting a standard policy of only allowing authorized persons in inventory storage areas. The concept can be extended to restrict access to the inventory records in the computer system. Sample policies are:

> Only authorized warehouse personnel are allowed access to the warehouse area. Non-authorized personnel must be accompanied by a warehouse staff person when accessing the warehouse area.

> Only authorized personnel are allowed access to inventory records. Access passwords for the record-keeping system shall be changed as soon as an authorized person leaves the employment of the company.

The first policy is difficult to enforce if a large part of the raw materials are stored in bins adjacent to the production area, as is common in a just-in-time production environment. If significant and unexplained inventory shrinkage occurs in these areas, it may be necessary to shift the inventory back to the more secure warehouse area.

Batch Sizing Policy

Within the production area, there may be a policy that a large container be filled with completed parts at one work station before it can be shifted to the next work station for additional production activities. This policy is usually enacted when there is a focus on improving the efficiency of materials handling equipment, where a forklift is only needed at relatively long intervals to shift filled parts containers from one work station to another. However, this policy is not useful from an inventory perspective, for it increases the number of partially-completed work-in-process units scattered throughout the manufacturing area. In addition, the use of batch sizing can starve a downstream work station of units to work on, since units must accumulate to a predetermined quantity before being shifted to the next work station. It is better to have no batch sizing policy at all, thereby encouraging the more rapid transfer of inventory between workstations.

There may be no formal batch sizing policy – instead, the containers used to shift materials between work stations are simply so large that the policy inherently exists. If so, the best way to tear down the implied policy is to move work stations close together and install conveyors between them, so that parts are individually transferred.

Production Run Size Policy

A business may operate under a policy that production runs for any product must be of a certain minimum size or larger. This policy comes from a cost accounting analysis that requires one to spread the setup cost of a production run across as many units as possible, thereby reducing the average cost of the production run. This is a false analysis, for most work centers have excess capacity, and so can easily handle a large number of setups with no impact on the overall production capacity of a business.

When a run size policy is used, or if a lot sizing formula is being used to derive the most economical run size, it is quite likely that the number of units produced exceeds the immediate demand for those units. This means the excess quantity produced will be stored for some period of time, thereby increasing the investment in inventory.

The run size policy should be replaced by a just-in-time "pull" system that only produces the amount required by a customer order. The result will be a large number of small production runs that yield no excess finished goods inventory.

Resource Maximization Policy

A common misconception is that all production equipment should be run at the highest possible production rate at all times, since doing so results in the highest level of "efficiency." In reality, this policy only results in a production area that is clogged with work-in-process inventory. Most production work stations can actually be run at a level well below their theoretical maximums, with only the production bottleneck operation having to be run at all times.

The elimination of the resource maximization policy is a difficult one, for many managers seem to find it necessary to run all parts of an operation "flat out" at all times in order to improve work station efficiency levels. It can require a notable amount of re-education to convince employees that equipment should only be operated when it is needed to fulfill a customer order.

Substitutions Policy

There may be instances where it is possible to substitute one item for another in a production order or customer order. However, this cannot be done without proper planning, for an undocumented substitution causes one inventory balance to decline, while the balance of the item being replaced unexpectedly does not change. Instead, all substitutions must be channeled through a single department that is experienced in properly documenting these changes. A sample policy is:

> Production substitutions must be authorized in advance by the engineering manager and recorded in the bill of materials by the materials management staff. Order substitutions must be authorized by the customer service staff, with related customer order changes being made by the same personnel. Under no circumstances are the warehouse personnel allowed to initiate substitutions without the authorizations just noted.

Customer Service Policy

An issue that has a major impact on the investment in inventory is the customer service policy. In this policy, management states the speed with which customer orders will be fulfilled, such as:

> 98% of all customer orders shall be filled within one business day of receipt.

Such policies are routinely posted on a company's web site and included in marketing brochures, with the intent of reinforcing with customers that the company is serious about serving its customers.

The problem with this policy is that the company must maintain a large stock of inventory in order to ensure that nearly all items ordered are currently in stock. This is a particular concern if the company offers a large number of products and product variations to its customers. The result could be an overloaded warehouse where many inventory items are kept in stock, on the off chance that low-demand items will be ordered.

A more prudent approach is to conduct an analysis of customer ordering patterns, and adopt a more reasonable fulfillment policy, such as filling 80% or 90% of all customer orders within a short period of time. If the company offers such a vast array of products that even meeting an 80% or 90% policy goal is a stretch, then it may be prudent to not advertise a customer service policy that states any fulfillment goal.

If it still seems advantageous to advertise some sort of fulfillment goal, a company could try some alternative approaches, such as:

- Use a two-stage goal, such as a 90% fulfillment rate in one business day, with the remainder fulfilled within five additional business days; or
- Offer blanket fulfillment within one business day, with all unfilled items refunded to the customer at once; or
- Offer a replacement goal, such as a 95% fulfillment rate using the exact items ordered or approximate replacement products.

Pricing Deals Policy

The use of coupons and other forms of discounting are a beloved marketing technique. However, they are much less appreciated in the inventory planning area, since they can cause fluctuations in demand that are not related to the inherent level of customer demand. Instead, customers buy in response to a low price point, and then stop buying for as long as it takes to consume what they purchased under the special deal.

The result of a pricing deal is a ramp-up in production to meet the estimated increase in sales resulting from the deal, followed by a decline in production in response to the sales drop that occurs after the pricing deal is over. This has the following negative effects:

- The production staff may have to work overtime to expand the on-hand reserves of finished goods prior to the start date of the pricing deal.
- It is not possible to exactly forecast incremental changes in sales resulting from a pricing deal, so too much inventory may be produced.
- The effects of the deal are also felt by suppliers, from whom more goods are ordered in anticipation of the pricing deal, followed by a decline in orders. This can cause forecasting confusion within the supply chain.

Given these issues, pricing deals are generally to be avoided. The one case where they can be useful is to eliminate inventory that is becoming obsolete. In this case, there is no effect on production, since the goods have already been produced, and are merely taking up space in the warehouse. A sample policy is:

> The company does not offer reduced-price deals to its customers, with the sole exception of deals intended to eliminate obsolete goods from stock.

Tip: Eliminate specific monthly sales goals. Otherwise, customers know there will be a month-end push by the sales force to make their budgeted targets, and will wait for the lowest-priced deals before placing orders. This timing bubble also means that the production department will be hit by a crushing production load just prior to the end of each month.

Returns Policy

When products have a relatively short shelf life, it may be necessary to restrict the ability of customers to return products. Otherwise, the seller may find itself overwhelmed with a large number of returned goods that it cannot resell for anywhere near the original price. The same problem can arise when products are being sold to retailers and distributors, since these entities routinely clear their shelves of unsold goods and attempt to return these items to sellers. In both cases, it makes sense to have a tightly-enforced returns policy. There are a number of variations on an effective returns policy, such as:

(1) All sales are final. Once sold, products cannot be returned.

(2) All goods may be returned within 90 days of the sale date, with a copy of the sales receipt.

(3) If you wish to return a product, please contact our customer service department for a return authorization.

(4) Returns will only be accepted if all original tags remain attached.

The sample policy requiring a copy of the sales receipt is intended to keep customers from returning goods that were actually purchased from a different seller. One of the sample policies requires that a customer obtain a return merchandise authorization (RMA). An RMA number is only issued when a customer has a valid reason for returning product, and is only valid for a certain period of time. This level of restriction is particularly effective for cutting back on the number of returns from retailers and distributors.

The policy requiring all original tags to still be present prevents customers from wearing clothes and then returning them (known as *wardrobing*). This is an especially useful policy when the tags are so glaring that customers could not possibly wear the clothes with the tags remaining on them.

> **Tip:** Consider adding a restocking fee to the returns policy, so the company can recoup some of its costs for testing and repackaging returned goods. A sufficiently high restocking fee may deter some customers from returning goods at all. A typical fee is 15% of the original product price.

> **Tip:** If there is no alternative use for goods that customers want to return, instruct them to throw away the goods, and still issue them a credit. Doing so eliminates the cost of return freight as well as processing in the receiving area.

It may take some testing to arrive at the best possible returns policy. The best version is the one that contributes to increased sales without triggering an excessive amount of returns. When testing different returns policies, consider altering the amount of time during which returns are accepted, whether a restocking fee is charged, the amount of hassle involved, exclusions to the returns policy, and whether cash or credit will be allowed when goods are returned. Typically, the absence of a restocking charge and minimal returns hassle tends to stimulate sales, while the other variables tend to reduce the amount of returns. Given the number of variables involved, a relatively complex returns policy may end up being the best choice.

Collections Take-Back Policy

When the collections department contacts a customer about an overdue account receivable, one collection option may be to take back goods sold to a customer, in settlement of the outstanding debt. However, this approach only works if the goods retain sufficient value to be resold at an adequate price to a third party. Consequently, it may be necessary to have a policy that either allows or restricts the take-back of goods. Allowing a take-back is most viable when the gross margin on goods sold is quite high, so that even a re-sale of the goods at a substantially reduced price will still earn back the cost of the goods. Conversely, if the margin is low, reselling at a reduced price means that the company will assuredly lose money on a take-back.

This policy can be designed to leave some wiggle room for the collections staff, so they can still offer a take-back, but only as a last resort after all other options have been investigated. This situation occurs when the company will otherwise experience a total loss on a receivable, and can at least reduce the loss through the return of inventory.

Summary

Altering a policy can have an immediate and highly beneficial payback by reducing the investment in inventory. Since a policy is really a conceptual issue, rather than a system or hardware change, it might seem simple enough to enact a change and see an immediate improvement in inventory levels. However, policies tend to be quite difficult to change, because they have the long-term support of employees. Only a vigorous, long-term re-education effort can completely squash an old policy; and even then, new employees who do not have a grounding in the company's inventory reduction efforts may attempt to re-introduce bad policies.

Chapter 4
Materials Planning and Forecasting

Introduction

The job of the materials planner is a difficult one, having to depend upon unreliable forecasts to predict when materials should be ordered and jobs scheduled for production. In this chapter, we outline just how unreliable forecasts can be, while also noting a variety of techniques for improving the accuracy of forecasts and sidestepping the need for forecasts. We also note several ways to improve the efficiency and/or effectiveness of how materials management can be operated, ranging from the use of modeling software to the manner in which finished goods are configured for sale. This chapter does not attempt to lay out all aspects of the materials planning and forecasting function, but rather to focus on ways to improve the function to optimize the use of inventory.

The Evils of Forecasting

Whenever a company bases its materials planning on a forecast of product sales, there is an increase in the amount of both raw materials and finished goods inventory. The problem arises from the very nature of a forecast – it is an estimate. Actual demand will almost never match the forecast. Instead, either too few or too many goods will be produced. If too few finished goods are manufactured, then the sales department will wail about lost sales, and demand an increase in the next forecast, so that all sales can be accommodated. Continual increases in the forecast will eventually end badly, when actual results dip below an especially exuberant forecast. If too many goods are produced, then the company is saddled with excess inventory that must be sold off at a loss.

If the forecast period extends a long ways into the future, the probability of a forecast not meeting actual sales levels is extremely high; and the further the forecast extends, the better the chance that actual results will vary substantially from forecasted results. In short, lengthy forecasts can result in major inventory management issues.

The best solution is to shrink the amount of time that a company requires for its forecasts. When there is an exceedingly short forecast timeline (such as one day), there is much less chance that the forecast will vary from actual results by very much. Given the small amount of the variance, a business can essentially produce to order, resulting in only a minor inventory investment.

If a company cannot get away from a lengthy forecast period, it should at least manage its own activities to dampen any swings in the sales forecast. For example, if the marketing department enacts a sales campaign that features a discount on certain products, the production department may see a sudden and unexplained spike in demand. The materials manager accordingly buys more raw materials and sets aside additional production capacity to deal with the situation, only to see just as large a decline in sales once the discount period ends. In effect, the marketing department has stuffed customers with goods, who no longer need to buy more goods until they have used up the amount they just bought. To avoid this problem, the marketing staff can either cancel the bulk of its discounted sales campaigns, or at least inform the rest of the company of their plans. In the latter case, production can be ramped up in anticipation of the sale, but there will be no assumption that sales will continue to rise for a prolonged period of time.

The Bullwhip Effect

The nefarious effects of forecasting can be particularly pernicious deep in the supply chain. In this area, a small change in a customer order can be amplified as the effects of the order ripple down through the supply chain. The result can be major swings in forecasted demand, which is known as the bullwhip effect.

The basic concept behind the effect is that when customers perceive that something is in short supply, they tend to order too much of it, in an effort to hoard the goods. Note how each step in the following hypothetical sequence triggers an expansion of the underlying order, until the supply chain has vastly over-forecasted its production needs:

1. A customer increases the size of an existing order by 100 units.
2. The retailer of these goods buys them from a distributor. In anticipation of additional demand, the retailer places an order for 250 units.
3. The distributor sees the order for 250 units from one retailer. On the assumption that there may be a buying trend to take advantage of, the distributor orders 500 units from the manufacturer. This quantity also represents a truckload quantity, which the distributor can take advantage of to reduce its freight costs.
4. The manufacturer sees the large order, and concludes that overall demand has increased on a permanent basis. Accordingly, the management team decides to invest a significant amount in fixed assets to increase the production capacity of the business.

In effect, the manufacturer is at the wrong end of the bullwhip effect, where an order for 100 units is quintupled. The effect also works in reverse. If the end customer cancels its order, this can trigger a cascading series of order cancellations through the supply chain of increasing size. Those suppliers furthest from the end customer are impacted the most strongly, with potentially wild swings in demand from their immediate customers that make no sense.

The main underlying cause of the bullwhip effect is the lack of communication up and down the supply chain. A company deep in the supply chain may not even know how its products are eventually used, and has no concept of ordering patterns among users. An additional cause is order batching. As noted in stage three of the example, the distributor increased the size of its order to take advantage of a full truckload freight rate. When both causes are combined, a supplier will find that the pattern of orders from its immediate customers does not appear to follow any rational pattern, which makes forecasting especially difficult.

> **Tip:** To mitigate the bullwhip effect, avoid using buyback contracts. This contract allows the buyer to order in large quantities at a volume discount, and then return unused goods to the seller. This contract provides an incentive to the buyer to order too many units, since the risk of obsolescence is largely shifted back onto the seller.

Forecasting for Style Items

The forecasting problems associated with style items are particularly difficult, for the amounts that may be sold are extraordinarily variable, can change in value suddenly, and may end abruptly. Common characteristics of forecasting for style items include the following:

- There is a selling season that is relatively well-defined. The period may be triggered by the onset of a flood of advertising or other scheduled events, covering an industry-standard range of dates.
- Goods must be on-hand in stores as of a certain date, to coincide with the start of the selling season. Otherwise, retailers will have no shelf space available for additional goods.
- Given the preceding two aspects of the selling season, a manufacturer has to guess at the extent of sales for its new product line, since there is no historical basis of existing sales to use.
- If the selling season is sufficiently long, it may be possible to produce enough additional goods to replenish stock in retail locations. The forecast of additional production is derived from early indications of sales, and so has more of a basis in actual sales than the original forecast. These replenishments may have high incremental costs, such as using air freight to retailers to prevent stockout conditions. Manufacturers are willing to incur these costs, since style items typically have high profit margins. Nonetheless, replenishment costs can be severe.
- Once the selling season is over, it is very difficult to keep price points up, so any remaining goods are usually sold off, either directly with massive price discounts or through discount distributors. Given the nature of the industry, there is little point in trying to retain unsold goods and sell them in the next season, since room must be made for a new line of products.

In summary, anyone in an industry strongly influenced by style is faced with highly irregular demand that may be well above or below expectations. The result is an on-going series of reactions to actual sales results to either trim away excess inventory at a loss or rush more goods to market at a high incremental cost.

Given the nature of this forecasting scenario, it should be of extreme interest to a producer to spend considerable effort creating a compressed cycle time for production activities. By doing so, initial job lots of goods can be produced in smaller quantities, since management knows it can rush additional units into retail stores in relatively short order. Also, with a compressed cycle time, replenishments can be delivered in a somewhat more leisurely manner, eliminating the need for overnight fright charges for deliveries to retail stores.

Forecasting Service Parts

A company that manufactures goods for long-term use will likely find that customers will occasionally order spare parts for their products, and may continue to do so for years to come. This can be an excellent business, allowing a company to earn generous margins simply because it is the sole provider of the parts. However, it can be difficult to forecast the amount of future demand for service parts for what may be an extended period of time.

There are essentially two problems with forecasting for service parts. If the forecast is higher than actual demand, then the company pays to produce too many parts, pays to store them for a long time, and then takes an obsolescence write-off years in the future, when the extent of the over-production is finally clarified. The alternative problem is that the forecast is too low, so there are no spare parts left, causing customers to abandon their products and turn to the offerings of competitors. Or, if there is still strong demand for an out-of-stock part, a third party may fill the need by producing it instead. Given these high-low problems, it is worth spending some extra time examining the current service parts forecast. Consider the following factors:

- *Expense.* The incremental cost of materials associated with many spare parts is negligible. If so, produce to an optimistic forecast. If actual demand turns out to be less, the associated obsolescence cost will be quite low.
- *Customer importance.* If a customer owns a large number of the company's products, and especially if the customer acts as a reference, by all means use an optimistic forecast. It is far more important to retain this type of customer than to save a small amount of money by shaving the number of spare parts kept on hand.
- *Batch size.* If a spare part can be created with a quick equipment changeover, then there is little need to keep a large quantity of parts on hand. Instead, manufacture small batches of parts when needed, which means that the forecast only needs to extend a short distance into the future.
- *Useful life.* If a spare part has a maximum useful life, only produce through the period of this useful life. Then forecast again as this end-of-period event approaches.

In general, it is better to produce more spare parts than less, if there is any emphasis at all on customer service. The greater danger in spare parts forecasting is that a low forecast will drive away customers, and not that a high forecast will incur extra costs.

Forecasting by Product Families

If a business offers a large number of products, it may require too much effort to forecast at the individual product level. If so, consider grouping products into product families, where the components used to construct each product are similar. Doing so can result in a massive decline in the amount of forecasting effort, especially if the company has already developed product families in order to offer a full range of product options and sizes to its customers. A further advantage of this type of aggregation is that demand tends to be less variable across an entire product family, which makes it easier to derive forecasts that match actual results.

To wring the greatest advantage from product family forecasting, only use it to plan demand for those product components that are shared amongst the products in each designated product family. This is useful for the purchasing staff, which can reliably procure components in greater volume than would be the case if forecasting were only used at the individual product level.

EXAMPLE

Milford Sound produces a broad range of speakers for home entertainment systems. For product planning purposes, all outdoor speakers are considered to be one product family, since they are comprised of all-weather components that are shared among the speakers in the family. Demand for each individual speaker product is difficult to predict, with variability from the forecast commonly exceeding 50%. However, when aggregated into a product family, variability from the forecast declines to just 10%. Consequently, the purchasing department uses family-level forecasts to order parts. The result is a close match between on-hand inventory balances and customer requirements, though no one is ever sure about exactly which products within a product family will be ordered by customers.

Forecasting Segmentation

Any forecast is inherently inaccurate, since it is impossible to precisely predict the future. However, this does not mean that some elements of a forecast represent more stable demand than others. For example, a company selling goods into four sales regions may find that the sales level in the southern region is incredibly stable, while the demand in the other three regions is much more variable. Similarly, certain customers can be expected to order the same goods in the same quantities, year after year. It is quite likely that there are numerous pockets of stable demand in a forecast, intermixed with other elements that are much more unstable.

A close examination of historical demand patterns may yield insights into where demand is stable. If these areas comprise a significant proportion of the total forecast, it is worthwhile to segment the forecast to separately project sales in the stable demand areas. By doing so, the uncertainty of the forecast as a whole improves, allowing for better planning of inventory levels.

> **Tip:** Concentrate forecasting efforts on those few products that comprise the bulk of all sales, since errors here can result in a significant excess investment in inventory, or stockout conditions that result in lost sales.

Forecasting Collaboration

As just noted, the accuracy of the forecast can be enhanced by segmenting it in multiple ways to discern patterns of more stable demand. Another way to improve forecast accuracy is through the collaboration of multiple people within and outside of the company. The following people with specific knowledge impacting future sales could be asked to review the forecast:

- *Chief executive officer (CEO).* The CEO is aware of any discussions to sell off parts of the business or terminate certain product lines, which can have a profound impact on projected sales and therefore the supporting inventory levels.
- *Engineering manager.* The engineering manager knows when new products are most likely to be ready for market.
- *Marketing manager.* The marketing manager has the best understanding of planned marketing campaigns, and when they will be launched and terminated.
- *Distributors.* If the company is a manufacturer with no direct ties to end customers, it can be extremely useful to discuss sales patterns with the retailers and distributors that buy the company's products.

The opinion of the sales department is always sought as part of the forecasting process. However, see the next section regarding issues that may arise from the participation of the sales staff.

Problems with the Sales Department Forecast

When the sales function is organized around sales regions, a common approach to forecasting is to have each sales team periodically aggregate their estimates of likely customer demand, and forward a grand total sales figure back to the factory. There are several problems with this approach. First, the sales staff takes the easiest path to forecasting and requests only those products that have historically sold in the highest volume. This is a problem for those customers interested in buying different product configurations, which will only rarely be available. When faced with only being able to buy standard configurations, these customers may be tempted to review the offerings of a competitor. Second, the sales staff is submitting estimates primarily based on historical sales results, which do not necessarily reflect what will happen in the future.

Both of these problems can be removed by giving customers the option to configure their own products. This can be done in a company showroom, or perhaps on the company website. By doing so, a business can replace forecasts with actual orders. In addition, because customers get to pick the exact product version that they want, they are more amenable to paying a higher price for the completed product. This approach requires that the sales staff be removed from the forecasting process, thereby allowing customers to interact directly with the factory.

Forecasting with Customer Linkages

All of the preceding forecasting systems are inherently incorrect, since they are all essentially guesses. At best, a forecast can be segmented into sufficiently small pieces that portions of it are likely to result in a reasonable approximation of actual sales results. Nonetheless, there will always be a variance between expected and actual sales.

One way to completely eliminate this variance is to convince the company's customers to give the company direct access to their ordering systems. This gives the company perfect advance knowledge of the exact amounts and types of goods that will be ordered. Not only do these linkages eliminate excess inventory and shortage situations, they also eliminate the wasted effort that goes into creating and recasting forecasts of customer demand.

Gaining perfect knowledge of customer orders does not always equate to a perfect materials management situation, for the following reasons:

- *Not the end user.* The customer may be several levels down in a supply chain, and so is itself subject to the variability of its own customers, which may create substantial gyrations in its internal materials planning systems.
- *Short planning horizon.* The customer's internal practices may involve planning within only a very short time horizon. If so, the customer's projections may be wildly inaccurate outside of the planning horizon, which gives the company little insight into its eventual orders.
- *Management plans.* The management team of the customer may constantly change its product planning strategy, in which case the materials planning system may be routinely uprooted and reconfigured on short notice. This is particularly common for a low-profitability customer that is continually in search of greater profits by altering its product mix.

There is a significant cost associated with setting up direct linkages with customers. Given the cost, a company may find that it can only do so for a few of its largest customers. If so, forecasts will still be needed for all other customers. However, if a company conducts the bulk of its business with a small number of customers, integration with even a few of them can vastly reduce forecasting variability, since so few remaining sales must be forecasted.

Modeling of Materials Planning

Thus far, the discussion has largely revolved around the evils of forecasting and how this problem can be mitigated. If a company uses a material requirements planning (MRP) system, the materials management staff can take a more proactive approach to the issue by examining the impact of a variety of factors on inventory levels. An MRP system is more fully explained in the Impact of Production on Inventory chapter, but is essentially a system for breaking down scheduled production into its component parts and matching those parts to current inventory levels and supplier lead times. The result is a determination of which items must be ordered by what dates in order to release a production job. Many MRP systems contain modeling modules, where the criteria under which the system operates can be adjusted to determine the impact on inventory levels and the production schedule. For example:

- A supplier requires a longer lead time for parts to be ordered. The system can determine the impact of this change on the company's own quoted lead times to customers, which may need to be extended. An alternative treatment is to determine the amount of extra inventory that must be kept on hand, if the company wants to keep offering compressed availability dates to its customers. If the results of this analysis are excessively negative, a result may be switching purchases to a different supplier.
- Management wants to reduce the amount of funds invested in inventory. The system can be used to model the impact on quoted production lead times if buffer stocks are eliminated, so that the company must wait for the full duration of supplier lead times before it can begin production.
- A supplier begins offering just-in-time daily parts deliveries. The system can be modeled to see what happens to the company's quoted production lead times if the lead times associated with purchased parts are eliminated. This modeling can lead to the transfer of other purchased items to the supplier, if these other items currently require lengthy purchasing lead times.

In short, an MRP modeling system can be an excellent tool for making adjustments to a variety of inputs to the materials management process.

Inventory Management by Classification

From an efficiency perspective, it may be possible to assign safety stock levels and replenishment methods to groups of inventory items. For example, fittings and fasteners can be designated to have a large safety stock level, since excess inventory in this area represents quite an inexpensive investment. Also, all fittings and fasteners can be designated to be replenished through a two-bin visual review process, thereby keeping these high-volume, low-cost items out of the inventory database and away from cycle counters. This aggregation concept works best when the computer system contains the following features:

- All inventory items can be assigned an inventory classification
- Safety stock levels can be assigned by inventory classification
- Any change to an inventory classification is automatically assigned to all of the inventory items linked to that classification

If these features are present, it is much easier to update service levels for large blocks of the inventory with just a few keystrokes.

Here are several variations on how inventory management by classification might be used to improve materials management:

- *Channel focused.* Management might decide that stockout conditions are more permissible for certain sales channels, such as an Internet store, than in other channels, such as retail stores. If so, and the items sold are different by channel or stored separately by channel, consider creating inventory classifications by sales channel.
- *Life cycle focused.* If products have just been released, they might be assigned to a separate inventory classification that requires a larger safety stock, in expectation of a sales surge. Conversely, late-life products could be switched to a different classification that allows for minimal reserve stocks, in the expectation that they will be terminated in the not-too-distant future.
- *Replenishment focused.* Certain items may be replenished in different ways, such as through a supplier-managed inventory system, a material requirements planning system, or the visual inspection of quantities on hand. Each one requires different flags to be set in the inventory management system, which can be most efficiently handled by linking them to separate inventory classifications and setting the flags through the designated classification.

Only those inventory items that will remain within an inventory classification for a reasonable period of time should be assigned to a classification. If an item were to be constantly moved between classifications, there would be little point in utilizing the classification system, since the whole point of using it is to reduce the manual labor of adjusting inventory settings.

Product Substitution Options

An interesting planning consideration is to set up product alternatives in the order taking system. When a customer places an order for an item that is not currently in stock, the system presents them with the substitute products as well as the original item that they want to order. By doing so, the company is more likely to retain customers and gain immediate sales, rather than losing customers to competitors. This approach also works well when the company is trying to eliminate slow-moving items from stock, and presents them as low-priced alternatives to customers.

To make a product substitution system work, it is necessary to set up in the item master file a linkage to other products that are closely related. The system must then pull up these items for presentation only if they are currently in stock; otherwise, the customer is merely being presented with multiple ordering options that will all result in backorders.

The main downside to using a product substitution system is that the proportion of customer orders that are returned for a refund may increase, since customers are ordering items that do not quite match their original expectations. Also, extra effort must be put into maintaining a linked set of products in the item master file.

Supplier Lead Time Adjustment

A key part of the grief experienced by the materials management staff is dealing with the ordering lead times required by suppliers. If a long lead time is required, the staff must plan well in advance for the production of goods that incorporate these components. An equally unpalatable option is to maintain a reserve of components on-site, thereby avoiding the lead time issue but requiring a large investment in inventory.

A concept that is rarely explored is the relevance of the lead times quoted by suppliers. In some cases, a supplier may be quoting a long lead time that has been used traditionally, but which has little basis in fact. There may instead be a considerably shorter actual lead time underlying the date range being quoted by a supplier's sales staff. When entering into a relationship with a new supplier, it can be useful to forcefully point out the company's need for a short lead time, so that it can maintain minimal buffer inventory and also quote short lead times to its own customers. This immediate emphasis on lead times may cause some suppliers to take themselves out of consideration, leaving only those suppliers capable of delivering on short notice. The same concept can be applied to existing suppliers, and may result in some turnover among those suppliers unwilling or unable to deliver within a short period of time.

> **Tip:** Issue purchase orders with very specific delivery dates and times, to focus attention on lead times. Also, create report cards for suppliers that emphasize their ability to deliver by designated dates, and make sure that the suppliers see these report cards.

Internal Lead Time Adjustment

When a company maintains safety stock, the intent is to protect the company against a stockout condition during the interval when a replenishment order is routed to a supplier and goods are delivered back to the company. What is rarely considered is the first part of that interval, when a replenishment order is routed to a supplier. If a company takes an inordinate amount of time to create and deliver a purchase notification, the company is paying for the delay by having to increase the amount of safety stock that it maintains. If a way can be found to reduce the time required to create and deliver a purchase notification, the amount of safety stock needed to guard against a stockout can be reduced. Here are several examples of ways to compress internal lead time:

- If an MRP system is used, allow the system to automatically issue replenishment orders directly to suppliers, or at most with a brief order review by a purchasing staff person.
- If a just-in-time "pull" system is used, use kanbans to automatically order goods from suppliers without manual purchasing intervention.
- If purchase orders are manually issued for each materials requisition, consider allowing purchase order issuance without supervisory overviews and approvals, to eliminate queue time.

- If purchase orders are mailed to suppliers, consider e-mailing them instead, perhaps with a hard-copy document following at a more leisurely pace.
- If materials requisitions are manually created, use a workflow management system to track the progress of orders through the purchasing department, so that someone can expedite any orders that appear to be delayed.

It is useful to formally track the time required to place orders, on the theory that anything being measured will be improved upon. Even if the result is a general decline in internal lead time, continue to pay attention to outlier requisitions that are delayed. All it takes is a delay in the ordering of a single item to halt a production order, and trigger renewed calls for more safety stock to guard against such lapses.

Job Releases to Production

A key factor in the ability of a business to produce goods within a short period of time, as well as to minimize its investment in work-in-process inventory, is to tightly control the release of new jobs into the production process. If this activity is handled in a non-controlled manner, too many jobs will likely be resident in the production area, which causes the following problems:

- There is an excessive investment in work-in-process inventory.
- The excess amount of inventory clutters the production area, making it more difficult to process jobs, and increasing the risk of damage to goods stored on the production floor.
- The production staff is uncertain about which job to process next, so that some jobs are delayed beyond customer expectations.
- Inventory record accuracy declines, because of the extra transactions required to track goods on the shop floor.
- Parts may be taken from one job kit in order to complete a different order, so the cannibalized jobs remain in the shop area longer, until they can be rekitted.
- There is a greater risk of theft

All of the preceding issues are eliminated by reducing the number of job releases to exactly match the ability of the production area to process the work. By doing so, there is a smoother production flow that results in a reduced period of time to complete the manufacturing process. This can translate into a short lead time that can be quoted to customers, which may result in more customer orders.

Store Finished Goods at Pre-Configuration Level

A common complaint of the sales department is that a company is not offering its goods in a sufficient number of product variations to maximize sales. If company management accedes to this demand and stocks all possible product variations, it will soon find that the investment in finished goods inventory has ballooned. Also, some variations will not be purchased in much volume, resulting in an increase in the reserve for obsolete inventory. A common reaction to this situation is a sharp cutback in the number of product variations kept in stock. However, there is an alternative that can be used to continue offering a full range of products, without investing in too much inventory.

This alternative is to only manufacture and store goods at a level of sub-assembly that can be converted into several different final product configurations. For example:

- Manufacture cell phones without the phone shell, and add shells with different colors only after customers place orders for specific colors.
- Manufacture lawn mowers without the engine, and add the engine only after customers order a specific engine configuration.
- Manufacture furniture without the final stain or paint color, and add this last step after the receipt of customer orders specifying their desired stains or colors.

It is likely that a company capable of following this approach will be able to store far fewer "finished" goods, while also minimizing the risk of incurring obsolete inventory write-offs. However, a downside is that deliveries to customers may be delayed for a short time, while a sub-assembly is configured for final delivery.

Tip: If it is important to offer immediate delivery to customers, consider maintaining a small supply of fully-configured goods in stock, and re-filling this small buffer from sub-assemblies. A variation on the concept is to charge a higher price for goods that ship immediately (from the fully-configured stock) and a lower price if customers are willing to wait for goods to be assembled from the sub-assembly stock.

The pre-configuration approach requires the deep involvement of the engineering staff, which must design product families to be adjustable as a final production step. Since it may require an entire product development cycle to implement the use of pre-configurations, expect several years to pass before it can be fully implemented.

Cost-Effective Inventory Reduction

The management team may conclude that the company is investing too much working capital in inventory, and issues a directive to the materials management staff to find a way to shrink this investment. Doing so in a prudent manner requires the examination of the characteristics of a great many inventory items, which can overwhelm the staff. There are simply too many inventory items to analyze.

A good way to engage in an inventory reduction effort in a cost-effective manner is to immediately eliminate from consideration all slow-moving inventory items. Since these items do not turn over very frequently, any steps taken to gradually shrink their unit counts will take a long time to show results. Also, the vast majority of all inventory items are relatively slow movers, so avoiding these items automatically concentrates the analysis on just a small number of high-turnover items. If steps are taken to reduce the on-hand quantity of high-turnover items, the initiative will show results almost immediately. Also, since the analysis now encompasses only a small number of items, the materials management staff can engage in a great deal of fine-tuning to minimize inventory levels without expending too much time on the effort. In short, a focus on high-turnover items can generate a rapid inventory reduction without the expenditure of an excessive amount of effort.

Reduction of Inventory Returns

When a business operates in the consumer goods marketplace, a high proportion of goods are returned at a later date. These items may be returned so late that they are no longer in season, or the goods are damaged and so cannot be sold at full price. The extent of these returns can be so massive that they cut deeply into the profits of a business. Here are several suggestions for reducing the amount of these returns:

- *Customers pay the freight.* Though competitive pressures may not allow for it, consider requiring customers to pay the cost of freight if they want to return goods to the company. This may prevent them from engaging in such behavior as ordering three sizes of an article of clothing in order to bracket their estimated size, and then returning two of the three items.
- *Revise size charts.* If there is a pattern of returns associated with the size chart supplied by a vendor, alter the size chart to more realistically portray the sizes being created by the vendor.
- *Avoid marketing mismatches.* If a customer has already bought items from the company, this represents a history of both purchases *and* returns. This information should be tracked. If certain sizes, colors, or brands have been returned in the past, alter the marketing materials sent to that person to not include these items. This would be easiest for e-mail distributions, where marketing campaigns can be tailored to the individual.
- *Track serial returners.* If certain customers return an inordinate amount of goods, stop all marketing to them. It may even be necessary to stop taking orders from them, or to refuse their attempts to return goods.
- *Monitor size returns by regions.* Customers in some geographic regions may have a propensity to buy smaller or larger sizes and then return them. If so, consider altering the store stocking levels for these regions to more closely align sizes with the sizing needs of shoppers in those areas.

The tracking requirements suggested for the last three items are extremely detailed, requiring expensive software to monitor customer returns. Nonetheless, these systems can pay for themselves by reducing returns by even a fraction of one percent, given the severity of the losses associated with returns.

Consigned Inventory

Inventory is consigned when the manufacturer of goods allows retailers or wholesalers to maintain physical control over the goods. Consignment arrangements are almost always restricted to finished goods. This type of arrangement may be required by the manufacturer, which wants to retain title to the goods, thereby making it easier to repossess the goods if the party maintaining physical possession goes out of business. The arrangement is especially common when the holder of the goods has such poor credit risk that it cannot be relied upon to purchase the goods outright. This arrangement may also be a desirable one for the retailer or wholesaler, which does not have to pay the manufacturer until such time as cash has been received from a third party buyer. However, these advantages may be obliterated if a consignment arrangement is not properly managed. Take the following steps to enhance the consignment experience:

- *Perfected interest.* The manufacturer creates a security agreement between the inventory holder and manufacturer that states the rights of each party in regard to the asset. The manufacturer then files a UCC-1 financing statement with the required government office (usually the secretary of state) to publicly reveal the presence of a lien on the asset. Doing so gives the manufacturer seniority over other creditors who might also file liens against the asset at a later date; this is known as *perfecting* the lien. The manufacturer should have a procedure in place to terminate each security agreement as the underlying assets are paid by their purchasers. There should also be a standard practice in place for how assets are to be repossessed under a security agreement. The most efficient approach from the manufacturer's perspective is to notify the buyer and reach a mutual agreement for the manufacturer to retrieve the goods. The manufacturer is also entitled to repossess goods without the cooperation of the inventory holder, as long as the manufacturer does not illegally break into any structures while doing so, or cause a public disturbance.

> **Tip:** The UCC-1 financing statement will expire after five years. Track all unexpired financing statements to see which ones will expire soon, to ensure that all related payments have been received from inventory holders, or to file continuation statements to extend the liens.

- *Linked systems.* The manufacturer can use a consignment arrangement to learn about sales at the retail and distributor level as soon as they occur. This can be done by using the excuse of inventory ownership to demand access into the sales databases of retailers and distributors. At a further level of systems integration, the manufacturer can use this information to automatically ship replacement goods when inventory is sold to third parties.
- *Manual systems.* A consignment arrangement may be an excessively burdensome and error-prone system when transactions are manual. In this situation, the materials management and accounting departments must use home-grown systems to monitor shipments to consignees, the subsequent sales of these goods to third parties, and the remittance of collected funds back to the company, along with deductions for consignee commissions. It is entirely possible that the incremental profit to be gained from these arrangements is less than the incremental cost of the staff needed to handle the transactions.

Consequently, see if some interlinked systems can be developed between the company and the consignees to streamline the inventory tracking process.

- *Powerful customers.* A powerful retailer or distributor may insist on a consignment arrangement under the guise of a long-term payment arrangement. For example, a lengthy payment period, coupled with an unlimited right to return unsold goods is essentially a consignment arrangement, but without the benefit of formal inventory ownership by the manufacturer. In this case, the manufacturer has no right to take back its inventory, and so bears the risk of counterparty failure. A manufacturer in a weak position may be unable to alter these terms. However, if the comparative power of the two parties is more equal, the manufacturer should strongly consider negotiating the use of a formal consignment arrangement.

Elevate the Materials Manager Position

When it comes to the management of inventory, there are a number of parties within a business that have conflicting interests in regard to the most appropriate inventory levels to maintain. The following table notes the various conflicts:

Opinions Regarding Inventory Levels, by Position

Position	Opinion	Reason
Chief financial officer	Reduce inventory	Wants to reduce the investment in working capital, as well as to avoid any obsolete inventory write-offs
Production manager	Increase inventory	Wants enough raw materials on hand to support the production schedule
Purchasing manager	Increase inventory	Wants to take advantage of volume purchase opportunities, which also reduces the number of individual purchase transactions
Sales manager	Increase inventory	Wants lots of finished goods to fulfill orders promptly, as well as many product models to satisfy the full range of customer needs
Warehouse manager	Reduce inventory	Wants to keep the warehouse from becoming cluttered with excess inventory

Given the large number of positions and perfectly valid reasons for pulling the inventory investment in different directions, it makes sense to assign overall responsibility to a single position. That position is the vice president of materials management, which is tasked with consolidating the various needs of the company into a consistent set of inventory policies. We suggest the following enhancements to the position to ensure that it has full control over inventory:

- The position reports directly to the chief operating officer, in order to keep it independent of the opinions of the chief financial officer, which might otherwise lead to excessive inventory reductions.

- The position should be entirely independent of the sales manager, thereby avoiding any undue influence to increase inventory levels.
- The position directly supervises the purchasing manager, to ensure that appropriate purchasing policies are followed.
- The position directly supervises the warehouse manager, picking operations, shipping, receiving, and materials handling, to ensure that materials storage and movement policies are followed.

These recommendations mean that the vice president of materials management will be on the "hot seat" when there are inventory stockouts or overages, but such grief goes hand-in-hand with any management position. The main point is to ensure that one person can balance the conflicting needs of a business when deciding upon the most appropriate inventory levels to maintain, even if doing so occasionally results in sub-optimal outcomes.

Summary

Managing materials based on a forecast is a losing proposition, since actual sales will always vary from expected amounts. In this chapter, we have noted repeatedly that the compression of lead times is an excellent way to mitigate this problem, since a shorter-term forecast is an inherently more accurate one. This calls for an ongoing and detailed review of the time required to order raw materials, receive goods, schedule production jobs, and manufacture goods. If time can be stripped from any or all of these activities, the forecasting horizon can be shortened, leading to a much easier life for the materials management staff.

In addition, we must strongly emphasize the need to minimize the number of production jobs released onto the shop floor. Too many jobs concurrently running leads to excess work-in-process inventory, the expediting of jobs, and general confusion. Minimizing job releases may require a strong constitution, for there will be pressure to initiate jobs as soon as possible, in the false hope that an earlier start date will lead to an earlier completion date, and therefore an earlier ship date to an anxious customer.

Chapter 5
Purchasing Activities

Introduction

The purchasing department does not just buy goods on behalf of the rest of the company. On the contrary, the manner in which it conducts purchasing activities, its methods for evaluating suppliers, and the motivational systems used all have a profound impact upon the amount of inventory kept in storage and the prices at which it is purchased.

In this chapter, we address several methods for examining potential suppliers, including total cost, product availability, quality, and other concepts. We then move on to several systems under which goods are purchased, such as manual and system-based, before noting a number of techniques for improving upon these systems, such as streamlining purchase approvals and matching contract lengths to pricing trends. We then finish with discussions of supplier delivery arrangements that can reduce the ongoing inventory investment, supplier measurement systems, and the impact of variance analysis on inventory purchases.

Total Supplier Cost

When evaluating whether a company should deal with a supplier, it is useful to view the situation in terms of the total cost of the supplier. Much more than the quoted cost per unit is involved in the total cost concept. Other costs that may arise include the following:

- *Unit cost*. This is the quoted price for goods or services. This amount should be adjusted for any full-year expected discounts from volume purchasing arrangements, or other types of discounts.
- *Freight in*. This is the charged cost of freight to ship goods from the supplier to the company. If the company uses its own freight service, then reduce the cost of freight by the projected amount of any volume discounts.
- *Duties*. There may be customs duties associated with imported goods.
- *Setup fees*. If the supplier has to acquire molds or tooling in order to produce goods for the company, it may charge an up-front fee for these items, which should be amortized over the projected number of units to be purchased.
- *Hedging*. If goods must be purchased in a foreign currency, it may be necessary to enter into a hedging transaction to offset any possible changes in the exchange rate before the company issues payment. The cost of the hedge should be included in the total cost.
- *Holding costs*. Once goods have been acquired, the company may hold them in stock for a long period of time. If so, include the interest cost of the funds

used to buy the inventory, as well as any projected costs for obsolescence, shrinkage, and damage to the inventory.

Of the costs just noted, pay particular attention to the cost of freight. Many organizations have been lured by low labor costs to shift some or all of their production overseas; as energy costs have risen, this means that the cost of the freight needed to shift those goods to the company's customers will likely follow an ascending cost trend. Consequently, it is useful to continually re-evaluate the distance of suppliers from the company's core markets.

If there are large setup fees involved in a purchase, consider modeling the fixed and variable cost components of the purchase to determine at what unit volume the average cost per unit of a pricing option becomes favorable. A hefty up-front charge may translate into a large purchase volume before a purchase from a particular supplier makes sense.

EXAMPLE

The purchasing department of Entwhistle Electric is considering the purchase of a plastic battery casing from two suppliers. Regional Plastics is quoting a straight $0.50 per case, which incorporates all costs associated with setting up the production run. Mountain Plastics is quoting $0.35 per case, plus an initial $2,000 setup charge. There is a $0.15 difference between the per-unit costs in these quotes. If Entwhistle were to accept the Mountain Plastics quote, it would require a purchase quantity of 13,333 units to bring the average cost per unit down to the price charged by Regional Plastics (calculated as $2,000 fixed charge ÷ $0.15 per unit). Thus, the company should order from Regional if the anticipated quantity is less than 13,333 units, and order from Mountain if the order size is larger.

Materials Sourcing Considerations

One of the greatest failings of materials sourcing is to only buy materials based on the lowest cost. There are many other considerations that are of much greater importance than cost. Consider the following:

- *Availability*. A supplier must be able to provide goods in a timely manner. If not, the buyer cannot properly schedule them into its own production processes. Needless to say, promises to customers may be severely impacted. This problem is most common among those suppliers that pare away their internal support staffs in order to offer the lowest possible prices to their customers. Availability is a massive concern when the materials are only available from a small number of suppliers, and the overall supply of goods is constrained. In this case, it pays to use the highest-availability supplier, rather than the lowest-cost one.

- *Capacity*. Does the supplier have the production capacity available to meet the buyer's requirements? In some cases, the buyer is not the supplier's highest priority, and so is only allocated a small amount of capacity once the needs of more important customers are met. In other cases, a supplier's capacity is maxed out, and so must put all customer orders on an allocation basis. In this situation, the best supplier may be the one that charges the highest price, but which can effortlessly provide large unit volumes on short notice.

- *Delivery*. If the company requires that materials be delivered within a specific time slot on a certain day, the supplier must be able to meet that requirement on a consistent basis. If not, the result is likely to be an inoperable production schedule. Alternatively, if the buyer is simply routing orders forward to customers with a cross-docking system, a delayed delivery will delay shipments to customers. This issue can arise from the supplier location – a long transport distance from a low-cost supplier in another country is nearly guaranteed to eventually result in a delayed delivery. In many cases, a strong emphasis on reliable delivery times may mandate that suppliers all be based near the company's production and/or distribution facilities. If so, the cost of materials is a lesser consideration.

- *Quality*. A supplier's goods must meet the buyer's specifications. This means that all specifications, such as for product dimensions, appearance, and material content, be met with such reliability that there is essentially no point in inspecting the goods at the receiving dock. If a supplier cannot meet this standard, being the low-cost provider is nearly an afterthought. Indeed, suppliers with the best product quality are in such high demand that they can routinely charge much higher prices than their counterparts – and buyers are willing to pay the price.

If price is the key consideration, many companies look to foreign suppliers, which have access to such low labor costs that they can routinely underbid domestic suppliers. However, a low-cost international supplier may not be the best alternative. If a foreign supplier demands payment in a local currency, the buyer is at risk of an unfavorable swing in foreign exchange rates. If the buyer does not want to incur this risk, then it must buy a foreign exchange hedge, which increases the cost of the overall transaction. In addition, the buyer may have to pay additional administrative costs to monitor the transaction, as well as customs duties. Consequently, it is useful to examine the all-in cost of international transactions before engaging the services of a supplier in another country.

There are situations where being the low-cost provider of goods is still the most important consideration for end users. This situation typically arises for a subset of customers that are willing to tolerate late delivery times and uneven product quality in exchange for rock-bottom prices. However, a much larger proportion of customers, comprising the majority of almost any market, have a higher regard for the other factors noted here, and so are willing to accept higher price points.

Manual Purchasing

The traditional purchasing method is where purchases are only made in response to specific requests made by other parts of a company. If someone needs to acquire goods or services, they let the purchasing staff do so on their behalf. A highly compressed version of the normal process flow is:

1. The person needing to acquire something fills out a purchase requisition, has the department manager approve it, and forwards the document to the purchasing department.
2. The purchasing staff investigates pricing for the item, initiates a bidding process if the item is sufficiently expensive, and then issues a signed purchase order.

Even this shortened version of the process requires a painful amount of labor; it can take hours to issue a single purchase order. To mitigate the effects of this manual process flow, several workarounds have been adopted. One is to allow the use of purchasing cards (i.e., credit cards) for smaller purchases, thereby keeping the purchasing staff away from small-dollar purchases. Another option is the master purchase order, where a large quantity is authorized with a single purchase order, and then releases are issued against the master purchase order whenever goods are needed. This combination of workarounds makes the demand-based system reasonably tolerable for the purchase of non-inventory items. However, the system is still inefficient and prone to error when used for repetitive purchases, as are needed for inventory acquisition. The following systems-based purchasing concept provides a better solution.

Systems-Based Purchasing

In a systems-based purchasing environment, there is a process in place that automatically generates a purchase notification. The notification can be produced in one of two ways, which are as follows:

- *Material requirements planning (MRP)*. There is a production schedule that runs on MRP software. The software explodes the planned production into its constituent raw materials to determine which items are needed as input to the planned production run. The system then compares these requirements to on-hand inventory to determine which items need to be ordered. Finally, the system incorporates estimates of supplier lead times to determine when required items should be ordered. The system can even issue electronic purchase orders straight to suppliers, or the purchasing staff can act as an intermediary, printing and reviewing proposed purchase orders and forwarding them to suppliers.
- *Kanban*. There is a manual notification system called a kanban that indicates a purchase is needed when a bin is emptied or reaches a certain on-hand balance. When this happens, a notification is sent to a supplier, triggering a pre-authorized order for a certain amount of replacement goods. This is an inherently manual process that does not require a computer system, but can use one to speed up the flow of information to suppliers.

In both cases, there may be master purchase orders that are used to settle the prices at which goods are being purchased, with each subsequent purchase notification being a release against a master purchase order.

These systems-based purchasing methods are far superior to manual purchasing, since there is a high probability that inventory will be requisitioned in a timely manner, and because the amount of paperwork required is vastly reduced. It can take a large amount of both up-front and ongoing effort to set up systems-based purchasing, but the enhanced efficiency of the resulting system is well worth the effort.

Spend Management

The preceding manual and systems-based purchasing methods form the basis for purchasing activities. Once these systems are in place, spend management can be used to pare back on the cost of purchased goods and services. Spend management involves the aggregation of information about a company's expenditures into a database, which can then be sorted in a variety of ways to uncover opportunities for cost reductions, primarily through the concentration of purchases with a smaller number of suppliers.

The spend management database lies at the center of the spend management system. Information from the company's purchasing departments in all of its subsidiaries is pulled into the database. Once the information is assembled, it must be cleaned up with the following techniques:

- *Name linkages.* It is extremely likely that each subsidiary uses a different supplier identification code for its suppliers, so the aggregated data probably contains information about purchases from a single supplier that are listed under several different names. A table must be constructed for the database that links all of these name variations to a single supplier name. Thus, purchases from ATT, AT&T, and AT&TWIRELESS would all be linked to the same phone company.

- *Description linkages.* As was the case for supplier names, the descriptions of items purchased may vary wildly from each other at the subsidiary level, and so must be standardized in the spend database. To do so, have the suppliers always load the official supplier part number for each item into their purchasing software, so that this can be ported into the spend database. Then attach a file to the database that contains all supplier part numbers and part descriptions. Once supplier part numbers are identified in the data feeds from subsidiaries, they can be linked to the supplier descriptions.

- *Commodity code linkages.* Every purchase made should have attached to it a standard commodity code, which assigns a spend category to the purchase. This information is useful for aggregating purchases by commodity type, which can then be used to concentrate purchases with preferred suppliers for volume discounts. It is best to have all subsidiaries record purchases using the same standard commodity code system, such as the North American Industry Classification System (NAICS). If commodity codes are not being entered, then there should be a feedback loop to the subsidiary purchasing departments to remind them to do so.

- *Credit rating linkages.* The database should include a data feed from a third party credit rating service, which contains the credit rating for each supplier. This information is useful for determining which suppliers may be in financial difficulty, so that spending can be shifted to more reliable suppliers.

A spend database can be enormous, which means that all of the preceding data cleansing and enhancement activities must be performed through automated routines. It is not even remotely cost-effective to engage in these activities manually.

> **Tip:** Have the company's purchasing staff review the information resulting from the various automated routines just described, and recommend additional automated routines to further clean up the information.

Once information has been fully aggregated into the spend database, sort the information by commodity code to determine spend levels for all of the various types of commodities. The resulting reports can be used to drive down costs by any of the following means:

- *Consolidate suppliers.* While each subsidiary may proudly point out that it has already consolidated its supplier base, each one may have consolidated around a different group of suppliers. The database can reveal that the subsidiaries have few suppliers in common at the commodity code level, which represents an opportunity for *all* of the subsidiaries to consolidate their purchases with the same group of suppliers. The net result can be a remarkable decline in the overall number of suppliers from which purchases are made. For example, if there are five subsidiaries and each one purchases from five suppliers, of which only 20% are commonly used by all subsidiaries, this means a total of 20 suppliers could potentially be stripped away from a pool of 25 suppliers, which is an 80% reduction.
- *Source through distributors.* The spend report may reveal that the company is spending a relatively small amount with a large number of suppliers in certain commodity code categories. When this is the case, the easiest solution may be to locate a single distributor through which all of the items can be purchased. The result could be a massive reduction in the number of suppliers, which reduces the administrative and accounting burden of the purchasing and accounting departments.

It can take a long time to gradually work through the information provided by a spend database, shifting purchases to a smaller and smaller pool of suppliers. Over time, the categories of unaddressed commodity codes will shrink, in which case the emphasis should always be on the next largest remaining spend by commodity code. It is possible that the lowest-spend commodity codes will never be addressed, because the potential savings are so small that they are not worth investigating.

Once purchases have been shifted to a small group of preferred suppliers, the company must ensure that it is obtaining the full amount of volume discounts from these suppliers. Accordingly, monitor the amount spent with each supplier and compare the aggregate spend with the contractual trigger points at which volume discounts will be achieved. The company should remind suppliers whenever volume discounts have been earned.

This level of spend analysis is made easier if the database contains a listing of the trigger points at which volume discounts and other rebates will be earned, by supplier. This listing is essentially a summarization of the key elements of each supplier contract. The primary data items to include in the listing for discount tracking purposes are:

- Contract start and stop dates
- Discount thresholds and amount of discounts
- Rebate thresholds and amount of rebates

When this contract information is matched against the spend database, you may find that suppliers are not following the terms of their own contracts, and that the company is entitled to volume discounts right now, before any supplier consolidation activities have commenced. Consequently, matching contract terms against the spend database should be one of the earlier activities to engage in, once the database has been created.

The construction of a spend management system is one of the more expensive database projects that a company can engage in. To accelerate the payback period, consider the following ways in which to roll out the system:

- Initially include in the database the purchasing information for just the largest subsidiaries. Doing so accumulates the bulk of the information needed for the database, without wasting an undue amount of time creating interfaces to the smaller purchasing systems.
- Estimate which commodity codes comprise most of the company's spending activity, and focus all of the data cleanup efforts on purchases within these codes. Doing so allows you to take more immediate action to engage in volume purchasing in these areas.

These actions should yield relatively rapid results, which may encourage management to provide additional funding for a more complete rollout of the system.

The Volume Purchase Discount Conundrum

A long-running goal of the purchasing department is to offer suppliers a sufficient amount of volume to warrant the granting of volume purchase discounts. These savings can be significant, and can contribute to a spike in earnings. However, the downside of volume discounts is that the company is committing to a large purchase volume – a volume that it may not need, based on future changes in its sales. Consequently, the production staff must be able to recognize situations where the discount should be pursued, and when it should not. Here are several scenarios to consider:

- *Min-max delivery range.* If the company projects a continuing need for large volumes of an item over an extended period of time, it can safely commit to a large purchase volume. To make the promised order quantities fit within its production schedule while still qualifying for the discount, enter into a min-max agreement with the supplier. This means that the company will maintain a certain range of production volume that will mandate deliveries from the supplier within a minimum and maximum unit range. By making this arrangement, the supplier can tailor its own production processes to manufacture goods at sufficiently high volume levels to still earn it a profit within the indicated volume range.

- *Contract-based purchases.* If the company is relying on a contract with a large customer as the justification for a volume purchase discount, only negotiate the discount for the volume of purchases indicated by the current contract. It can be exceedingly dangerous to commit to a larger quantity in expectation of a contract renewal, which may not happen. An alternative is to make a supplier aware of the situation, and then negotiate for a lower volume discount based on the current contract and a higher discount if the company gains a renewal of the contract.

- *Expanded purchases.* It may be possible to obtain a volume discount by committing to a broad range of purchases, rather than to the purchase of just one or two specific items. It is much more likely that a company can follow through on a commitment of this type, as opposed to being forced to buy large quantities of just a few items for which demand has declined.

> **Tip:** The expanded purchases concept can be broadened to include the purchases of other company subsidiaries. See the Spend Management section for more information.

- *After-the-fact discounts.* If the company cannot make a binding commitment to a specific purchasing volume, an alternative is to wait until the end of the annual measurement period, and retroactively calculate the volume discount based on whatever the volume turned out to be. This may not yield as large a discount, since the supplier cannot rely upon steady demand from the company through the contract period.

The Auction Option

In most cases, a company certainly wants to buy from suppliers with which it has developed in-depth relationships, since doing so yields the best mix of delivery times, product quality, and price. However, there are a few situations in which a business is looking for commodity parts that are available from a number of suppliers. If so, a possible option is to post the company's requirements on an Internet auction site, and let participating suppliers bid on the proposal. The result can be a notably lower price than the purchasing department can obtain from its normal stable of suppliers.

While costs can be lowered by using auction sites, these sites must be used with care, for the following reasons:

- *Delivery times.* A delivery of goods by the winning bidder may not be as timely as a delivery from a long-term supplier that understands the company's receiving requirements.
- *Quality.* If parts have unusually tight specifications, an auction is not the best place to source them. The delivery of out-of-spec parts might terminate a scheduled production run.
- *Supply chain systems.* A company may have tied its regular supply chain members into a closely-integrated information system that relays purchasing needs back to the various suppliers. This system is not available to bidders on an auction site. Instead, the purchasing staff must take a more direct interest in forwarding information about purchasing needs, which is labor-intensive.

In brief, auction systems are useful from a cost-reduction standpoint, but a company should not attempt to construct a supplier base around these systems. Instead, auction-based purchases should be carefully defined only for specific parts that are commoditized and which have no special delivery or customization requirements.

Match Contract Length to Pricing Trends

If there is a long-term downward trend in the price of a particular commodity, expect suppliers to offer longer-term contracts, which allows them to garner larger profits over time as the company is locked into a fixed price while their costs decline. In such cases, it is better to steer clear of these offers. Alternatively, if there is a long-term upward trend in the price of a commodity, attempt to lock in the longest-term pricing arrangement possible. However, doing so may put a supplier at risk of becoming unprofitable, so consider including a cost-sharing clause in the contract that allows the supplier to continue to be financially viable.

It is more important to maintain a mutually profitable, long-term arrangement with suppliers than to reduce their profits with clever anticipation of pricing trends. Nonetheless, this is an area to consider when devising ways to reduce the cost of inventory.

Streamlined Purchasing Approvals

A company may have a number of different ways in which it purchases goods and services, ranging from the petty cash system to the multi-tiered approval process for fixed asset purchases. These systems are all designed to ensure that a business maintains a proper level of control over its assets. Unfortunately, a detailed review of every inventory purchase hopelessly slows down the buying process. A slower purchasing process means that more safety stock must be kept on site, to guard against the approval delays of the purchasing department.

The obvious solution is to remove all approvals from the inventory purchasing process, and to rely upon the underlying materials management system to issue notifications to suppliers whenever it is necessary to acquire more goods. However, the need for more control is one that dies hard, especially when there are isolated circumstances where the system fails and goods are purchased by mistake. A reasonable approach that deals with this reaction is to re-task the purchasing department away from the laborious creation of an individual signed purchase order for each purchase, and toward a new role of monitoring the purchasing system.

The purchasing staff can use either a reactive or proactive approach to its monitoring of purchases. In reactive mode, the department looks for clear instances of purchasing errors, where the system triggered a purchasing transaction (or not) that yielded an incorrect inventory balance. For example, the use of an incorrect unit of measure results in the purchase of several pallets of goods, when only individual units were needed. Or, there is a stockout condition for an item because the automatic reorder flag was not set in the item master file for that item. In both cases, there is a clear problem that is readily apparent, and which the purchasing staff can investigate and correct. This is the easiest way to monitor purchases, though the downside is that problems have already occurred.

The most effective method for monitoring purchases is to do so in a proactive mode, before the system has generated any actual problems. This is a more difficult approach, since the staff must hunt for potential errors amidst a sea of perfectly normal transactions. Here are several ways to engage in proactive monitoring:

- *Pause automated orders prior to release*. This gives the purchasing staff a brief window to scan through the orders before they are released to suppliers.
- *Flag out-of-bounds orders*. If an order is for an unusually large dollar or unit amount, the system flags these items for manual review.
- *Flag return and shortage transactions*. If parts are returned to the warehouse from the production area, or additional units are requested, these are indicative of incorrect bill of material records, and so should be investigated.
- *Flag work stoppage transactions*. If production cannot begin due to a missing part, this indicates a flaw in the ordering system, probably due to a part not being included in a bill of materials, or an item master record not being set for automatic reordering.

In essence, a streamlined purchasing approval system is one that focuses on how well the automated purchasing system is functioning, keeping a light touch on the flow of transactions to highlight unusual transactions that may require a more in-depth investigation. This is an effective use of the purchasing staff's time, and also allows for the rapid ordering of goods.

Purchase Order Shutdowns

There are many instances where subsequent events show that existing purchase orders are no longer needed. For example, a production schedule may be changed because a customer withdrew its order, or because the absence of some other raw material forced the cancellation of a production job. Another strong possibility is that an error in the inventory records is corrected, revealing that the company has more stock on hand than it realized, and no longer needs a replenishment order. There may also be situations where only part of an order was fulfilled by a supplier, leaving a residual authorized balance still sitting on a purchase order. In these situations, the company has authorized the delivery of more goods, but no longer needs them. The purchasing department should have a system for detecting these purchase orders, so that it can terminate them before the company accepts more inventory than it needs.

A good way to detect unwanted purchase orders is available to a business that uses a material requirements planning (MRP) system. The system can be configured to run a daily report that matches the following items:

- The amount of materials required, based on an explosion of the current production plan, and netted against on-hand and un-allocated inventory; and
- The amount of materials ordered and not yet delivered on currently open purchase orders.

If there are more goods arriving due to open purchase orders than are needed, the disparity represents opportunities to shut down or modify the underlying purchase orders, resulting in less unneeded inventory. This report can also be used in reverse, to see if there are any items needed for which there are insufficient goods on order. Thus, the purchasing staff can use this report as a control, to ensure that the MRP system is placing orders as intended.

Supplier Delivery Arrangements

The traditional delivery arrangement with a supplier is a simple one – the buyer issues a purchase order to have goods delivered, and the exact amount stated in the purchase order is delivered. While simple, this approach does not minimize the amount of on-hand inventory for the buyer, nor does it minimize the amount of purchasing paperwork. In this section, we present several alternatives that may be more palatable from the perspectives of pricing, inventory investment, and administrative hassle. The alternatives are:

- *Split deliveries*. If the buyer knows that it will buy a certain quantity of goods over an extended period of time (such as a year), it can negotiate for a volume discount with a supplier and demand that the goods be delivered only as needed. The supplier is willing to accept this split delivery schedule, since it will eventually earn a large amount of sales during the period covered by the agreement. The buyer benefits from only having to pay for inventory as it is needed, and also can operate from a single purchase order and a series of release notifications that are tied to the purchase order. The main risk to the buyer is that it will not need the full quantity to which it committed. If this is the case, the buyer will need to issue a termination or penalty payment to the supplier.
- *Phased deliveries*. In cases where the buyer is not interested in obtaining a long-term price reduction in exchange for a commitment to buy a large

quantity of goods, it may still be possible to break a normal purchase into several deliveries, thereby delaying payment on at least a portion of the ordered goods. This approach is most amenable to a supplier when it is already making an ongoing series of deliveries to the buyer, and so does not incur any additional incremental cost for delivering an order in several parts. This concept works best with suppliers that have been working with the buyer for some time, and so are heavily involved in the just-in-time delivery concept already.

- *Just-in-time deliveries.* A company's production system may be set up under the "pull" system (see the Impact of Production on Inventory chapter). If so, the production cells are only authorized to produce in small unit quantities to match customer orders. Under this arrangement, suppliers are only asked to deliver in small (and possibly irregular) unit quantities. Suppliers do not like this arrangement, since deliveries may be in far less than full truckload quantities, but may accede to it in exchange for sole supplier status that grants them a higher volume of company purchase dollars.
- *Sequenced deliveries.* When the buyer has approved a supplier to deliver goods directly to the company's production line, the goods may be delivered into a mixed production line, where each unit in line is different from the ones around it. In this situation, the supplier must deliver goods that are sequenced to exactly match the order in which goods are flowing through the production process. Thus, a leather-upholstered seat must be delivered for one vehicle on an assembly line, while a plastic-upholstered seat must be delivered for the vehicle directly behind it. This level of precision is greatly rewarding to the buyer, which can then avoid having to sequence the goods on-site with its own staff. The supplier is willing to do this in order to be the sole source supplier. Sequenced deliveries are only possible if the computer systems of the buyer entity and the supplier are closely interlinked, so the supplier knows what the sequencing order must be, and exactly when the goods must be delivered to the production line.

Measure Suppliers

A crucial part of the purchasing function is to ensure that suppliers are performing at the level needed by the company to meet its cost, quality, and delivery targets. This is a particular concern if a business is engaged in a long-term program to gradually consolidate the number of suppliers that it uses, since marginal performers will be dropped as part of the consolidation. To ascertain which suppliers are not meeting the company's standards, consider installing a supplier measurement program. This program can review a range of issues, including the following:

- *Timeliness of deliveries.* Suppliers should deliver exactly within the time slots granted to them. This means that an excessively *early* delivery is also flagged, since the company must find room in which to store inventory that it does not yet need.

- *Quality issues*. If delivered goods do not meet the company's specifications, this is a major flaw, since it can shut down the manufacturing process for lack of raw materials. Consequently, this issue may be weighted as more important within the scoring system.
- *Prices charged*. If the prices charged by suppliers are higher than the rate at which the goods were ordered, flag the differential.
- *Incorrect deliveries*. This is the delivery of the wrong goods, or delivery to the incorrect company location.

A company can put this ratings system to very specific uses. For instance, it can be used as a database, into which users can drill down to obtain the specifics of supplier failures. The system can also be employed as a certification tool, where a supplier scoring above a certain level is certified to bypass the company's receiving process and send their goods straight to storage or the production area.

The information in a supplier rating should always be shared with suppliers. They can use this information as the basis for their own internal improvement programs. Also, if the company issues them a warning that it is considering dropping them as a supplier, there will be no question about the reason for the warning.

In addition to the points just noted, there may be additional qualitative ratings for suppliers that are used in the decision to drop a supplier entirely, or to shift purchases to a more willing partner. For example, there can be an evaluation of whether a supplier is willing to participate in product planning meetings, to repackage its goods specifically for the company, or to engage in drop shipping to the company's end customers.

While the supplier rating system is an excellent concept, it is not always an easy one to implement. Information about deliveries, pricing, and quality must be collected from around the company – through either manual or automated systems – and input into the rating system. The resulting information must then be aggregated for reporting purposes, and issued to suppliers. In addition, there should be a process in place for dealing with customer complaints that their ratings are incorrect. Despite these issues, it is still worthwhile to measure suppliers at a detailed level.

Negative Effects of the Purchase Price Standard

A common method for judging the purchasing department is to compare the prices at which goods are bought to a standard price. This is known as the purchase price variance, and is calculated as follows:

$$(\text{Actual price paid} - \text{Standard price paid}) \times \text{Actual quantity purchased}$$
$$= \text{Purchase price variance}$$

The purchase price variance is easily circumvented using either of two techniques. First, the purchasing manager can negotiate the highest possible standard prices against which actual prices paid will be compared. This issue can only be avoided by completely excluding the purchasing staff from the setting of standards.

The second circumvention is for the purchasing staff to buy in large quantities, thereby gaining volume discounts. While doing so may result in a favorable purchase price variance, it triggers an excessive investment in inventory. The volume purchases not only translate into an excessive amount of inventory, but also an increased risk of inventory obsolescence, since it may be a long time before the amount purchased can be consumed.

Given the negative impact on working capital, the use of a purchase price standard should be avoided. If management decides to continue tracking it, then at least disassociate it from any purchasing department evaluation systems, so there is no incentive for them to buy excessive quantities of goods.

Summary

To achieve a state where the purchasing staff is most effectively using its time, a manual system of placing orders for inventory must be abandoned. Instead, there should be a system-based process that issues requirements, with little participation by the purchasing staff. The department can then use its time in other areas that generate more value for the business, such as monitoring the flow of inventory orders for errors, evaluating suppliers, and ensuring that purchases are being concentrated with a small number of suppliers to maximize volume purchase discounts.

Chapter 6
Inventory Receiving

Introduction

Goods enter a company through the receiving dock. The receiving area is responsible for ensuring that all received goods are authorized, that they are stored properly, and that the received items are correctly recorded in the company's computer system.

If the receiving process is conducted incorrectly, it can have a profound impact on a number of downstream activities, including production, putaways, picking, and shipping. Conversely, a well-run receiving function that employs the correct floor plan, processes, and technology can achieve a near-seamless introduction of goods into a company. In this chapter, we address the concepts of touch reduction, advance shipping notices, data collection, alternative routings, and several related topics that all contribute to the formation of a well-run receiving function.

Touch Reduction

One of the key goals in the receiving function is to reduce the number of instances in which received inventory is handled. Each of these instances increases the probability of inventory breakage, incorrect data entry, and additional warehouse staff time. Consequently, the following should be considered best practices in receiving goods, in descending order of priority:

- *Drop shipping.* Goods are routed directly from suppliers to customers, and never flow through the receiving dock at all. See the Warehousing Efficiencies chapter for more information.
- *Cross docking.* Goods are routed directly from the receiving dock to a shipping dock, for immediate delivery to customers. No time is spent in storage. See the Warehousing Efficiencies chapter for more information.
- *Putaway to primary pick location.* Received goods are sent immediately to the bin location from which they are picked. This means there is no additional movement later on to shift these goods from a secondary storage location to replenish the primary picking location.
- *Buffer storage.* There are situations where there is not an immediate need for received goods, but there should be shortly. If so, moving these items to storage and then back out again for their final use represents an unnecessary touch. Instead, consider setting up a small buffer storage section in the receiving area where goods may be held for a short time until their use has been clarified.

In each of these best practices, the number of inventory touches is reduced or eliminated entirely. These approaches can be compared to the traditional handling of received goods, which places every receipt in storage, from which goods are later shifted to a primary picking location, and then picked, packed, and loaded for delivery to customers. In the latter case, the opportunities for errors and breakage to occur are heightened, while labor costs are increased.

Advance Shipping Notices

An advance shipping notice (ASN) is an electronic message sent from the seller to the buyer, stating which items have just been shipped to the buyer, when the goods left the seller, when they are expected to arrive at the buyer's facility, and even the specific locations of goods within the trailer. This message is extremely useful, because the receiving staff can preposition unloading equipment and a crew at the designated receiving door. If any of the items listed on the ASN are needed immediately, they are assigned a forklift operator for immediate movement elsewhere in the facility. All other items in the load are pre-assigned a storage location by the warehouse management system, which directs the unloading crew to the noted locations. Thus, ASNs are useful for streamlining the receiving workload by giving advance warning of deliveries.

The ASN is not just a workflow management tool. Since it provides early notice of which goods will arrive and when, this reduces the uncertainty of the materials management staff in estimating the amount of safety stock that should be kept on hand. Since there is certain knowledge of incoming deliveries, it is now possible to selectively reduce the safety stock investment. In short, expanding the use of ASNs among all company suppliers can reduce a company's investment in inventory.

Delay Low-Priority Receipts

The receiving area can be a bottleneck when there are a number of high-priority receipts arriving at approximately the same time, especially if pallets are being broken down and then cross-docked to nearby trailers for immediate shipment to customers. In this environment, any receipts that do not have a high priority are only interfering with the timely handling of more critical inventory items. Ideally, these low-priority items should be delayed and then handled during off-peak hours. There are two ways to do so:

- If the purchasing staff knows in advance that items to be delivered do not have a high priority, note in the purchase order that the goods must be delivered during an off-peak time slot. It is then up to the supplier to time the delivery appropriately.
- If the priority of a delivery is only known when received, log the contents of the trailer into the warehouse management system, and then move the trailer to yard storage. The trailer can then be moved back to the receiving dock at a more convenient time and unloaded in a more leisurely manner.

Minimize Travel Time with Dock Assignments

A warehouse may have many dock doors from which to choose, when a driver wants to position a trailer. The choice of which door is assigned can have a surprisingly large impact on the travel times of the warehouse staff. Ideally, a trailer should be assigned to the dock door nearest to where the goods it contains will eventually be dispositioned. For example, if the goods are to be cross-docked straight across the warehouse to a trailer intended for a customer, then the door selected should be as close to the cross-docking area as possible. Or, goods intended for reserve storage should be routed through a dock positioned close to the reserve storage area.

The best way to minimize travel times in this manner is to require suppliers to forward ASNs to the company, so that the warehouse manager knows in advance what goods are arriving on which trailer, and can plan accordingly. Without this advance knowledge, the warehouse manager will only be able to assign docks based on what is immediately available, which may not be the optimum solution.

Dock assignment is not usually a significant issue if there are only a small number of adjacent dock doors, since the impact on travel times within the warehouse if one dock is selected over another is relatively small.

Organize around Length of Delivery Time Slots

Not all supplier deliveries can be unloaded within the same period of time. Some trailers are of different sizes, and so will contain different quantities of goods. Others contain less than full truckloads to be delivered. Other trailers may be filled with highly-organized pallets that are easy to unload, while other loads contain large numbers of individual cases that must be removed by hand. Thus, unloading times can vary drastically for each type of load.

To be properly organized, the receiving manager should make note of the unloading time for each type of load from each supplier, as well as the number of receiving staff and equipment used. Since the same types of goods are likely to be delivered from the same suppliers in the same manner in the future, it is possible to organize the handling of new receipts based on these historical records on an ongoing basis.

To properly apply these historical records to incoming deliveries, it is especially useful to obtain advance shipping notices, so that enough resources can be allocated to each delivery before trucks arrive.

> **Tip:** It can be quite useful to install several telescopic boom conveyors in the receiving area, which can be extended directly into trailers to assist with the unloading of case loads. This equipment significantly reduces unloading time.

Affix Labels at Receiving

Much of the information gathering for inventory relies upon the presence of detailed labels that accurately depict the contents and unit of measure of goods. The best place to affix such a label is the receiving area, since all purchased goods must enter the company through this natural choke point.

The receiving staff could make mistakes in identifying goods, quantities, and units of measure for these goods, resulting in incorrect label information. Instead, have suppliers create labels in accordance with the company's specifications for label size and content, and affix them to goods prior to shipping them to the company. These labels can then be used in place of any labels that would otherwise be generated as part of the receiving process.

> **Tip:** Conduct an audit of the warehouse bins and note which items are not being labeled in advance by suppliers. If these suppliers are unwilling to provide labels, this should be a consideration in identifying which suppliers the company wants to work with over the long-term.

Initial Data Collection

If suppliers have not provided a complete set of information with delivered goods (typically on a bar coded label), then the receiving staff is responsible for attaching and logging this information. This can include the summarization of receipt information into bar coded tags, as well as determining the cubic volume and weight of received goods.

Initial data collection at the point of receipt is important, since the materials management staff needs to know as soon as goods have arrived, so that any shortages related to customer orders or production jobs can be addressed at once. This information is also needed by the accounting staff, which uses it as evidence that a supplier invoice for delivered goods is valid, and so should be paid.

Weight and cubic volume information is stored in the warehouse management system, which uses it to determine where goods can be stored in the warehouse while maximizing available cubic storage space. The information can also be used for shipment planning, if the received goods are simply being trans-shipped to a customer. Weight information can be automatically collected with deck scales or load cells. Also, there are a number of cube scanning systems on the market that use infrared beams to measure the dimensions of received goods.

In short, timely data collection can be considered one of the main activities of the receiving function, since the resulting information is needed in many parts of a business.

The Need for Receipts Inspection

The traditional view of the receiving function is that the receiving staff must inspect all received goods to ensure that they are authorized, in the correct quantity, and are not damaged. While this may appear to be a reasonable control, inspection is not an efficient activity. A large and complex order may require a considerable amount of time to inspect, thereby clogging the work queue in the receiving area. Still, there is a need to ensure that non-standard and unauthorized goods are not purchased. How do we balance these conflicting issues?

The vast majority of all goods received comply with the buyer's purchase order in all respects. If the unit quantities delivered are slightly different from the authorized amount, then the difference is negligible. There is no need to inspect these goods. Instead, they can be accepted upon receipt and immediately sent to storage or other intended uses. To identify which suppliers' goods are not in need of inspection, assign a team to engage in the following steps:

1. Identify those suppliers sending the largest number of deliveries to the company. This group should be reviewed first, since granting any of them an inspection waiver will have an immediate positive impact on the receiving department.
2. Review the inspection reports for this group of suppliers for the past year, as well as any records of returns sent back to these suppliers. The returns information is particularly useful, since it provides evidence of additional problems that may not have been found during a cursory inspection.
3. If no inspection or return issues are found, grant these suppliers an immediate inspection waiver, and notify the receiving manager.
4. If inspection or return issues are found, notify the supplier at once and assign a team to work with the supplier to remediate any issues found.
5. Move to the next-largest group of suppliers and repeat the process.

In addition, have an ongoing review process in place that identifies any additional returns that crop up after a supplier has been granted an inspection waiver. These returns are of particular concern, since they may require that an inspection waiver be withdrawn.

It may not be cost-effective to completely eliminate inspections. At some point, the review team will find that there are a number of suppliers from which only incidental items are ordered at long intervals. In these cases, the cost of reviewing inspection reports and following up with suppliers probably exceeds the cost of inspecting goods. Thus, even a seriously streamlined receiving department may find that a modest number of inspections must still be made.

Tip: If inspections are needed, be sure to flag received items in the warehouse management system as not yet being available for picking. A warning sign in the inspections area helps, too. Otherwise, someone looking for a high-priority SKU may inadvertently pick an item that has not yet been cleared for use.

Repack at Receiving

When a customer places an order, the company's order fulfillment policy may leave little time in which to fill and ship the order. If the quantity ordered is not in the amount in which goods are currently stored, this means the picking staff must spend extra time assembling the correct number of units, possibly from a mix of broken pallets. This results in extra-long picking times, which can interfere with the timely delivery of orders. To mitigate this issue, determine which quantities are most commonly ordered by customers, and repack a number of incoming supplier deliveries at the receiving dock into the anticipated order size.

The receiving dock can be a good location for this repacking task, since there is comparatively more time available for the receiving staff prior to inventory putaway than is available to the picking staff. However, this approach only works if the receiving department is sufficiently staffed to have the time for repackaging, and if there is enough space in the receiving area for repackaging work to be completed.

Route Goods Directly to Production

The traditional path that incoming deliveries follow is to arrive at the receiving dock, wait for inspection, and then be parked in a warehouse bin until needed in the manufacturing area. The time required to inspect incoming goods can be substantial, especially if the receiving staff is overwhelmed with a sudden influx of deliveries. To avoid this issue, consider having a select group of pre-qualified suppliers deliver goods directly to the production line.

To do so, the deliveries of these suppliers must be examined closely. The deliveries must meet all buyer specifications, and be consistently delivered within the required time slot. If a supplier has been certified as meeting these requirements, then a routing straight to production is reasonable. Only suppliers whose deliveries have been tested in this manner can be certified for a direct routing. The deliveries of all other suppliers should still run through the receiving department, and be subjected to the normal examination process.

Tip: If certain deliveries absolutely must run through a receiving inspection, tag them as being on hold subject to quality review. This should be a prominently-displayed tag that makes it quite unlikely that the goods will be inadvertently forwarded to the production area.

It is only possible to bypass the warehouse and deliver direct to the production area if there are adequate delivery locations set up on the periphery of the production floor. Thus, it may be necessary to construct special production docks and localized storage areas before the receiving function can be bypassed.

Route Remaining Goods to Storage

If goods are not being cross-docked straight to the shipping area or forwarded to production, then the remaining movement alternative is to the formal storage area. Putaways to storage should be conducted as rapidly as possible after goods have been received. Doing so reduces the risk of a massive pileup of inventory in the receiving area, as successive loads of goods are delivered. Immediate routing to storage can be accomplished with the following preparations:

- Require customers to send advance shipping notices that detail exactly which goods are stored in incoming trailer loads.

- Assign suppliers specific time slots within which to make deliveries.
- Use the ASNs and time slots to calculate in advance the number of putaway staff required at various times of the day, as well as the storage locations in which received items are to be stored.
- Use some form of advanced data collection, such as RFID, bar coding, or voice entry, to store receipts and putaway information in the warehouse management system in real time.

Clearly, the ability to route goods to storage in a timely manner requires supplier cooperation, an effective warehouse management system, and good management of staffing levels. If there is a breakdown in any of these three elements, the ability to conduct rapid putaways from receiving will decline.

A more efficient way to move goods straight from the receiving area to storage locations is to aggregate received items by putaway zone. This means shifting received items to specific areas on the receiving floor that are serviced by materials handlers that specialize in putaways in different parts of the warehouse. For example, all case deliveries may be routed to a case staging area, from which a person using a pallet jack moves goods to picking-height storage bins. Also, pallets designated for reserve storage are moved to another staging area, where someone operating a forklift equipped to service double-deep racks is employed to move goods. The use of putaway zones requires additional coordination in the receiving area and perhaps more space, but can pay off by shortening the time required to move goods away from the receiving area.

Time-Phase Shipping and Receiving

The shipping and receiving functions involve inherently different activities. Receiving requires the collection of more information than is the case for shipping, while receiving may involve an inspection activity that is not needed for shipping. Similarly, receiving must deal with returned goods, staging, and repackaging. Despite these differences, the two functions share use of the same types of materials handling equipment and they both employ dock doors. To take advantage of the latter items, it may be possible to combine the shipping and receiving functions in a single facility, even when there are relatively high incoming and outgoing unit volumes.

To merge the shipping and receiving functions, the best approach is to time-phase incoming and outgoing shipments. For example, suppliers could be required to only make deliveries during the morning hours, while deliveries are only scheduled for the afternoon hours. However, this approach only works under the following circumstances:

- Suppliers are willing to limit deliveries to a specific time block. Otherwise, there is a risk of traffic jams in front of the dock doors.
- There is minimal fixed equipment, such as automated conveyor systems, in the receiving/shipping area. Such equipment may work well for one aspect of the combined functions, but will likely interfere with the other function.

- The warehouse layout must be in a "U" shape, so that incoming goods are intended to be shipped back out through the same side of the warehouse.

Reverse Logistics

The receiving department may also be tasked with the receipt of goods sent back by customers, which is known as reverse logistics. If a company operates its own retail stores, then goods may be returned to the stores by customers, and then batched at the store level and forwarded to the warehouse. In addition, a company may encourage its customers to return re-usable packaging materials, such as pallets, roll cages, trays, and so forth. No matter what is being returned, reverse logistics requires the receiving function to engage in a number of additional activities that are not part of the normal receiving routine. These activities can include:

- Review goods to see if they can be reworked, and tag them for indicated re-work
- Repackage goods for resale
- Notify the purchasing department that goods must be disposed of through an alternative discount sales channel
- Designate the goods as scrap and dispose of them accordingly
- Tag the goods as hazardous materials and dispose of them in accordance with regulations

An essential point is that items returned through a reverse logistics program be processed quickly. Otherwise, an inordinate amount of inventory will clog the receiving area. In addition, goods that have not been properly dispositioned are not generating any residual cash flows for a business. For both reasons, the backlog of unprocessed returns should be monitored regularly, and extra resources assigned if the backlog threatens to become excessive.

Rapid processing of returns is especially important when the market values of goods decline rapidly, as is the case with consumer electronics and high fashion clothing. In these cases, it can be cost-effective to staff the returns area with well-trained specialists who are adept at quickly sizing up returned products based on their condition and value, and routing them to the appropriate market for resale.

Since these activities vary so markedly from normal receiving functions, it may be useful to shift them to a third party that has more experience with reverse logistics. Another option is to set up an entirely separate function within the warehouse or as a separate warehouse that handles returned goods.

Summary

The sign of a well-run receiving department is one that efficiently accepts and disperses goods throughout a company, while accurately logging all incoming goods into the corporate computer system. To achieve this nirvana, management must pay close attention to:

- How the receiving area is laid out to accept and process goods;
- How materials can be rapidly shifted away from the receiving area; and
- How information about received items is recorded

It is impossible to elevate the performance of the receiving area without paying attention to all three of these concepts. At a minimum, there must be enough receiving space to avoid bottlenecks, there must be enough materials handling personnel to handle the work load during peak periods, and information about received goods must be entered into the computer system in real time – not in a batch at the end of the shift. More advanced concepts can be employed in higher-volume receiving operations, but these are the minimum requirements for a successful receiving function.

Chapter 7
Putaways and Picking

Introduction

Putaway and picking tasks comprise the bulk of all warehouse labor, and so are of interest from a management perspective. This interest has been enhanced in recent years, as the advent of just-in-time concepts have vastly increased the number of receipts and deliveries that a company must deal with. To make matters worse, there is increased emphasis on timely deliveries to customers to keep a company competitive – an issue that makes picking activities crucial to corporate success. In this chapter, we address the types of equipment needed to maintain effective putaway and picking operations, the extent to which mechanization should be used, and the operational improvements that can be used to improve the effectiveness and efficiency of these crucial functions.

Putaway and Picking Equipment

A central part of the putaway and picking functions is deciding what types of equipment to use for the movement of inventory. There are a large number of options available, each one designed for a different inventory layout. In the following tables, we make note of the different types of equipment, and the situations in which they can be used.

Small Item Putaway and Picking Equipment

Equipment Type	Discussion
Picking cart	Non-motorized cart available in many configurations, excellent for manual picking and putaway activities in narrow aisles. Can be customized for different-sized storage bins, weighing scales, computers, and so forth. Very low cost.
Manned ASRS	An automated storage and retrieval system (ASRS) in which a picker rides. This is useful for picking at a variety of heights within an aisle. A single picking trip may accommodate picks for multiple orders, depending on the space available in the manned part of the ASRS. An ASRS can fit within a narrow aisle, and so is good for dense storage configurations that are many feet high. Given the slow picking speed, this approach works best when there are a large number of slow-moving items. The system can also be used for putaways. However, a manned ASRS is very expensive.

Equipment Type	Discussion
Robotic picker	A rail-guided system that uses a robotic arm to extract items from storage drawers, or to extract entire storage drawers. The system delivers the picked items to an output location for further manual handling. This is a very expensive option, and so is only cost-effective in dense storage situations where inventory items are small and expensive. Can also be used in reverse for putaways.

Case-Size Putaway and Picking Equipment

Equipment Type	Discussion
Pallet jack	A motorized pallet transporter, with the operator riding in front. There is no lift capability, so the pallet jack only works for floor-level storage. Quite inexpensive and widely used.
Pallet train	As the name implies, this is a group of pallets that are pulled behind a motorized vehicle. Suitable for larger transfers of pallets at floor level.
Order picker truck	A truck that moves the stock picker vertically to access upper bins. Useful for work in high-density locations where cases are stored several levels high. Not a fast solution.

Pallet-Size Putaway and Picking Equipment

Vehicle Type	Discussion
Counterbalanced lift truck	This lift truck includes a counterbalance in the rear of the vehicle to offset the weight of loads carried in front. The driver rides in the vehicle, so it can be used to cover long distances. Loads can be accessed and putaway up to heights of about 25 feet. Requires a relatively wide aisle to accommodate its turning radius. This is the standard vehicle used in most warehouses.
Sideloading truck	A lift truck that loads from one side, thereby allowing access to narrower aisles. Since it is configured to only load from one side, the operator must access an aisle from the correct end in order to access a rack location; this can increase travel times.
Straddle truck	This lift truck offsets load weights by integrating outriggers at floor height that straddle the pallet being moved. Proper balancing requires that the truck be driven into a storage rack, so the outriggers are directly beneath and to either side of the pallet being moved. Can operate within a slightly narrower aisle than the counterbalanced lift truck.

A variation on this concept is the straddle reach truck, which extends into a rack for putaway and picking functions; that is, the truck is not driven into the storage rack. This version is more expensive than the standard straddle truck. |

Vehicle Type	Discussion
Turret truck	A lift truck that loads from a mast. This approach allows for loading from either side of an aisle, and use within narrow aisles. This configuration works well in high-density locations, but the turret truck is one of the most expensive storage and retrieval vehicles.
Walkie stacker	The most minimal type of forklift. The operator walks next to the stacker, rather than riding on it. It can be used to stack pallets up to three loads high. Best usage is when travel distances are short, rack locations are low, and equipment costs must be minimized.

The typical warehouse employs a mix of this equipment. The most common mix is the counterbalanced lift truck and the pallet jack, since they allow for ready access to upper-level storage locations, as well as manual access to cases stored at ground level. In a more dense storage environment where aisles are narrow, the most common mix is the sideloading truck and the pallet jack, since they can access loads in tight operating environments.

Other solutions are available that only apply to picking operations. These systems are designed to reduce the amount of travel time by inventory pickers. Consider the following systems, which can be linked together to provide a completely automated solution:

- *Automated dispensers.* Goods are stored in gravity flow racks (see the Warehouse Storage Systems chapter), which automatically drop goods onto a telescoping conveyor when an order is received. The process can also work in reverse to putaway goods in storage locations.
- *Conveyors.* A conveyor belt can run the length of an aisle, and is used by pickers to transport picked goods to a downstream sortation area. Pickers remove items from bins, attach identification bar codes to the items, and place them on the conveyor. The conveyor moves the goods to a sortation area, where the goods are aggregated by order. This approach greatly improves picking efficiency, but requires the capital cost of the conveyor system and the downstream sortation area.
- *Automated sortation.* If goods are coming into a sortation area from a series of conveyor belts (see the last bullet point), bar code scanners can review each item to determine the customer order for which it is intended, and use an automated shunt to divert goods into the correct accumulation lane.
- *Robotic palletizing.* Once goods have been sorted for delivery to a customer, a robotic palletizer can be used to stack the goods on a pallet for shipment. This approach is faster and safer than having a person stack cases. However, robots are extremely expensive and must be maintained, so this approach is usually limited to areas where labor costs are extremely high.

Taken together, the preceding items can be used as a completely automated picking solution. However, full automation is also quite expensive. It may make more sense to begin with the conveyors to reduce picker travel time, and see if there is a reasonable financial return. If so, the dispensing, sortation, and palletizing components can also be considered.

Automated Storage and Retrieval Systems

An automated storage and retrieval system (ASRS) accepts a pallet that is dropped off at the end of an aisle and automatically deposits it in a designated storage location via a system of rails and lifts. Similarly, the system can remove a pallet from stock and deliver it to the end of an aisle for pickup. The better systems can accomplish both a putaway transaction and a pick transaction before returning to the front of an aisle. There are also variations on the concept that can access pallets stored in double-deep locations, and carry two pallets at once. This approach has the following advantages:

- *Labor reduction.* An ASRS limits the need for forklifts to the front of the warehouse, thereby cutting down the amount of travel time by the warehouse staff. There is also no need for staff to putaway or pick items within the aisles.
- *Aisle size.* The system does not require the full width of an aisle that a forklift operator needs, so aisles can be compressed to about five feet, leaving more room in the warehouse for storage.
- *Rack height.* The system can putaway and pick goods in very high rack locations, so the cubic volume of the warehouse is maximized.
- *Damage reduction.* An ASRS does not damage goods being moved, which is not always the case with a forklift operator.

Despite this high level of automation, the following issues may prevent a business from installing an ASRS:

- *Cost.* A company must invest a large amount in the rail and lift system needed for an ASRS.
- *Maintenance.* As is the case with any automated system, there is a certain amount of maintenance cost required. Also, since this is a mechanical system, there is a risk of equipment downtime, which can halt warehouse operations.
- *Warehouse configuration.* The configuration of the warehouse is essentially fixed once an ASRS is installed, since the labor required to subsequently alter the layout is massive.

The disadvantages of an ASRS are considerable, limiting its use to specific situations – typically where the costs of land and labor are high. In this case, an ASRS can maximize the use of the warehouse space and staff to the greatest possible extent.

Automated Storage and Retrieval Vehicles

An automated storage and retrieval (ASR) vehicle is an automated forklift that runs along a grid of wires installed beneath the warehouse floor. They can be directed through the wire grid to engage in putaways and picks. An alternative version of the ASR vehicle dispenses with the wire grid, instead using onboard positioning systems.

A system of ASR vehicles is quite expensive, especially when the cost of the wire grid is considered. Consequently, these vehicles are only used in situations where the cost of warehouse labor is high, and where there is a need for a high volume of inventory moves on a continual basis. They can also be of use in refrigerated warehouses, where the operating environment is uncomfortable for human workers.

A system of ASR vehicles makes little sense if a warehouse location is to be shifted in the near future, since the cost of installing the wire grid cannot be adequately recouped in a short time. Also, the racking system cannot be reconfigured without also altering the wire grid. Consequently, this approach is only recommended when there are long-term warehouse leases, and where the storage layout is extremely stable.

The Impact of Mechanization

A progressive management team may decide to introduce a high level of mechanization into the warehouse, employing a variety of automated storage and retrieval systems to increase the efficiency of operations. Is this level of mechanization truly effective? In many cases, the level of efficiency actually declines, for the following reasons:

- *Complexity*. A highly complex system is more likely to fail. Thus, a warehouse can be created that largely automates a variety of warehouse functions – but it may suffer from persistent downtime. This is a particular concern when mechanized systems are assembled from several suppliers, and do not mesh together very well.
- *Cost transfer*. A high level of automation may initially appear to reduce the overall costs of the warehousing function. However, it is entirely likely that a portion of those saved costs have actually shifted into different costs. For example, it may now be necessary to employ a full-time maintenance staff, as well as purchase a stock of repair parts. Also, it may be necessary to invest in additional equipment that is held in reserve, in case some equipment breaks down and requires immediate replacement.
- *Bleeding edge systems*. Given the level of complexity just noted, it makes little sense to install a system that is the first of its kind. These systems contain hidden bugs that will take time to become apparent and be remediated. Instead, this is a situation in which being the technology follower is extremely logical – wait to see how a system operates somewhere else and view it in operation before actively considering a purchase.
- *Training*. Mechanical systems require significant amounts of staff time to operate and maintain. This can require an upgrade in the training regimen of the warehouse staff, and possibly staff turnover when management discovers that

the educational level of warehouse employees must be increased. An uncomfortable discovery may be that pay rates have to increase to reflect the increased skill level of the work force.

- *Inflexibility.* Once a mechanized solution has been installed, it is no small matter to move the system. Instead, the equipment becomes a monument around which the rest of the warehouse is configured. This can be a concern if it later becomes apparent that a different warehouse layout should be implemented.

In addition to the preceding issues, a mechanization project may fail because it was never financially viable in the first place. This situation most commonly arises when those responsible for capital improvement projects do not conduct a sufficient amount of investigation into what should be installed or how a company will gain a return on its investment. In this situation, even the most perfect installation will still not yield a profitable outcome.

Given the issues noted here, we suggest that all other improvement alternatives be pursued prior to adopting an enhanced level of mechanization. Also, even when the decision is made to proceed in this area, consider implementing a pilot installation first in a segregated portion of the warehouse. Only after a mechanization project has been installed and reviewed should the decision be made to roll out the concept through the entire warehouse. Otherwise, a company may spend an inordinate amount introducing systems that yield no payback.

Tip: Before installing mechanization, simply streamline warehouse operations to the greatest extent possible. When mechanization is then introduced, it will build upon the simplified systems, resulting in a low level of complexity that is simpler to maintain.

EXAMPLE

The warehouse manager for Country Fresh Produce has done a poor job of running the warehouse staff, resulting in at least $250,000 of excess annual labor costs and more than $100,000 of spoiled vegetables that were not shipped out to customers in a timely manner.

The production manager is a great believer in automation, having successfully installed industrial robots in several parts of the manufacturing area. He vigorously advocates investing in a more mechanized warehouse, in the belief that much of the $350,000 of excess costs can be eliminated.

The warehouse manager is fired and replaced by a more hands-on manager. She investigates the claims of the production manager, and concludes that the company would invest $2,000,000 in fixed assets in order to eliminate the $350,000 of identified excess costs. Or, she can install better management practices and procedures in order to streamline warehouse operations, and achieve the same cost savings – with no expenditures for fixed assets. The situation illustrates how initial streamlining activities should be completed before attempting any significant investment in mechanization.

Putaways

The act of putting received inventory away in the warehouse can have a major impact on the efficiency of warehouse operations. Putting received goods away in the nearest accessible rack space may minimize the current travel time of a fork lift operator. However, if the goods do not closely match the cubic volume of the storage location in which they are placed, then the cubic utilization of the warehouse will decline. Also, if an item is frequently used but is stored near the back of the warehouse, this vastly extends the time required to travel to and retrieve goods. Given these concerns, consider using one of the methods for putting away inventory in the most effective manner, as stated in the following table.

Putaway Methodologies

Method	Advantages and Disadvantages
Usage frequency	Goods are stored near the front of the warehouse if they are accessed continually, and progressively further back in accordance with declining frequency. Does not account for the cubic volume of stored goods, which can result in inefficient storage.
Usage and cubic volume	Storage is based on both usage frequency and the cubic size of the goods to be stored. Thus, goods that are frequently used and which are assembled in a pallet configuration are stored in those pallet racks closest to the front of the warehouse. There may be pallet racks at the front of the warehouse that are specifically designed for these goods.
Dynamic	A warehouse management system (WMS) automatically calculates the best storage location based on the preceding criteria, and sends a message to the putaway person, directing that received goods be sent to a specific bin location that is currently open. Requires a WMS and a high level of inventory record accuracy.

Within any of the three preceding putaway methodologies, it may also be possible to putaway goods by warehouse zone. For example, it may make sense from an organizational perspective to putaway all sizes of a particular garment in the same area, rather than scattering the various sizes throughout the warehouse. This makes it easier for the picking staff to locate goods.

The preceding putaway schemes are predicated on knowledge of the size, weight, and demand characteristics of goods. More specifically, the following information should be stored in the warehouse computer system in order to engage in appropriate putaways:

- Size of unit loads
- Weight of unit loads
- Crushability (i.e., can pallets be stacked on top of each other?)
- The product family with which goods are associated
- The usage level of unit loads

In addition, the system must store information about the size of storage locations and their weight-bearing capacity. This information is used to determine the locations in which goods can be safely stored.

An additional putaway consideration is reducing the total number of inventory touches that goods will experience during their time in a company. Every time goods are handled, there is an increased risk of data entry errors and material breakage, while extra labor costs will also be incurred. To mitigate these issues, consider giving top priority to putaways being routed to the primary picking location first. By doing so, subsequent touches are avoided that would otherwise have been needed to route goods from a secondary storage location to the primary picking location.

The type of putaway methodology employed can be severely constrained if the inventory tracking system only allows for the use of a single, fixed inventory location. In this situation, inventory items are always stored in the same place, even if that location is not an optimal one from the perspectives of picking frequency and cubic storage volumes. If this recording issue is present, the tracking system must be replaced by one that allows for on-the-fly changes in storage locations, as well as multiple locations, before any additional putaway improvements can be made.

Reslotting

The demand for the goods stored in a warehouse constantly changes, so it is impossible for the configuration of a warehouse to be perfect for more than a few moments. Over time, the locations in which goods have been putaway will diverge significantly from their optimal locations. This variance makes it necessary to periodically engage in reslotting to shift goods to their most optimal locations. The trigger for a reslotting event may be the simple passage of time, such as reslotting once a year, during a traditional slow period in customer orders. Here are several other scenarios in which reslotting may be warranted:

- *Catalog issuance.* A company issues a certain number of catalogs per year, each of which offers significantly different sets of goods for sale. The warehouse should be reslotted just prior to the issuance of each catalogue, in anticipation of selling the items listed in the catalogue.
- *Seasonal.* A company offers different mixes of goods in its retail stores, depending on the time of year. The warehouse should be reslotted in anticipation of changes in demand for each upcoming shift in seasonal sales.
- *Zero balance.* When inventory levels drop to zero, there is no longer any on-site inventory to be moved to a new location. In this case, a better location can be designated in advance of the next batch of goods being produced or received.

Picking

As the name implies, picking involves taking items from stock locations, with the intent of either shipping them to customers or forwarding them to the production area. There are many ways to conduct picking, depending on the size of the items picked, the number of line items in an order, and the amount of travel time required to reach goods held in storage. Another significant consideration is the cost of more automated solutions, which can be prohibitive for a smaller organization.

We have divided this section into discussions of each type of picking. While perusing them, consider that a combination of solutions may work best for your company. Thus, a highly-automated solution could work well for those items picked with the greatest frequency, while a lower-cost solution might be more cost-effective for items that are picked with less frequency and which are stored further away.

Single Order Picking Tours

A single order picking tour occurs when a picker is assigned to retrieve all of the line items in an order placed by a single customer. This approach is usually considered too labor-intensive, since a great deal of travel time may be incurred to fill a single order. However, picking to a single order enhances the integrity of an order – that is, items picked cannot be mixed with orders placed by a different customer. This can be a major issue when there are many line items in an order, or when the integrity of orders have been a problem in the past, or where a customer is so important that its orders must be picked perfectly every time. In these situations, it can make sense to use single order picking.

Single order picking tours may be necessary in emergency situations where a customer is in great need of an order. The customer may be waiting for the order on the company's premises, or have arranged for special transport of the goods. If so, any of the more complex picking systems that are designed to enhance the overall efficiency of picking operations may yield an excessively slow total picking time for an individual order. Though emergency picks are essentially a form of expediting that interferes with regular picking operations, they are occasionally necessary. When demanded by a customer, consider increasing the price of the order, to reflect the extra labor cost of the order pick, as well as the disruption inflicted on the rest of the company's picking operations.

If a single order picking tour is considered necessary, at least have the computer system print out a picking ticket that is sorted in order of aisle-rack-bin location, so that pickers can engage in the shortest-distance warehouse tour to pick the mandated items.

If there is no warehouse computer system that automatically prints out a picking ticket for each order, the next best alternative is to take a photocopy of the original customer order, and use it as the picking ticket. Doing so eliminates any problems that might otherwise arise from transcribing the order information onto a formal picking ticket. The main risk in using the customer order for this purpose is when the original order was filled out by hand, and is illegible.

> **Tip:** Revise the order entry form to include a check-off box next to each line item. This can be used to contain the initials of the picking crew, which sign off on each box as they pick goods.

Pick to Shipping Container

There may be situations where the cubic size of a customer order is relatively small. If so, consider placing the shipping container directly on the picking cart, so that the picker can pack goods directly into the shipping container. However, this requires that correctly-sized shipping containers be selected in advance and distributed to pickers.

Single Line Picking Tours

In some organizations, a number of customer orders may only include a single line item that must be picked. This is especially common when a customer needs a specific replacement part, or is ordering in response to a specific marketing promotion. In these situations, it can make sense to separate out all single-line orders from the multi-line orders, and then sort the single-line orders in warehouse location sequence. This information is then handed to the picking staff, which can efficiently work their way through the warehouse in the indicated location sequence and pick all of the single-line orders. This approach assumes that single-line orders will be handled by a small number of experienced pickers that are very familiar with the goods being ordered, and who can efficiently work their way through the warehouse. Given the higher level of picking knowledge required, these single line picking tours are usually assigned to the more senior warehouse staff.

Batch Picking Tours

If the warehouse area is so large that picker travel times represent a major cost, consider assigning a batch of customer orders to each picker. Pickers will then fulfill all these orders during the same picking tour. The primary advantage of doing so is a substantial reduction in the total amount of travel time.

Some companies prefer not to use batch picking, despite the reduced cost, because there is a notably increased risk of picking errors. In particular, order line items may be picked and then mistakenly assigned to the order of a different customer whose order is in the same batch. This problem is particularly common when the orders in a batch are comprised of many line items. The error rate experienced will determine whether batch picking should be used.

Dedicated "C" Level Picking Tours

A common method for designating inventory as high-traffic or low-traffic is to assign an "A" code to inventory items picked with high frequency, a "B" code to those picked somewhat less, and a "C" code to the slowest-moving items. "C" items are then stored in a distant part of the warehouse, since they are accessed relatively less frequently. The trouble is that "C" items are still picked, and require someone to travel the extra distance to fetch them. Rather than requiring the picking staff to make a separate trip for each "C" item picked, consider one of the following alternatives:

- Separate the "C" inventory line items from the daily set of customer orders, and assign a picker to make a special tour of the "C" level inventory area to pick these items.

- If there are enough "C" level picks in a day to warrant the employment of a dedicated "C" picker, set up the "C" storage area for zone picking. A person is permanently assigned to this area, and picks all of the "C" items noted in customer orders.

In both situations, items picked from the "C" area are then forwarded to the packing area, for re-integration with the related customer orders.

Wave Picking

Wave picking involves the timed release of orders into the warehouse, with the intent of deriving a consolidated cluster of picked customer orders. The usual reason for wave picking is to consolidate customer orders by delivery region, so that a full truck-load of orders can be issued from the warehouse at the same time. The result is the reduced shipping cost associated with a full truckload delivery. Otherwise, a business that does not focus on delivery costs will merely assign customer orders picking priority in the order in which they are received, resulting in a scattering of more expensive less-than-truckload deliveries.

For a wave picking system to work properly, there must be an order consolidation area near the shipping point. This area is responsible for sorting through the various picked items, assigning them to specific customer orders, and packing them for delivery.

Forward Picking

There may be situations where a company is constantly receiving a stream of customer orders for small amounts of goods, for which a large crowd of pickers are employed to move through the warehouse and conduct picks. This results in a massive amount of employee travel time, as well as many inventory transactions to record, and a serious housekeeping problem from the large number of broken cases that the pickers leave behind.

A solution to this scenario is to periodically summarize a number of these small orders into a single picking document, and have one picker remove all of the indicated items from stock. The aggregated pick is then moved to a forward picking area, where the items are separated into individual orders. This approach massively reduces both employee travel time and the number of inventory transactions, while still avoiding the need for much automation or fancy computer systems.

An enhanced version of this approach is to maintain certain frequently-ordered items in the forward picking area, rather than in the formal warehouse storage area. Doing so eliminates the need for any travel time by pickers to locate and pick these items.

Zone Picking

When the warehouse manager assigns a single customer order to an inventory picker, that person may be required to move throughout the warehouse to locate all of the items noted on the order. This is not efficient, in terms of the large amount of travel time involved to move from bin to bin. Further, all of these removals from stock require a large number of transactions in the inventory database, which present the risk of data entry errors.

A solution to single-order picking is to use zone picking. With zone picking, an entire batch of customer orders are combined into one master order, for which the computer system prints a picking report that is sorted in order by warehouse bin location. The warehouse manager apportions this list among the picking staff, so that each picker only picks within a small section of the warehouse. Doing so vastly reduces the travel time required to pick goods for orders.

The pickers then forward their picked items to a central location in the warehouse, where the items are separated and matched to specific customer orders. Not only does this approach reduce travel time, but it also reduces the number of inventory transactions to be recorded, since picks are being conducted for multiple units at the same time. Here are two variations on the concept:

- *Progressive order assembly*. The applicable line items in one order are completed in a picking zone, after which the picked items are shifted forward in a carton to the next zone for which additional picks are needed. This approach retains the integrity of an individual order while the order is gradually assembled as it moves through the various picking zones. Picking accuracy tends to be higher, since picks are always identified with a specific customer order. It also avoids the cost of the next variation, which is downstream sortation. However, progressive order assembly requires the presence of a conveyor system that moves partially-filled cartons from one picking zone to the next. Also, if there are many small orders, the picking system can be overwhelmed by a massive number of cartons to be filled.

Tip: An advanced form of progressive order assembly is the automated conveyor system, which automatically sends a partially-filled customer order carton to the next zone containing applicable goods. All intervening zones are bypassed. This approach avoids the buildup of picking carton queues in the other zones, where an operator has to decide whether there are any pickable items to place in a carton.

- *Downstream sortation*. Order line items picked in a zone are transported to a central sortation area, where they are assigned to specific customer orders, packed and shipped. This process is computer-dependent and can be largely automated, resulting in a significant incremental expenditure over a progressive order assembly system.

Zone picking creates the largest number of efficiencies when there are many customer orders, but is much less effective when customer orders arrive relatively infrequently. Additional efficiencies associated with zone picking are:

- *Familiarity*. A picker assigned to a specific part of the warehouse will become very familiar with the locations of the items in his or her area, and so will be better able to pick, both more accurately and at a higher rate of speed.

- *Housekeeping.* A person assigned to a picking zone is fully responsible for that zone, which can lead to a heightened level of housekeeping that makes it much easier to putaway and pick stock.
- *Traffic interference.* There are no problems with stock pickers blocking aisles and getting in the way of other pickers, since there is no reason for anyone to stray outside of their assigned area.
- *Location changes.* Pickers will become so familiar with usage patterns in their assigned areas that they may reshuffle bin locations to locate high-frequency items where they can be more easily picked.
- *Socializing.* Since pickers are assigned to specific areas, there is a reduced amount of socializing among the warehouse staff, which can equate to an increase in picking efficiency.

Despite the significant advantages of zone picking, there are also a few issues to consider, such as:

- *Central picking area.* There must be a method for efficiently reshuffling picked items into their designated customer orders, which may represent a level of organization that does not currently exist within the company.
- *Responsibility.* It can be difficult to track down the reason for a picking error, since a large number of pickers may be involved in each order.
- *Lumpy demand.* The content of customer orders may change over time, resulting in some pickers being intensely busy and others looking for work to do. This issue can be mitigated by periodically rebalancing workloads in the warehouse, based on picking frequencies.
- *Information system reliance.* Zone picking relies upon zone picking software that functions correctly and has excellent up-time. If there are flaws in the system or it is unreliable, the entire picking process may be halted for extended periods.

Tip: Consider posting the picking accuracy and inventory record accuracy for each zone at the end of the zone. This can spur picker competition to see who can achieve the best scores.

In general, the main problem with zone picking is its overall level of complexity. We are deconstructing customer orders, picking in aggregate, and then reconstructing orders for delivery. The increased efficiency of the system should more than offset the increased level of complexity; if not, consider one of the less complex picking methods described in this section.

Tip: Conduct a cost-benefit analysis of zone picking and the best alternative picking method, perhaps using a pilot test, over a sufficient period of time to arrive at a reasonable estimation of the best picking method to use.

Field Picking

Field picking is employed in the more distant reaches of a warehouse – both horizontally and vertically. If there are goods located in higher-level mezzanine storage, or in a far corner, schedule someone to pick these areas, and then house the picked items in bins near one of the more-frequented picking zones. The goods are picked up at this location as part of someone else's scheduled picking duties, and transported from there to the front of the warehouse.

Picking by Experience Level

Some warehouses store dissimilar items adjacent to each other to save space. Research has found that an experienced picker is significantly more efficient than newer workers at sorting through bins of disparate items. Consequently, it can make sense to adjust computerized routing algorithms to send the most experienced pickers to the highest-density bins, even if these workers are not the closest pickers to the bins.

> **Tip:** In situations where the storage environment is relatively chaotic, retaining highly experienced pickers is more important, so it makes sense to increase compensation, benefits, and working conditions to reduce the turnover of pickers.

Additional Picking Efficiencies

This section contains a number of additional concepts that can be used to enhance picking activities. These improvements include reconfiguring storage, the use of certain types of technology, changes in the picking software, and even the prepackaging of goods into standard picking quantities.

Separate Forward-Area Picking

It is not very efficient for pickers to go to reserve pallet storage areas to obtain required goods. These locations are scattered throughout the warehouse, and so maximize the amount of travel time. A better alternative is to shift individual cases and broken cases to a concentrated area in the front of the warehouse, and have the pickers access goods solely within this area. Doing so results in a massive reduction in picker travel time that far outweighs the additional labor required to occasionally refill these forward areas from reserve pallet storage in the rear of the warehouse.

An alternative to this concept is to bring the inventory to pickers with a carousel operation, which is discussed next.

Carousel Picking Pods

In those instances where the picking frequency for certain items is high and the goods occupy a small cubic space, it can make sense to bring inventory to the pickers. This is accomplished by setting up a cluster of carousels (see the Warehouse Storage Systems chapter) that surrounds a picking station. An inventory picker removes targeted items from one carousel while the other carousels are rotating to the correct locations where additional items are to be picked. The number of carousels used depends on the speed with which the carousels can rotate to the next picking position. Typically, there are two or three carousels for each picking pod. This approach minimizes the picking time per order, though at the price of investing in a number of carousels for inventory storage. Also, since the picking process is computer-directed and operates at a predetermined pace, it is relatively easy to predict the amount of picking labor required for a given volume of customer order line items.

Robots Move Mobile Shelves to Pickers

The traditional approach to picking inventory is to send designated pickers into the warehouse, where they spend most of their time walking down the aisles, looking for the correct goods. A different approach is to keep the pickers in centralized packing stations, and instead send robots into the warehouse, with instructions to bring the correct bins to the pickers. This approach requires a significant commitment to reconfiguring the warehouse area, and purchasing a multi-million dollar automated system. Thus, the approach only works well in situations where there is a substantial picking cost that can potentially be reduced.

An additional advantage of this system is that the locations in which bins are stored can be reconfigured on the fly, with high-velocity items being stored close to the picking workstations. If velocity declines over time, these bins can be shifted further away from the pickers. The result is a reduction in the amount of robot travel time, which reduces the need for robots and increases the speed with which orders can be filled.

In addition, mobile shelves and robots are extremely easy to reconfigure into a new work space. This means that a company can shift to an entirely new warehouse within a short period of time; the system essentially rolls itself out in the new warehouse facility. Consequently, a user of this system is much more likely to engage in warehouse relocations to optimize its financial and operational results. For example, it may be necessary to shift a warehouse to follow a customer, take advantage of lower labor costs, or avoid an area that is prone to natural disasters.

EXAMPLE

Smithy Ironworks produces a broad range of iron garden curios. A large customer is Green Thumb Garden Centers, which operates separate distribution centers for five sales regions. Green Thumb changes the location of its regional distribution centers once every five years, to optimize transport costs to its retail stores. Given the importance of this customer, Smithy always positions its own regional warehouses within one mile of the Green Thumb distribution centers. Smithy purchases a robotic mobile shelving system in order to more easily move into new warehouse facilities on an ongoing basis.

Prepackage Goods in Picking Increments

When very small items are stored loose, pickers must either count items individually or use a scale to determine the correct quantity to pick. The first approach in particular takes a large amount of time. To avoid this issue, consider prepackaging goods in the most common picking increments. If goods are being purchased directly from suppliers, this can be accomplished by requiring the suppliers to implement the prepackaging before shipping goods to the company.

> **Tip:** If the counting of individual items is especially laborious, do not even offer individual unit quantities to customers as a pricing option. Instead, the only pricing option is for the prepackaged unit quantity.

Picking with Scales

A warehouse may contain a large number of small items that are stored loose. For example, there may be thousands of washers in a single bin. When these items are scheduled for picking, a picker must spend an inordinate amount of time laboriously counting out the required number of units. This is a poor use of picker time, especially in comparison to the low cost of these items.

A reasonably cost-effective way to deal with these high-volume, low-cost items is to install count scales on picking carts. To use a count scale, a picker places one unit on the scale to ascertain the weight per unit. Once this weight is established, the picker dumps a pile of additional units onto the scale and then adds or subtracts units until the required number is sitting on the scale. This approach is vastly more efficient than hand-counting.

There are only two problems with count scales. One is that they are rather expensive. The more important concern is that inattentiveness on the part of a picker can result in the wrong number of units being pulled from stock. Consequently, from an accuracy perspective, it is better to limit the use of count scales to the more experienced staff. This may require picking tours to be designed around whether count scales are needed to pick certain items from stock.

WMS-Directed Picking Issues

If a warehouse management system is directing pickers to pick goods via remote terminals, there are a few programming issues to be aware of that can impact the efficiency of picking operations. They are:

- If there are breaks in the racks, they can be used as short cuts between aisles. Their existence should be noted in the WMS, so the system can direct pickers through them as part of their picking activities, thereby saving travel time.
- The WMS may be designed to first empty the case and broken case areas, and then direct pickers to the reserve area for additional picking. This approach does not work well when the total amount to be picked equates to more than one pallet load, since the result is a broken pallet in the reserve area. Instead, alter the logic to first pick a complete pallet load if the amount to be picked equals or exceeds the amount of a full pallet.

The Cost of Picking Errors

No matter how efficient a company's picking operations may be, they still form the largest part of the costs of a warehouse operation. The situation is exacerbated when there are picking errors, since the number of additional steps required to correct a mistake can consume an extraordinary amount of staff time. Consider the following picking costs:

- *Processing.* The customer service staff handles the call from the customer, pointing out that an incorrect item was shipped, and issues a return merchandise authorization.
- *Freight.* The incorrectly-picked item must be shipped back from the customer, with the company bearing the cost of the freight return.
- *Receiving review.* The receiving staff opens and inspects the returned item for damage.
- *Damage.* If the returned item was damaged, the company dispositions it at the best possible price.
- *Picking and packing.* The correct item is picked, packed in a new shipping container, and shipped to the customer.
- *Cost of cash.* If the customer has elected to not pay the company's invoice until the incorrect part is replaced, the company loses interest income on the receivable for the period during which payment is delayed.

Several of the costs just noted are fixed costs, and would be incurred even if there were no picking error. For example, there is probably no actual increase in the costs of processing, receiving review, or picking. Nonetheless, a company will certainly incur the incremental cost of freight, as well as the risk that the returned goods are damaged and cannot be re-sold.

Given the extent of picking error costs, it should be evident that driving down the number of picking errors is a major target when selecting a picking methodology. In many cases, the cost of picking errors may drive a company to adopt a slower picking system, as long as it can deliver higher rates of picking accuracy.

Kitting

The assumption thus far has been that all picking activities are intended for shipments to customers. It is also possible that goods are being picked from stock for delivery to the production area – this is known as kitting. When all items to be kitted are available, they are shifted to a container, which is prominently labeled with the associated job number, and forwarded to the manufacturing area.

> **Tip:** When setting aside kitted parts in a bin, the main goal is to ensure that the parts are not intermixed with or mistaken for the parts intended for other jobs. This means the bin must be prominently identified and have sufficiently high sides to prevent intermixing. To forestall the loss of identifying paperwork, put job documents in a secure sleeve that is permanently affixed to the bin.

The warehouse management system times the release of kitted goods to production to be just prior to the scheduled job start date, so that not too many kitted jobs are cluttering up the shop floor. This is the standard approach to kitting, and results in the following benefits:

- The presence of all required goods is verified before a job begins, so there are no production stoppages caused by missing raw materials.
- Work-in-process levels are reduced, since there is no reason for jobs to be halted partway through production because of missing raw materials.
- Since parts are removed from stock and sent to production in one batch, there are fewer inventory touches, resulting in less parts damage.
- Machine operators do not have to waste time going to the warehouse to request missing parts.

There are several variations on how kitting is conducted, each with its own advantages and disadvantages. The following table notes kitting options:

Types of Kitting

Kitting Technique	Advantages	Disadvantages
Directed by warehouse management system	Keeps kitting duties away from production staff	Subject to inventory record inaccuracies. Parts shortages require production staff to obtain missing parts from the warehouse.
Kitting at point of use; inventory stored locally	Operators do their own kitting from readily accessible inventory	Machine operators pick parts. This approach requires extra floor space near the production area. Also requires extra machine operator training.
Kitting at point of use; rapid replenishment	Operators do their own kitting from readily accessible inventory	Can have shortage in local inventory if counts are not accurate, resulting in late replenishment. Also requires machine operator training.
Outsourced kitting; suppliers deliver parts on just-in-time basis	Pushes labor costs to suppliers	No direct control over materials sent to the production area; requires excellent cooperation from suppliers.

Technically, kitting consumes extra inventory, for goods are set aside for specific jobs until used at a later date. However, the alternative is to have machine operators conduct their own kitting by taking raw materials from nearby stocks – and that can interfere with the productivity of the production process. Consequently, the decision to implement a particular type of kitting depends upon a variety of factors, including the following:

- The amount of excess space in and near the production area. More space allows for local inventory storage.
- The distance between the warehouse and the production area. Longer travel distances do not allow for economical replenishment of local stocks, or at least require that local storage be in larger quantities.
- The accuracy of inventory records for local inventory. Highly accurate records for locally-stored inventory make a rapid-replenishment solution more viable.
- The existence of production bottlenecks. The operator of a bottleneck operation does not have any excess time to locate inventory items in nearby storage locations.

Replenishment

The bins from which the warehouse staff picks goods must be replenished at regular intervals. How is this accomplished? Here are several alternatives, in order of increasing sophistication:

- *When empty*. When a picker notes that a bin is empty, he notifies the replenishment staff, which shifts replacement goods into the bin from the reserve storage area in the rear of the warehouse. This approach creates an immediate crisis, since the bin is empty and therefore no longer available for picking purposes until the replenishment task is completed.
- *Periodic*. Bins are deliberately overloaded with goods, so there is no need for replenishment staff during the picking shifts. Once the pickers go home, the replenishment staff visually inspects the bins, determines which ones require replenishment, and reloads the bins. This approach avoids stockout conditions, but requires more on-hand inventory and the scheduling of a separate shift when pickers cannot be used.
- *Anticipated – manual notification*. When a picker notes that the remaining amount in a bin has dropped below a marked fill line, he notifies the replenishment staff. This approach avoids an immediate crisis, since there are still some goods on hand that can be picked. However, it relies on an alert picker to initiate the replenishment process.
- *Anticipated – automatic notification*. If there is a computerized tracking system that maintains an updated register of unit quantities, then this system issues an automated notification to the replenishment staff, telling them which bins require replenishment and the number of units to add to the bins.

The final option is strongly recommended, for it shifts the replenishment notification burden away from the pickers, who should be more concerned with their picking chores.

The Simultaneous Replenishment and Picking Conundrum

As may have been evident from a perusal of the last few sections, there is intense interest in creating a highly efficient picking environment. Doing so ensures more rapid order fulfillment and less travel time by the picking staff. However, the picking staff cannot operate if the locations from which they pick are not replenished at regular intervals. This can lead to conflict, since the putaway staff must co-inhabit the same aisles as the pickers while adding inventory to the shelves. When there are too many people in an aisle at the same time, travel times may increase as everyone maneuvers around the various packing crates and picking carts. However, there are some ways to circumvent this conundrum. Consider the following alternatives:

- *Separate shifts.* Picking is usually needed during the day shift, so that picked items can be sorted and packed for shipments during the day. This leaves either the second or third shift for the replenishment staff. Thus, the two functions are split into different time periods.
- *Separate aisles.* It may be possible to assign picking duties for a certain set of aisles, while a replenishment team works in all other aisles. This approach is quite difficult to achieve, especially in a zone picking environment where the picking staff is employed in every aisle, all of the time.
- *Separate breaks.* If the picking staff is allowed break periods, the replenishment staff can update their aisles during the breaks. This approach is limited by the duration of the break periods, but can be useful for replenishing bins whose contents have become extremely low.
- *Multiple picking locations.* A warehouse can be designed to have more than one picking location for an SKU, so that replenishment can occur at one location while picking is taking place at another location.
- *Gravity-flow racks.* As described in the Warehouse Storage Systems chapter, gravity-flow racks allow the replenishment staff to add goods at the rear of a rack. The goods then roll down a ramp, to be accessed at the front of the rack by the picking staff. This excellent approach separates the replenishment and picking employees, so that they can both work during the same shift without interrupting each other's flow of work.
- *Combine functions.* In a small warehouse environment, it may be possible to have the picking staff also work on replenishment activities. This scenario usually only works where the customer order volume is so inconsistent that stock pickers have large blocks of unused time within which to engage in replenishment activities.

Interleaving

A problem that applies to both putaways and picking is the concept of *deadheading*, where a person is sent to putaway or pick goods, and is not performing any useful function during one leg of the trip. For example, a forklift operator tasked with picking a pallet from a far corner of the warehouse will not be carrying a load while moving to the location where the goods are stored. This issue can be resolved with interleaving, which is the practice of assigning an additional task to a person in transit. To continue with the same example, a forklift operator can be assigned to putaway goods from the receiving area to a rack location near where the goods designated for picking are located. This fills one leg of the operator's trip, while the picking task fills the other leg. This approach can result in a massive increase in the productivity of the putaway and picking employees, likely resulting in a reduced staffing requirement.

Interleaving is most effective when automatically managed by a warehouse management system (WMS). The WMS communicates with the warehouse staff on-the-fly via radio frequency terminals, sending them an ongoing series of picking and putaway instructions.

Summary

If a company wants to reduce its warehouse costs, a good place to look is in the putaway and picking functions. These tasks absorb the bulk of all warehouse labor costs, especially in the amount of travel time required to move goods around the warehouse. Consequently, a warehouse and its WMS should be set up to either bring high-turnover goods and human operators as close together as possible, or to increase the efficiency of staff time.

Putaway and picking tasks generate nearly all of the inventory transactions in a warehouse, and so represent the main source of errors in the inventory records. For a discussion of inventory accuracy and how it can be improved, see the Inventory Record Accuracy chapter.

Chapter 8
The Impact of Production on Inventory

Introduction

Much of the discussion of inventory tends to involve the warehouse, where inventory is most easily found. However, it is the production system and the policies that drive the production process that are the foundation for the amounts and types of inventory stored in the warehouse. An extremely advanced production system that is combined with a tightly-clustered group of suppliers can result in an exceedingly small warehouse, and therefore a very small investment in inventory. Conversely, a company that continues to produce to a forecast and employs long lead times will likely find it necessary to invest in a large amount of inventory.

In this chapter, we explore the push and pull production systems, and the necessary components of a pull system. We also address a number of other production issues relating to inventory, such as the relationship between a production bottleneck and inventory, how the length of a production line impacts inventory levels, and how expediting alters the amount of in-process inventory.

The Produce to Forecast (Push) System

The most common production system is one in which a forecast of expected customer demand is generated, and is used to schedule production. This is known as a push system, since a production planner is pushing production orders into the manufacturing process.

The production module used to plan production around a forecast is called material requirements planning (MRP). MRP links computer-driven planning with the bills of material for all items to be produced, records of on-hand inventory balances, and a production schedule. The output of this system is a listing of dates on which orders are released for production, as well as a set of purchase orders issued to suppliers for raw materials to be delivered to the company in order to support the planned production. An MRP system is a marvel of interlinked schedules, and can yield significant output improvements over a less organized system. However, it is also highly dependent upon having accurate inventory records and bills of material; if there is a data error anywhere in the system, MRP planning breaks down.

The use of a push system has a profound impact on the amount of inventory in a company. The following areas are affected:

- *Finished goods*. The accuracy of the forecast used to schedule production directly impacts the amount of finished goods on hand. If the forecast is lower than actual demand, finished goods inventory levels will be near zero. If the forecast is too high, these inventory levels will be quite high as well, and there is an increased risk of having obsolete inventory on hand. These issues can be mitigated by producing to a very short-term forecast, for which the accuracy is likely to be higher than a long-term forecast.

- *Work-in-process.* There can be a substantial amount of goods in the production process, depending upon the extent to which the system assumes that goods are batched at a work station prior to being moved to the next work station for additional processing. There can also be significant queue times in front of each work station, allowing work-in-process to pile up.
- *Raw materials.* If large safety stocks are built into the MRP system, there may be substantial raw material inventory balances on hand to guard against shortages. This can result in obsolete raw materials, if the products for which the raw materials are intended are cancelled.

The preceding points indicate that inventory levels are relatively high under a push system. While true, an MRP system supported by accurate information can be tweaked over time to reduce the inventory investment to modest levels. For a more substantial inventory reduction, see the following Produce to Order section.

The Produce to Order (Pull) System

One of the more significant reasons for excessive quantities of finished goods inventory is that companies estimate customer demand, and produce to that forecast. When they do so, some products will inevitably be over-produced, since it is impossible to precisely determine the amounts that will be ordered. In addition, other products will be under-produced in comparison to demand, resulting in backordered goods, lost sales, and customer dissatisfaction.

A possible solution is to produce goods only after an order has been received from a customer, which is called the just-in-time (JIT) system. The result of producing to order is that a company can vastly reduce the amount of inventory that it must keep on hand in anticipation of customer orders, while the incidence of losses from inventory obsolescence should plunge. Further, because producing to order can exactly match customer requirements, this approach tends to improve customer satisfaction, which in turn leads to customer retention over the long term.

However, it is not an easy matter to switch from the traditional produce-to-forecast method to the produce-to-order method. The initiation of production orders must be reversed, from a push system to a pull system, where the receipt of a customer order triggers the manufacturing process. Also, though the ultimate goal might be to only produce to actual customer orders, it is usually more practical to create a uniform work load in accordance with a production plan, thereby preventing demand spikes from overloading the production system. The result is some finished goods inventory that acts as a buffer between customers and the production area.

It is critical to minimize work-in-process levels in this environment, so that a company can quickly react to a customer order. To do so, the manufacturing process must be clustered around production cells that can rapidly complete all required processing of goods. A cell arrangement is a cluster of people and equipment that are brought together to focus on the construction of a small group of related products. A production cell is configured in a "U" shape, which is an efficient flow path for unfinished parts to follow as they move through the various conversion stages. This arrangement requires employee training, since they are expected to operate multiple work stations in sequence; the higher level of job complexity tends to foster an enhanced level of employee morale.

To do this effectively, the equipment in each cell must be capable of a fast changeover to handle different products in rapid succession (see the Fast Equipment Changeovers section). The ordering of goods between production cells is handled by an authorization to produce a specific quantity of goods, which is called a kanban (see the Kanban Notifications section). Once kanbans are in place, the amount of work-in-process should decline precipitously, since the kanbans only authorize the production of just enough units to ensure that a customer order is completed.

A company is typically faced with a roughly predictable number of units that it can expect customers to purchase within a given period of time. If so, the team in a production cell must ensure that they maintain an average pace of unit production that ensures the number of items to be sold can be created. This concept is called operational takt time, which includes all downtime expected; downtime may include such factors as stoppages for maintenance, equipment breakdowns, holidays and so forth.

To measure operational takt time, calculate the average amount of time that a cell is actually in operation each day, and divide by the number of units that must be built each day in order to meet demand. If the number of units actually produced falls below the operational takt time, then management can take steps to increase production, such as by authorizing a third shift or by outsourcing work. Takt time is typically posted in a production cell, so that employees can see how closely they are adhering to production requirements.

A pull system can only work if the quality of first-pass production is extremely high. Otherwise, so many goods will be rejected that additional production orders must be run through the system, thereby delaying the fulfillment of customer orders. See the First-Pass Quality section for more information.

Once a pull system has been properly installed, a company is likely to experience the following improvements in its operations and inventory investment:

- A reduction in the amount of factory space needed, since equipment is positioned closer together.
- A reduction in materials handling costs, since inventory is handed off between adjacent production cells, rather than being allowed to accumulate and then shifted with a fork lift.
- A reduction in inventory of all types, since it is being gradually bled out of the system in order to make the production process more reactive to customer orders.
- Much higher quality levels, since faulty goods are noted at once and the causes are corrected before too many parts are similarly afflicted.
- A reduction in lead times, so that customers can be promised delivery much sooner than had previously been the case.

In brief, if a pull system can be properly configured, the amount of inventory reduction that can be achieved is profound.

3-D Printing

A production technique that is having a profound impact on inventory management is 3-D printing. This is a process that makes three-dimensional solid objects from a digital file. This is done using additive processes, where an object is created by laying down successive layers of material until the object is created. Each of these layers can be seen as a thinly-sliced cross-section of the object. This approach is available using a variety of source materials, including resins, cement, glass, metal alloys, and ceramics. 3-D printing has multiple positive effects on inventory management. Consider the following:

- Since parts and entire products can be printed on demand, there is less need to keep finished units in stock.
- Since only a small number of base materials are needed to supply the printers, there is significantly less raw material and component inventory to manage.
- It may make sense to operate printers in regional warehouses, so that goods can be produced and shipped from those company locations closest to the customers who ordered them.
- Since parts and products are only being made when there is a customer order, there is no risk of having residual obsolete inventory on hand.

In short, the use of 3-D printing should result in a much lower investment in inventory, both in terms of raw materials and finished goods, while warehouse managers may find themselves engaged in 3-D printing within their warehouses.

Organize the Factory around Products

The traditional factory arrangement is by functional area, where a cluster of similar work stations are placed in one location and tasked with handling a single processing step. Inventory is sent to each of these functional areas in turn for additional processing steps. For example, a furniture factory may run all jobs through a cluster of lathes, followed by carving machines and then sanders. When inventory is run through this process, it is done in batches, with a routing sheet attached to each batch. When processing is completed in one functional area, the batch is moved to the next area. The trouble with this layout is that batches are placed in queues in front of each area, which can result in inordinately long wait times. It is common for the total time spent in the production area to be comprised of at least 95% wait time.

To avoid these wait times, organize the factory around specific products. This means that small production cells are organized, where each unit in process is taken from work station to work station without any wait time, until processing is complete. This approach calls for the use of smaller and less-complex equipment that can be easily moved and reconfigured into different production cells. The product-centered approach eliminates nearly all of the work-in-process in the production system.

Switching from a function-focused to a product-focused factory calls for a change in mindset. The production manager must be persuaded that it is not necessary to maintain a high rate of usage for all work stations, since this mindset means that longer production runs are needed. The product-focused arrangement does not focus on work station usage levels at all, but rather on pushing small numbers of units through the factory as quickly as possible.

> **Tip:** Only a small number of employees are needed in a production cell, and each one may be trained to work on multiple machines. To improve employee familiarity with the parts being produced, assign groups of similar products to each production cell. Not only does this increased volume eventually lead to more cell efficiency, it also reduces the number of defective parts.

Fast Equipment Changeovers

The use of very short production runs is a good way to produce to customer orders, which may only require a small number of units. However, doing so means that some equipment will experience downtime while they are changed over to produce the goods specified in customer orders. This problem is a major one, for equipment changeovers can consume a large part of the time available to the production staff, effectively reducing the capacity of a production facility.

The problem can be reduced by instituting a number of upgrades to shorten the time required to change over equipment. This program involves videotaping the current process and going over each step to see which activities can be altered to compress the change over time. Common changeover techniques are to preposition dies and tools next to equipment, eliminate all non-essential activities during the changeover period, and replace nuts and bolts with hand knobs and levers that are easier to position and tighten. The examination process may go through a number of iterations before an acceptably short changeover period is achieved.

> **Tip:** The reduction of changeover time is a substantial effort, so focus the review team on the equipment that represents a bottleneck in the production process. If a machine has lots of excess capacity, it is less critical to reduce its changeover time.

If the changeover period can be shortened to a few minutes or even less than a minute, this means that the production staff can easily shut down production intended for one customer and switch to the production of different products intended for someone else. This capability means that there is less need to stockpile finished goods in anticipation of customer orders, thereby reducing the investment in working capital and shrinking the risk of having obsolete inventory.

Kanban Notifications

A kanban is an authorization to produce goods in an environment where the consumption of goods is the trigger to produce more goods, rather than a forecast of possible consumption that may never occur. A kanban can take many forms, such as a colored card, a bin, an e-mail, or some alternative form of visual signal. A colored card is perhaps the most common form of kanban now in use, though electronic notifications are increasing in importance. A kanban card typically contains information about the item that requires replenishment and the amount to be replenished.

Here is an example of how a kanban card might work:

1. There is a bin full of parts on the production floor, to be used by the work station to which it has been delivered. The bin contains a kanban card.
2. When the bin is empty, it is sent to the upstream work station that provided the original workstation with parts. The upstream work station immediately sends one full bin of parts back; this bin is the only amount of inventory that the upstream work station has thus far been authorized to produce.
3. The upstream work station is now authorized to fill the empty bin to the extent of the quantity stated on the kanban card.
4. The filled bin is then held, pending the return of an empty bin from the downstream work station.

Kanbans are employed in conjunction with a pull system, so that each downstream work station authorizes an upstream work station to produce a certain additional amount of parts that are then sent to the downstream work station for further processing. In essence, the concept is used to ensure that only enough parts are manufactured to fulfill a customer order. Once that order has been completed, no additional kanbans are issued, so no upstream work stations are allowed to produce any more goods. The result is an extremely low investment in inventory.

A kanban system may be incorporated into a computer-controlled production system, or it can be an entirely manual notification system. The use of kanbans can also be extended to suppliers, so that suppliers, in effect, become the upstream work stations of a business.

Achieve First-Pass Quality

When production runs are as small as one unit, it is critical that the quality of these goods be perfect on the first pass. Since there is no reserve of extra goods to draw upon, an additional round of production activities must be initiated to supply replacements to damaged or out-of-specification parts, which can quickly bog down the production process.

To detect out-of-specification parts as soon as possible, the workers at the next downstream work station should examine incoming goods closely to detect issues; if found, they must immediately notify the issuing work station that there is a problem. By taking this approach, only a tiny number of units will be out-of-specification before remedial action is taken.

First-pass quality must be the job of the production staff, rather than quality inspectors. Inspectors only review a small sample of the total number of units that pass through a facility, while the production staff handles every unit. Consequently, the risk of having a large number of out-of-specification parts pass through the production facility before detection is much higher with inspectors.

Unfortunately, the first-pass quality concept works best only in a cellular manufacturing environment, where the amount of work-in-process inventory is minimal, allowing for more rapid detection of problems. In a more automated long production run environment, there is less opportunity for employees to personally review goods in process, so that low quality goods can more easily creep into the inventory.

Enhance Feedback Loop to Suppliers

As just noted, products passing through the production area must meet all specifications on the first pass, or else the production process will require more inventory to replace nonconforming goods. This principle also applies to suppliers. A supplier is essentially an upstream work station that feeds goods into the factory. If the goods being forwarded from a supplier do not meet specifications, then the situation should be dealt with in the same manner in which non-conforming goods are handled in a factory – via immediate notification.

Immediate notification is best accomplished by establishing a direct line of communication between the person discovering a problem and the production staff of the supplier. This direct line is needed in order to inform the supplier that it has a problem that must be corrected at once. Otherwise, if the issue goes through channels to the company's purchasing department and then on to the supplier's sales department, it could be days or even weeks before the issue is corrected – and in the meantime, out-of-specification goods are continuing to be shipped to the company.

Move Cells Closer Together

When there is some physical distance between production cells, parts completed in an upstream cell are typically allowed to pile up for a time, after which a materials handling person arrives with a forklift and shifts the parts to the next downstream production cell. There are several problems with this. First, the amount of inventory that is allowed to pile up represents an extra investment in inventory. Second, the materials handling person could damage the parts while transporting them. Third, a defective process in the upstream production cell might not be noticed until the entire batch is moved to the downstream process and used by the staff at that production cell, resulting in the entire batch being declared defective. The solution is to move the cells closer together and connect them with conveyors. By doing so, units can be shifted to the next production cell at once, there is no need for any materials handling staff, and the production area requires less floor space.

> **Tip:** When part of the production process involves an immovable piece of production equipment (a monument), consider setting up the production cells that use the monument's output adjacent to the monument. Doing so minimizes the amount of materials movement.

Inventory In-Process Identification

It is accepted practice to identify an inventory item when it is first received, usually with a label that includes an identification number, name, quantity, and unit of measure. This information is needed to maintain an accurate system of inventory records. However, what is not always understood is the need to also document the stage of completion of goods that are moving through the production process. This means that it may be necessary to attach a routing sheet to the goods, on which work center operators note the various stages of processing completion, before moving goods on to the next production stage. In the absence of this information, the level of production processing is not always clear, so goods may be routed to the wrong workstation or held to one side until their status can be ascertained. In either case, there is a production delay, which effectively increases the amount of inventory in process.

> **Tip:** Always attach work-in-process documentation to goods in such a manner that the paperwork cannot possibly be lost. This usually means enclosing the materials in a plastic sleeve, which is securely affixed to the goods, perhaps riveted to the container in which the goods are stored. Simply taping documentation to the goods is not sufficient, since paperwork can easily be lost or damaged.

Reduce In-Process Container Sizes

In some applications, workstation operators are issued trays, bins, or boxes that they are told to fill up with processed parts before handing them off to the next scheduled work station. If these containers are large, it means that more work-in-process inventory is building up within the production area. Simply reducing the size of these containers reduces the amount of inventory buildup between workstations, which in turn reduces the investment in work-in-process inventory.

An extension of this concept is to install conveyor belts between production work stations, so that individual units are transferred. However, this approach is significantly more expensive than the use of containers. Also, depending on the types of conveyors used, it can be more difficult to readily reconfigure the shop floor around different cells. Further, a motor-driven conveyor can break down, thereby interrupting the flow of goods between machines. An alternative that avoids the use of motors is to install rollers that shift goods down an incline to the next work station.

Locate Cells near Common Inventory

In a cellular production environment, it makes sense to stock raw materials as close to the cells as possible, within easy reach of the production staff. However, what if two cells located far apart on the factory floor both need the same raw materials? In this case, the materials manager is faced with the equally unpalatable choices of stocking the same inventory next to two cells, or of keeping the inventory in the warehouse and periodically having a forklift operator shift goods to those cells requiring the materials.

A longer-term solution that may be more palatable is to compare the production cell layout on the shop floor to the individual raw material requirements of each cell, and gradually alter the cell layout to more closely align those cells jointly using the same materials. These closely-aligned cells can then share inventory that is stored in a single adjacent location.

There is no perfect solution, since adjacent cells may only share demand for certain raw materials. Also, the mix and uses of production cells are continually in flux, so the ability to share raw materials will improve and decline over time. At best, this issue is one of several concerns that should be addressed when production cells are formed, reconfigured, or moved.

> **Tip:** When there are raw materials currently being used by a production cell, store it between the cell and the most adjacent aisle. Doing so protects employees from being injured by any materials handling equipment that may inadvertently veer out of an aisle. Damaging inventory is better than damaging people!

Purchase Less-Complex Machinery

An inherent requirement of a production cell is that it be comprised of a small number of machines that can be configured over time to match the changing needs of a business. Ease of configuration means that a machine be on the smaller and lighter side, so the objective is to avoid acquisitions of larger and more complex equipment that is typically positioned once and never moved again. This latter type of machine is called a *monument*, and leads to several types of suboptimal results. Consider the following:

- *No backup.* When a large investment is made in a monument machine, this usually implies that there was only enough cash to buy one unit. Therefore, when this machine is down for maintenance, there is no backup unit available to continue production, resulting in a complete stoppage.
- *Production runs.* Since a monument tends to take longer to set up, there is an inclination to have longer production runs, to justify the time required for the set up. The result is more inventory than a company actually needs.
- *Breakdown rate.* A more complex machine is more likely to break down, so expect it to have more down time and more maintenance staff time applied to it than would be the case if a simpler machine had been acquired.

> **Tip:** It can make sense to purchase as many machines of the same type as possible from a single supplier. By doing so, a small number of spare parts can be kept in stock that are applicable to a large number of machines, thereby reducing the investment in spare parts.

In short, the replacement of monuments with smaller and more configurable equipment results in more predictable and shorter production runs.

Manage Inventory around the Bottleneck

In many manufacturing environments, there is a bottleneck work station. This area constrains the company from producing more goods, and so impedes its ability to earn a profit. A bottleneck arises when a work station does not have sufficient capacity to handle the demand for its services. When a bottleneck is recognized, management should support it with extra staffing, off-hours preventive maintenance, and selective outsourcing to work around the constraint.

There is also an inventory management issue related to bottleneck operations. Ideally, there should be a large buffer of inventory positioned immediately in front of the bottleneck. This buffer is needed to ensure that there is always enough work to keep the bottleneck operation running at all times. Since the work station is a constrained resource, any work stoppage will have a direct negative impact on company profitability. Thus, this is one of the few cases in which having extra inventory on the shop floor is to be encouraged.

How much inventory should be stored in this buffer? Ideally, any work stoppage upstream from the bottleneck should not completely exhaust the inventory buffer. Thus, a historical analysis of work stoppages will indicate the appropriate amount of inventory to position in front of the bottleneck. Here are several variations on the buffer concept to consider:

- *Expedite zone.* A portion of the inventory buffer may be designated as an expedite zone. This is the final tranche of inventory that is accessed before the buffer is emptied. As soon as inventory is accessed from this part of the buffer, the management team is notified to expedite an accelerated rate of production in the upstream workstations, so that the buffer can be refilled. If there is no expedite zone, management has to continually monitor the entire buffer to see if there will be any incipient shortages.
- *Buffer holes.* When there is a sudden decline in the unit count in the inventory buffer, this is called a hole in the buffer. Such a hole is caused by a production failure at an upstream workstation that delays the arrival of parts. Every buffer hole should be investigated in detail to ascertain the reason for its existence, which is then documented in a buffer penetration report. A sample report follows.

Sample Buffer Penetration Report

Date	Delay Duration	Source Work Station	Problem
Feb. 13	8 hours	Splitting	Cutter saw blade broke; no replacement on site
Feb. 14	6 hours	Sanding	Staff reduction due to injury
Feb. 15	4 hours	Bleach bath	Incorrect bleach concentration
Feb. 18	2 hours	Drilling	Drilling template damaged

The information in the report is used to locate and correct the problems causing buffer holes. If the occurrence of these items can be contained, the number and severity of buffer holes will drop, allowing a company to reduce its investment in the inventory buffer.

- *Assembly buffer.* If there is a final assembly function where materials arrive from several sources and are assembled into a final product, it will also be necessary to place a buffer in front of that area. The issue is not a shortfall of parts arriving from the bottleneck – after all, the bottleneck is the most heavily monitored operation in the company. Instead, the buffer is used to guard against shortages of all other types of parts. The assembly buffer operates under the same principles used for the bottleneck buffer – that it provides sufficient unit quantities to guard against shortages caused by upstream workstations. This may involve the use of an expedite zone to warn management of impending shipment delays. By having an assembly area buffer, it is easier to establish a rapid flow of parts from the bottleneck, into the final assembly area, and out through the shipping dock to customers. In short, this additional buffer is needed to ensure that there is no final hitch in the production process that can interfere with the realization of revenue.
- *Dynamic buffering.* Under this approach, the production planning staff attempts to strike a balance between the amount of extra upstream capacity needed and the smallest possible investment in the inventory buffer. Doing so requires constant oversight of the level of buffer inventory. This approach is usually only necessary when the cost of upgrades in upstream capacity is considerable, and there is a large monetary investment in inventory. The amount of monitoring work required may mean that a full-time staff person is needed.

Another consideration is the speed with which the inventory in the buffer can be rebuilt, if it is depleted from an upstream work stoppage. The replenishment speed is based on the sprint capacity of the upstream work stations. *Sprint capacity* is the ability of a work station to generate excess inventory. A work station with a large amount of excess production capacity has a large amount of sprint capacity, and so can rebuild the bottleneck inventory buffer in short order. Consequently, a company with excellent sprint capacity requires a smaller inventory buffer, since it can rely upon the upstream workstations to rebuild inventory. Conversely, poor sprint capacity means that it will take a long time to rebuild the inventory buffer, which presents a strong case in favor of maintaining a larger inventory buffer. In short, the size of the buffer is based on both the upstream work stoppage history and the sprint capacity of upstream work stations.

The amount of upstream capacity needed to initially build and then maintain an inventory buffer does not necessarily require an inordinate investment, if a proper analysis is conducted to determine the exact amounts of additional capacity needed. The correct amount of capacity can be determined over time by gradually increasing the capacity level in response to actual buffer penetrations, or by modeling such penetrations to see where capacity needs to be bolstered. Another option is to increase capacity in those areas where labor is needed, rather than fixed assets, by engaging in cross-training and then calling in the extra staff when there is a sudden need to increase production volume.

A theoretical alternative to the inventory buffer is to maintain a skimpy buffer, but a large investment in upstream production capacity. This would mean that any inventory shortfalls could be fulfilled quite rapidly. However, the cost to maintain an inventory buffer is not especially large, while the cost of the fixed assets needed to maintain a comprehensive level of upstream capacity can be inordinately large. Consequently, the briefest financial modeling will usually indicate that a larger inventory buffer should be maintained.

Adjust Batch Sizes

A potentially significant issue is the number and duration of the batches that are scheduled to run, both upstream from the bottleneck and at the bottleneck. The issues are:

- *Proportion of setup time*. If there are a large number of small jobs, and those jobs require a significant amount of setup time, this reduces the number of minutes in the period that are available for actual processing work. This is more of an issue at the bottleneck (with its limited availability) than at the upstream workstations, which have more time available to accommodate numerous setups.
- *Delivery speed*. The speed with which batches of parts are delivered to the next downstream workstation is increased when the size of each batch decreases. The reason is that it takes less time for a workstation operator to complete a batch when a smaller number of units must be placed in the shipping container. The concept is explained in the following sample batch sizing exhibit, where there is an inventory buffer for which the unit quantity is mandated to be 50 units. If the unit count in the buffer declines to 25 units, the expedite zone (see the last topic) will be accessed, which will trigger a notification to the production manager that there is a problem. In Situation 1, the batch size being delivered is 25 units, which will be drawn down to zero before the expedite zone is accessed, due to the longer periods required to complete a batch of 25 units. In Situation 2, the batch size is cut to 15 units, which means that batch deliveries are made about twice as fast. Because the replenishments occur so much more frequently, there are less drastic declines in the buffer inventory between deliveries. In short, smaller batch sizes allow for a smaller investment in work-in-process inventory, while still maintaining an adequate buffer stock.

Sample Batch Sizing Scenarios

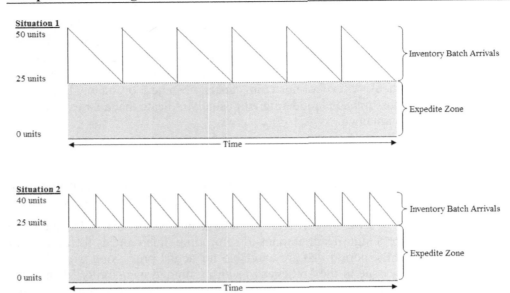

There are two production issues to take away from this discussion of batch sizes, which are:

- It is acceptable to have small batch sizes upstream from the bottleneck, since these workstations have excess capacity that can absorb the extra time required for the many machine setups associated with small batch sizes. These small batch sizes are useful for reducing the size of the inventory buffer. Consequently, consider an ongoing program of scheduling ever-smaller batch sizes until the burden of the additional setups begins to cut into the excess amount of sprint capacity available upstream from the bottleneck.
- It is less acceptable to follow the same philosophy for the bottleneck, where there is no excess time to waste on additional setups. If there are many setups and the setups are time-consuming, the total amount of units processed will decline. Instead, if setups at the bottleneck are lengthy, focus on larger batch sizes just in this one area. A larger batch size can be created when several customer orders are combined for production purposes. If a larger batch is authorized that cannot be immediately sold, one must balance the saved setup time against the cost of holding the inventory.

Shorten the Production Line

When a company installs a long production line, more space is allowed for employees to move around. However, it also means that there is space *between* employees. If parts are traveling down the line at a steady pace, the extra space means that there are a large number of work-in-process parts on the line at any one time that are not being worked on by employees. These extra parts represent an increase in the company's investment in inventory. This investment can be reduced by shortening the production line. The ideal arrangement is when the number of parts traveling down the line equals the number of employees on the line, which means that every item in process is being worked on at any given moment. Shortening the line to this extent will require some work load balancing by the industrial engineering staff, and may not be achievable at once. However, continual attention to this issue can reap benefits, not only in inventory reduction, but also by reducing the space taken up by the production line.

A variation on the concept is to remove some tasks from each production line, so there are more production lines that are individually responsible for fewer tasks. Fewer people and machines are involved in each production line, so a problem with either one will result in a smaller number of faulty units being produced.

Segment the Production Line

If a company uses a production line, it may have given its employees the right to stop the entire line if they see a problem that requires immediate correction. While the stoppage concept is a laudable one, an employee may be less inclined to use it if doing so results in a massive production line creaking to a halt. This can also be a concern from the financial analyst's perspective, who is undoubtedly calculating the impact on revenue of stopping a production line.

A possible solution is to divide the production line into segments, with each segment operating independently from the other segments. By doing so, an employee-authorized stoppage will only impact the segment on which that employee is working. All other segments will continue to operate in the normal manner. This approach will not impact the surrounding line segments, as long as there is an inventory buffer located between the segments. This buffer can be drawn upon by a downstream segment when there are no goods flowing from an upstream segment.

The reduction of work-in-process inventory is a central goal of inventory management, and this recommendation goes against that goal. However, it may be necessary to use line segmentation in error-laden production environments, so that the entire facility is not being continually shut down by production problems. In this environment, the use of line segmentation and inventory buffers may be the lesser of two evils.

Process Control

In many production processes, there are key points in the process where the operator must make an adjustment to the equipment in order to correctly manufacture goods. If this adjustment is incorrect, then a large amount of inventory may be rendered unusable. Consequently, exercising proper control over the production process can have a major impact on the amount of inventory used. The steps required to ensure that a proper system of process control is in place are as follows:

1. *Identify key variables in the process.* This is the machine settings and procedures that can alter the specifications of finished goods. A key variable has an impact on the dimensions, appearance, and/or performance criteria of a

product. All of these key variables should be identified. Machine operators are an excellent source of information when reviewing key variables.

2. *Develop a control plan.* This is the complete documentation of every machine setting and procedural step required to manufacture a product to specifications. The plan also includes allowable tolerances and the locations and extent of quality tests. The plan should be designed to incorporate how any changes in the various settings and procedures impact each other, so that the sum total of the plan will result in products that meet specifications.

3. *Verify the plan.* Walk through the production process with the control plan and verify that the ordering of steps is correct, that all settings and procedures are accurate, and that there is no missing information that might otherwise result in incorrect product specifications.

Tip: If the inventory being used is expensive, or if a lengthy production run is contemplated, pause a production line after the first batch has been produced. Test the batch for compliance with customer specifications, and then require a process sign-off by a qualified person. Then continue the production run. This approach is designed to contain the risk of destroying an expensive batch of inventory.

---

4. *Analyze the process.* Examine the production process to see if it is capable of producing goods consistently within specifications on an ongoing basis. Outcomes that routinely fall outside of the indicated specifications can be a sign of excessively tight specifications, as well as a variety of equipment and training problems. A process analysis should be conducted at timely intervals, to see if the production process is yielding results that are gradually diverging from expectations.

Tip: If a periodic process review always reveals a notable divergence in production results, test more frequently. If there is minimal divergence, it may be acceptable to test at longer intervals.

Assign Parts to the Same Machine

When a product or part is needed, the production planning staff will likely assign it to the next available machine. However, that machine may have slightly different tolerances or setup characteristics from the machine on which the item is usually produced. Consequently, the equipment changeover person assigned to the machine will likely have to engage in additional testing to ensure that the changeover is properly set up to produce the new item within allowable specifications. To avoid this extra work, the scheduling staff should try to run the same items on the same machines on a repetitive basis, so that a consistent set of changeover notes can be relied upon to produce an in-specification unit with minimal machine fine tuning.

This recommendation only applies when the production area is set up along functional lines with a push manufacturing system, rather than in a cell arrangement. Under this system, the production planning staff assigns jobs to specific machines.

Unfortunately, assigning the same parts to the same machines makes it more difficult to maintain equipment utilization levels, since some machines may have a queue of jobs lined up in front of them, while other machines stand empty. This issue can be mitigated by assigning all parts having short production runs to the same machines, so that these jobs can be readily swapped into the same machine on a recurring basis.

> **Tip:** Assign the best equipment setup staff to those jobs for which a setup is being made on a different machine from the usual one, since it is more difficult to achieve in-specification products in this situation.

Unscheduled Downtime Avoidance

The optimal use of inventory arises when production is completed in accordance with a specific schedule of production. For example, in a push production environment, a certain amount of goods are planned for production, in accordance with a forecasted amount of customer demand. If equipment unexpectedly breaks down at any point in the production process, this plan is interrupted. Instead, the work-in-process that was created prior to the equipment breakdown is held in abeyance until such time as the equipment can be brought back on line. If the production schedule is altered to work around the breakdown, then the incomplete work-in-process may be shifted to the warehouse and held in reserve until such time as the production equipment can be rescheduled to complete the remaining production steps. In short, equipment failures lead to an excess investment in inventory.

Unscheduled downtime can be avoided by scheduling both routine and preventive maintenance into production activities. Routine maintenance is comprised of all the activities that a company engages in to optimize the operation of production equipment, such as the ongoing lubrication of parts. Preventive maintenance is the replacement of parts before they fail. For example, the periodic replacement of hoses in a vehicle keeps the engine from suffering a catastrophic failure. Both routine and preventive maintenance can be included in the production schedule. By doing so, time can be set aside in an orderly manner to deal with these issues, in the midst of regular production operations. This approach keeps equipment from failing just when it is needed as part of a critical production activity.

If scheduled maintenance involves a major maintenance project, the pre-planning concept can be taken even further by itemizing each step of the project to determine the following items:

- That the amount of time blocked out for each step is adequate;
- That the replacement parts needed for the project are available and allocated to the project; and
- That the staff assigned to the project will be available during the designated maintenance period, and have the skills needed to complete their assigned tasks.

This level of project review may seem like overkill, but doing so can prevent snafus in the maintenance process that might otherwise keep a machine from being brought back on line by the expected date and time.

The key point regarding the avoidance of unscheduled downtime is to replace unscheduled downtime with scheduled downtime, so that equipment can be taken offline in an orderly manner. Doing so not only ensures that production is completed in a timely manner and excess inventory is avoided, but also that a company avoids rush expenditures, such as for maintenance staff overtime and the incurrence of overnight delivery charges for replacement parts.

> **Tip:** Scheduling maintenance means that one can reduce the investment in maintenance parts inventory. When preventive maintenance replaces catastrophic repairs, maintenance parts are purchased for the next scheduled maintenance routine. If a company simply waits for equipment to fail, it must maintain a larger stock of maintenance parts, since it does not know which parts will fail, or when they will fail.

In addition, it is much easier for the maintenance staff to maintain equipment when the company uses the same machine model throughout the production area. There are several reasons for this, including familiarity with the supplier's maintenance manuals, having the same preventive maintenance routines for all of the equipment, and acquiring a history of maintenance issues and how to fix them. In addition, the company can invest in a smaller amount of spare parts for these machines, since the same part is used in every machine. Further, there is less chance that spare parts will never be used and end up being classified as obsolete, as would be the case if a stock of spare parts were to be maintained for a wide range of different machines from different suppliers. Thus, standardization is an excellent goal from the perspective of maintenance costs and maintaining an inventory of maintenance parts.

> **Tip:** Minor lubrication and adjustment work can be handed off to the production staff, since they are constantly monitoring the equipment for which they are responsible, and may have enough downtime to manage this extra task without much trouble. This approach creates more time for the maintenance staff to handle more complex maintenance activities.

Mistake Management

In a typically complex production environment, there are a vast number of opportunities to make a mistake. When a mistake occurs, there must be a system in place for dealing with it immediately. Otherwise, the issue will travel up and down the management chain, and may be resolved weeks later; meanwhile, the mistake still exists, and is likely causing product defects or production inefficiencies. In some production environments, employees are authorized to halt production if they see a serious issue, and a repair team swarms over the problem until it is resolved. Alternatively, it may be sufficient to note the problem on a nearby whiteboard, which is closely monitored by repair teams. The key element in whatever solution is adopted is the *immediate* recognition and correction of problems. An elaborate reporting system is not needed, and could even introduce so much bureaucracy that it slows down the correction of mistakes.

A key outcome of a fast-response mistake management system is that parts are not being continually produced with a known manufacturing flaw. Instead, production is shut down until the flaw is corrected. By doing so, the investment in inventory is minimized.

Eliminate Causes of Rework

A business may require a significant amount of additional inventory if the manufacturing process is continually churning out goods that require rework. These items are ones that can be recovered, but which require additional labor to bring within the company's designated performance specifications. Since the labor required for rework is separate from the normal production process, it is quite common for items requiring rework to be set aside and not addressed for a long time, if ever. If items needing rework are not actually reworked, a company must invest in replacement inventory, as well as storage space for the designated rework items, and will probably take a write-off on the goods.

If rework is a significant problem, create a team to review the reasons for rework, and engage in remedial activities to eliminate these issues at the source. If there are many rework problems, it can be helpful to create a database that itemizes types of rework problems found, resolution status, cost of remediation, and so forth. Also, the team should be comprised of members from the purchasing, engineering, and production departments, since the ultimate cause of rework issues can arise within any of these areas. For example, a rework problem may be caused by poor-quality raw materials, which must be corrected by the purchasing staff. Or, excessively tight tolerances specified by the engineering department may be causing a large number of products to not meet specifications, resulting in rework.

Even a highly successful rework analysis effort cannot be considered a one-time project. Instead, there should be an ongoing analysis of new rework issues, to see if new problems are arising that could potentially impact a large amount of inventory.

Expediting

There are times when a customer may demand the immediate production of an order, or else the customer will take its business elsewhere. When this happens, an expediter walks the order through the production process, giving absolute priority to his job. This means that other in-process jobs are stopped and set to one side, setups are made for the expedited job, the work is completed, and then setups are re-configured and the old jobs are restarted. Now imagine this happening with an entire staff of expediters. The result should be chaos in the manufacturing area, with debris from interrupted jobs scattered everywhere – or is it?

In a push environment, the result of expediting jobs is exactly as just described. Production schedules are ruined, jobs are routinely completed later than expected, and the overall productivity of the shop floor plummets. Even if we examine the situation from the viewpoint of constrained resources, it may be possible to run expedited jobs through low-capacity operations, but there will still be problems ramming expedited work through the bottleneck operation. Consequently, requests to expedite jobs should most certainly be rejected in a pre-planned production environment.

The situation is different in a pull environment. In this case, production is only triggered if there are customer orders – and a customer's request for an expedited order is essentially just a production initiator. In this case, an expedited job is not really expedited – the system processes orders so fast that the order is simply slotted in with every other customer order, and manufacturing is completed within a relatively short period of time. There is no chaos in the production area, for there is no crisis. The only issue here is that the pull system may not yet have compressed its production response time enough to be immediately triggered by a customer order – that is, there may still be some delay before an order is produced. If so, the company can at least quote a shorter production date to a customer than would have been the case in a push environment.

When comparing the effects of expediting on the push and pull environments, the differing impacts on the inventory investment are startling. Inventory levels undoubtedly increase in a push environment, whereas inventory levels are unchanged in a pull environment.

Delay Final Assembly

If a company has many products that are slight variations on each other, build inventory only to the point at which the variations are added to the products, and then complete the products once customer orders arrive. By using this postponement concept, a business can avoid having committed too much of an investment in finished goods for very specific product variations that then sit in the warehouse until an order arrives.

EXAMPLE

Green Lawn Care builds electric lawn mowers. The company has three products, each involving the same blade width and electric motor. The only difference is the size of the battery and the tray in which the battery is stored. Orders for the three models have proven to be highly variable, so that some products are overstocked and others are out of stock.

After discussions with the company's distributors, it is determined that the distributors are willing to accept a one-day delay on order deliveries; this gives the company enough time to add the correct battery tray and battery to a partially-completed mower, and ship the reconfigured finished product. This approach allows the company to essentially manufacture just one product, with final configuration activities expanding the product range to three products.

Move Production to Raw Materials

There may be cases where a product is largely comprised of just a small number of raw materials. If so, and the transportation costs for these items are high, it may make sense to relocate the production facility closer to the source of supply. This technique is most applicable when local markets are served by local production facilities, rather than from a small number of central production locations.

Human Resources Issues

There are two areas in which human resources issues can have a profound impact on inventory levels. Altering the indicated concerns can spark a decline in the inventory investment:

- *Terminate volume incentives.* When the production staff is paid a bonus based on the number of units it can churn out within a certain period of time, the focus is on unit totals, rather than the quality of what is produced. The inevitable result is an increase in the amount of scrap and rework, since employees will do whatever it takes to meet their goal, including producing goods that are on the edge of being out of specification. Also, a volume incentive can result in having too much finished goods inventory on hand, which increases the working capital investment in this area.
- *Terminate efficiency incentives.* The goal of a production system is to generate the goods required by customers, not to maximize the use of every machine on the production floor. And yet many companies judge their employees based on how well they can maintain a high rate of production at every work station. This is a valid measurement only for a bottleneck operation that must be run at maximum capacity at all times. In all other cases, work stations should not be operating if there is not a valid customer order to support the work. Consequently, employee measurement systems should not include consideration of the efficiency levels of the equipment they operate.

Summary

A central theme in this chapter has been the need to reduce the total amount of time required to produce goods. If a lengthy production period is required, one or more of the following negative effects are likely to arise:

- The longer inventory is held on the shop floor, the higher the odds that it will be damaged by passing materials handling equipment or incidental contact.
- As long as goods are on the shop floor, there is a chance that they will be repurposed for another more critical job. A result is that partially-completed jobs are scattered about the production area.
- The value of inventory usually declines over time, so a lengthy production interval can result in products being sold at a lower price point.

To monitor this issue, track on a trend line the average time period required to complete a job. This information can be used as a feedback loop for the production staff, which can work through the various recommendations in this chapter to arrive at a shorter production period.

Another theme has been the need to produce to customer orders whenever possible. Doing so drives down the amount of inventory, since only enough inventory is produced to meet the requirements of immediate orders. This option is not always available, but the benefits are so great that it should always be considered the preferred form of process flow for a manufacturing operation.

Chapter 9
Inventory Shipping

Introduction

From the perspective of inventory management, shipping goods to customers might not initially appear to represent much of an opportunity for improvement – after all, goods are simply handed off to a third party freight carrier. Or is there more? In this chapter, we explore a multitude of concepts that can impact the condition of shipped inventory, load planning, freight costs, improved customer service, and several related issues. By the end of this chapter, it should be apparent that a number of techniques are available for improving inventory shipping.

Match Production to Full Truckload Requirements

When a company is shipping goods to more distant regions, it is much more economical to do so using a full truckload than making several less-than-truckload (LTL) deliveries. However, if there are not enough orders to fill a truckload, it would initially appear that LTL deliveries are the only answer. One possible option is to rejigger the production schedule to produce goods within a short period of time for a block of orders intended for one delivery route. This may mean that some orders are accelerated, while others are held back in order to arrive at a cluster of completed orders within a narrow time frame.

The end result should be an increased use of full truckload deliveries, thereby reducing total freight costs. However, this approach may not work well under the following circumstances:

- Customers do not appreciate having their orders held back in order to be included in the next full truckload.
- Rejiggering the production schedule in this manner may cause delays for the orders of other customers not located along the targeted delivery route.
- This concept relies on relatively short lead times for component parts, so that the production schedule can be altered on short notice to create full truckloads.

Tip: It may be possible to charge some customers a rush fee for accelerating their orders into the next full truckload delivery, despite the company's plan to do so anyways in order to fill the truck.

Shipping Container Considerations

Considerable efficiencies can be gained by engaging in a close examination of the containers used to ship goods to customers. Consider the following issues:

- *Weak construction.* If the sidewalls of containers are too weak, they cannot withstand the pressure of additional containers stacked on top of them, which will result in the crushing of goods while in transit or while being stored at customer sites. A likely outcome is customer claims for product replacement.
- *Stacked storage optimization.* Containers should be configurable on a pallet to maximize the cubic volume of space used. Otherwise, the company is paying a shipping company to transport a certain amount of unused cubic space.
- *Container reusability.* If a container is sufficiently robust, it may be possible to enact a returns program, where customers send the containers back to the company for reuse. This can yield a significant reduction in packaging costs, while minimizing the impact on the environment.
- *Container nesting.* Shipping containers should break down or nest for storage in the smallest possible space.
- *Container security.* Containers can incorporate locks, to prevent in-transit pilferage.

When using the preceding list to arrive at the optimal shipping containers, consider the *total* cost of the containers. This means compiling the estimated costs of the following factors:

Total Container Cost

+	Initial container cost
+	Incremental handling costs
+	Incremental storage costs
+	Cost of maintenance for reusable containers
+	Cost of replacing goods damaged in transit from inadequate packaging
+	Losses from inadequate container security
=	Total container cost

For example, the cost to construct a durable and reusable shipping container may appear to be much higher than the cost of purchasing a standard single-use cardboard box. However, the more robust construction of the reusable container means that in-transit product damage will be eliminated. Also, since the container can be locked, in-transit pilferage can also be eliminated. Based on these additional considerations, the cost of reusable containers may be lower than for cardboard boxes.

Pallet and Case Load Planning

When a trailer arrives that will transport shipped goods to the customer, the warehouse management system should assign a bay to the trailer that is as close as possible to where the ordered items have been aggregated for shipment. Doing so reduces the time required to move goods into the trailer, while also reducing the time needed to begin shipment to the customer, and also freeing up the bay for use by some other trailer.

There should be a grid marked out on the warehouse floor in front of each loading bay, indicating the dimensions of a trailer. Items designated for delivery in a trailer can then be positioned in advance in this grid in the exact layout in which they will be stored in the trailer. This allows the forklift operator to then shift goods into the trailer in accordance with the pre-planned layout, so that the trailer can later be unloaded in the order desired by the customer.

Container Load Planning

Even if goods are perfectly configured for shipping with optimal container sizes, it is also necessary to pre-plan the loading of those pallets. A customer may want to obtain certain goods first, so they should be loaded last onto a trailer. There may also be a need to balance the weight distribution within a trailer. To this end, an optimized loading plan can be provided by a high-end warehouse management system.

> **Tip:** As part of the order-taking process, see if customers want a particular loading configuration, or if they want the actual loading configuration sent to them as part of an advance shipping notice.

Dunnage Usage for In-Transit Inventory Protection

Dunnage is any materials packed around and between storage containers, to protect inventory from damage while in transit. The ideal type of dunnage is environmentally friendly, while also minimizing the amount of weight being transported. The ideal type of dunnage that meets both goals is the air bag. It is nearly weightless, and if constructed of a sufficiently durable material, can protect inventory from significant shifting while in transit. If these dunnage bags are not an option, then Styrofoam pads and polystyrene peanuts can be used. In all cases, make an effort to use the most recyclable dunnage materials.

Shipping Data Automation

When goods are shipped to a customer, the most common approach is to put them on a truck and send them off. The customer receives notification of the delivery when the truck arrives at its receiving dock. A more proactive approach is to create a data logging system that creates an advance shipping notice (ASN) for the customer. Under this system, the forklift operator loading goods onto a truck scans a bar code on each pallet that identifies its contents, as well as a bar code that identifies the shipping door at which the trailer is parked. The warehouse management system combines this information to create an ASN, which identifies the trailer in which the pallets are being delivered, the date and time when the trailer left the shipping dock, and the estimated arrival date and time. The ASN may also include a listing of the position of each pallet in the trailer. The ASN is then transmitted as an electronic message to the customer. Since the ASN is configured in a standard format, it can be integrated directly into the customer's computer systems, and so provides automated warning of exactly when goods are expected to arrive.

The use of ASNs does not directly impact a company's investment in inventory. However, since it gives customers excellent visibility into the flow of incoming goods, they may elect to retain less safety stock. If so, there is less of an inventory buffer on the customer's premises between the purchases of its customers and the replenishment orders it issues to the supplier. This means that the supplier has better visibility into the ordering patterns of the ultimate customer, which allows it to better forecast demand.

Frequent Delivery Service

If a company uses the recommendations in this book to accelerate its responsiveness to customer orders, a logical outcome is to deliver goods more frequently to customers. This can cause problems if the existing delivery fleet is comprised of larger trailers that are designed for full-truckload deliveries. Instead, it may be necessary to downsize these vehicles in favor of smaller trucks that can make less-than-truckload (LTL) deliveries to customers on a more frequent basis. If so, it is entirely possible that the company must switch to a different freight carrier that uses these smaller vehicles, or even invest in its own fleet.

Tip: If the exact configuration of a revised LTL fleet is uncertain, consider leasing trucks for the first year to determine usage levels, and then purchase the correct vehicle types once the proper vehicle mix is apparent.

Transportation Management Systems

A typical shipping department treats the subsequent transportation of goods as something that exists outside of the control of the company. In this situation, the final point of contact with the customer – the delivery truck – is not being monitored. Also, without proper attention to the transportation system, a company is probably not minimizing its transport costs. These issues can be addressed by installing a transportation management system (TMS).

A TMS is designed to manage a company's transportation operations. The system usually includes the following features:

- Batch customer orders to minimize freight costs
- Optimize travel routes for delivery vehicles
- Determine the optimal mode of transportation

- Pick the best freight carrier for a given route
- Track vehicles during their delivery routes
- Track transportation costs

Ideally, a TMS should sort through the historical performance of the various carriers and highlight those with the best results, while also reducing total freight costs and ensuring that customer orders are delivered on time. If customers are allowed to access the system, they can see which carriers are used for various loads, the contents of those loads, and when they are expected to arrive. A Web-based solution may be easier for customers to access than a package stored in-house on a company's servers.

Track Shipper Performance

Most organizations do not ship goods to their customers in their own truck fleets. Instead, they use third-party freight carriers, of which there are multitudes available. If a company elects to use a third-party carrier, keep in mind that this carrier represents the last point of service that a customer will see, and that this point of service is entirely out of the control of the company. This is a particular problem if the carrier loses or damages goods, or delays delivery for any reason. In these situations, the customer blames the seller, not the carrier.

Besides the obvious customer service ramifications, poor carrier performance also impacts the inventory situation for the seller. Here are two applicable scenarios:

- *Damaged in transit.* Goods are damaged in transit, so the company must ship replacement goods for free. Not only does this represent an extra cost, but it also shifts goods away from another customer to which the goods had originally been allocated.
- *Delivered late.* The customer complains that goods were not delivered, so the company ships a replacement, only to find that the original delivery arrived late. The company must now pay to have the customer return one of the deliveries. This also keeps the duplicate goods from being sold to someone else in the meantime.

To reduce the number of these situations, tie back all customer complaints regarding delivery problems to specific freight carriers. Use this information to gradually eliminate substandard carriers. Even if the remaining carriers charge higher rates, the resulting increase in customer satisfaction and reduced inventory issues should make the cost well worthwhile.

Summary

The shipping-related issues noted in this chapter should make it clear that a business must rigorously examine every phase of its operations that involve inventory – even after the goods leave the company's shipping dock. This means that proper attention must be paid to shipment schedules to reduce costs, to loading arrangements to reduce damage, and to carriers to ensure the timely arrival of goods. Only by attending to all of these issues can a business minimize its costs while maximizing customer satisfaction.

Chapter 10
Obsolete Inventory

Introduction

Nearly every organization is burdened with obsolete inventory – those items that are no longer needed, and which seem to be tucked away in every corner of the warehouse. This problem can be so severe that the warehouse manager demands a larger warehouse, just to accommodate the vast amount of unused inventory. In this chapter, we address every aspect of obsolete inventory – how to identify it, how to dispose of it, and how to prevent it from occurring in the first place.

> **Related Podcast Episode:** Episode 66 of the Accounting Best Practices Podcast discusses obsolete inventory. It is available at: **accountingtools.com/podcasts** or **iTunes**

Obsolete Inventory Identification

A common complaint among warehouse managers is that they need more space to accommodate the inventory. In reality, there is usually too much inventory, and probably because a large part of it is obsolete. Obsolete inventory must be identified at regular intervals, so that it can be targeted for disposal at the best possible price. The usual process for identifying obsolete inventory is:

1. *Assign review responsibility.* An inventory review will not be conducted unless the responsibility for doing so is specifically assigned to someone. A group known as the Materials Review Board (MRB) is usually assigned this task. The MRB is comprised of the warehouse manager, purchasing manager, and engineering manager, or a designated subordinate. The controller may also be included, in order to quantify the cost of the obsolete items identified by this group.
2. *Set review intervals.* The MRB should conduct a formal review of the inventory at intervals of no less than every three months. This review should be set in the corporate calendar of activities, with a senior-level manager ensuring that the reviews take place.
3. *Investigate inventory.* There are a number of methods available for reviewing inventory. One or more of the following methods may prove to be effective:

   - *Where used report.* If a company uses a material requirements planning (MRP) system, the software should produce a "where used" report, which identifies any inventory items that are not specifically called out in a company's bills of material. If an item is not being identified anywhere, it is unlikely to be used, and so should be considered obsolete.

- *Usage report.* Construct a report that compares the amount of inventory on hand to its usage level over the past year. This report should be used with caution, for it is based on historical usage levels, rather than forecasted usage. However, it can at least identify inventory items that are overstocked, so that some of the inventory can be eliminated.
- *Old count tags.* If there are no computer records of usage, a reasonable technique for manually identifying obsolete inventory is to spot inventory items to which old inventory count tags are still attached. These tags are added to the inventory as part of the physical inventory counting process. If inventory has not been used since the last inventory count, the tag is likely to still be attached.
- *Date review.* If there are no computer records and there have been no physical inventory counts, then inspect the inventory containers to see if there is a delivery date. If so, old delivery dates are strongly indicative of obsolete inventory. If there are no dates on the inventory, consider having the receiving department stamp incoming goods with a date, so that this information will be available for future inventory reviews.

4. *Formalize the obsolete inventory list.* Once all obsolete items have been identified, include them in a formal list, including the locations, quantities, and descriptions of all items. This report serves as the basis for follow-up disposition activities, as noted next.

5. *Assign disposition actions.* All obsolete items are to be cleared from stock. This may involve having the purchasing staff sell them off at a loss, return them to suppliers for a restocking fee, or donate them to a not-for-profit in exchange for a tax credit. Alternatively, the engineering manager may attempt to design them into a new product, or they may be scheduled into a production run for an existing product. The expected outcome of these disposition actions should be noted in the report, so that the accounting staff can estimate the amount of the resulting loss that should be recorded.

6. *Distribute results.* The obsolete inventory list and the statement of assigned duties is formally distributed to all members of the MRB, as well as to the senior-level manager who is responsible for the inventory asset. This step formalizes how the company plans to deal with its obsolete inventory.

Obsolete Inventory Disposal

An inventory item that has been designated as obsolete is not automatically thrown in the trash. On the contrary, there are a number of alternatives available by which inventory can be dispositioned while still providing some return to the company. The following alternatives are presented in order by the size of return that will be generated, with the first alternatives being the most productive:

- *Reserve as spares.* If there is a history of spare parts orders from customers, set aside a sufficient amount of the inventory to deal with these orders. This is one case where full pricing can still be obtained from sale of the goods, and probably for a fairly long period of time.

> **Tip:** Create an annual calendar reminder to review the amount of inventory being held as spares. It is possible that demand is lower than expected, so that some of the inventory can be declared obsolete and removed from stock.

- *Move to different location.* If the company has multiple locations, it is possible that demand is higher at a different location. If so, estimate the long-term demand in the alternate location, and shift a sufficient amount of inventory there.
- *Return to suppliers.* Suppliers are typically reluctant to take back goods, especially if the value of the goods has declined over time. Still, it may be possible to do so in exchange for a restocking fee. This option is most attractive when a supplier is willing to pay the company for any credit granted. Conversely, if a credit is granted and the company no longer does business with the supplier, the value of the credit is minimal.
- *Marketing campaign.* If the obsolete inventory is finished goods, the marketing department can roll out a discount program that offers the goods to customers at a steep discount. This approach should be used with caution, in case the goods being sold at a lower price will cannibalize sales of the company's full-price products.
- *Product integration.* If the obsolete inventory is raw materials, the engineering manager may be able to design them into new products. However, this is quite a long-term proposition, and is usually only feasible for a small number of items.
- *Third party reseller.* A number of third party resellers maintain cut-rate distribution channels through which they sell obsolete inventory. They may be willing to buy obsolete inventory, though only at a large discount. In this case, there is a risk that goods resold through these alternative distribution channels will cannibalize sales of the company's full-priced products.
- *Donation.* It may be possible to donate obsolete inventory to a not-for-profit entity. By doing so, the company can recognize the fair value of the donated goods as a tax credit. This approach works best for supplies and foodstuffs, for which there are a number of charities willing to accept donations.

- *Break down.* It may be possible to break down finished goods into their con- stituent parts, which can then be used in other products. However, doing so can damage the parts salvaged from this process.
- *Sell to salvage contractors.* There are third party salvage contractors that will periodically pick through a company's unwanted inventory and offer to pur- chase selected items. The price obtained will be low, but may be higher than what can be obtained from a scrap dealer. If you take this route, consider of- fering goods in batches, rather than allowing contractors to buy only the best items. Doing so may not result in much additional revenue, but will clear out a fair amount of valuable storage space in the warehouse.
- *Scrap.* A small amount of cash can even be gleaned from scrapping inventory, if it contains a sufficient amount of residual metal to be worth selling to a scrap dealer. Scrapping inventory may also make sense if the company wants to prevent its branded products from appearing in the marketplace.

Obsolete Inventory Prevention

The best way to deal with obsolete inventory is to keep it from becoming obsolete. One way to do so is after-the-fact, by investigating the reasons why inventory became obsolete in the first place. If this approach is taken, review underlying problems in order by the issues causing the largest inventory write-offs. Doing so concentrates attention on those issues that can generate the largest profit improvement.

Here are several more specific ways to prevent inventory from being designated as obsolete:

- *Engineering change order management.* The engineering staff may periodi- cally issue an engineering change order (ECO) for a product, which specifies that the configuration of a product will change as of a certain date. If an ECO is issued without regard to inventory on hand, it is possible that some compo- nents used in a product will be stranded in inventory, since they are no longer used in the product. A better approach is to examine the impact of an ECO before setting a date for its release, so that any remaining components can be used up before the ECO goes into effect.
- *Orderly product shutdowns.* When the management team decides to shut down a product or replace it with another one, part of the decision should be a review of all raw materials and finished goods related to the product termi- nation. The engineering staff should determine which raw materials are unique to the product being terminated, and itemize the best ways to dispose of these items. Possible options are to send them back to a supplier for a re- stocking fee, build them into one last production run before the product is shut down, design them into another product, or simply write them off. The main point is to give due consideration to the impact of a shutdown on inventory, rather than terminating a product and *then* considering the ramifications.
- *Shelf life tracking.* Some products have a limited shelf life, after which they must be thrown out. The obvious example is food products, but the same issue

113

applies to other products, such as gaskets, that will become unusable over time. Similarly, adhesives and epoxies are no longer effective after a certain period of time. All products that have limited shelf lives should be flagged as such in the computer system, and removed from stock on a first-in, first-out (FIFO) basis, thereby ensuring that the oldest items are consumed first. This is a good place in which to use gravity-flow racks (see the Warehouse Storage Systems chapter), which always present the oldest items to stock pickers, since the racks are loaded from the rear, pushing the oldest goods towards the picker.

Tip: If the receipt dates of received goods are noted in the computer system, it should be possible to derive a computer report that flags all products approaching their end-of-life dates. If the company cannot use or sell these items by the flagged date, then at least the purchasing staff should have sufficient warning for disposing of the goods before they have no residual value.

- *Reworking of returned goods.* If goods are returned by customers, do not let the goods sit in a pile, untouched. Instead, institute an active program of reviewing returned items at once, flagging any required rework, repackaging products as necessary, and selling them off as "B" stock at a somewhat reduced price. The key issue is to flip returned goods back into the market as soon as possible. Otherwise, returned products will age, become obsolete, and retain no value.

- *Reorder flags.* The item master record for each inventory item contains a flag that directs the computer system to automatically reorder more units when the on-hand unit level drops below a preset level. This can be a problem when the materials management staff is attempting to terminate corporate use of a certain inventory item, since their actions will reduce inventory levels and trigger an automatic reorder. To prevent this from occurring, create an inventory item termination procedure, in which one of the steps is to turn off the reorder flag in the item master record.

- *Match purchases to customer orders.* The purchasing staff may be accustomed to ordering raw materials in standard unit sizes that exceed the quantities actually needed, in order to receive price breaks. They may be further tempted to buy in even larger quantities in order to achieve volume purchase discounts. These practices may appear to reduce costs in the short run, but can result in unused and therefore obsolete inventory. A better practice is to order in small quantities and mandate frequent supplier deliveries, so that purchases more closely conform to the requirements of customer orders.

NCNR Inventory Reduction

When inventory is considered to be obsolete, the materials management staff may decide to send the items back to suppliers, accepting a modest restocking fee in exchange. However, a number of inventory items are classified by their sellers as noncancellable and non-returnable (NCNR), which usually means that the inventory is so heavily modified for the customer that its seller will be unable to resell it to other customers.

Since restocking is not an option for NCNR inventory items, the materials management group must explore other alternatives for reducing the risk of writing off these non-returnable items. The following are all reasonable options for reducing a company's investment in NCNR items, thereby reducing potential inventory losses:

- *Field flag.* Assign a field in the inventory item master file to be a flag to identify inventory items as being NCNR. Activate it for any items that cannot be returned.
- *Manual review.* If the company has an automated order placement system, have it use the NCNR flag to identify prospective NCNR purchases and route them to the purchasing staff for manual review. Doing so may result in less ordering of these items.
- *Hanging NCNR report.* Create a report that identifies the unit quantities and costs of all NCNR items that will be affected if an engineering change order is triggered. This report is useful for adjusting the timing of a change order to minimize the amount of NCNR items left in stock.
- *Forecasted NCNR report.* Use the same NCNR report just described to identify the quantities and costs of all NCNR items to be used in forecasted production. Management can use this report to determine whether it should reduce the forecasted amounts to reduce the risk of carrying too much NCNR inventory.

The preceding steps represent useful ways to more closely monitor the usage of and investment in NCNR items.

Summary

The amount of obsolete inventory hiding in the warehouse can be enormous, and much more than anyone will readily admit to. If so, the proper question is not how to dispose of it, but rather how it arrived there in the first place. The principal issue in dealing with obsolete inventory is to turn off the spigot, so that only a trickle of goods can be considered obsolete. Doing so involves constant attention to many issues that fall outside of the normal process of manufacturing and selling goods, and which are therefore ignored in all but the best-run companies.

Having pointed out the importance of cutting off incoming obsolete inventory, we must also focus attention on the *rapid* identification and disposition of obsolete inventory. Its value declines by the day, so a well-managed operation should be smothering this part of the business with continual activity to hand off inventory to someone else for the best prices that can be obtained.

Chapter 11
Product Development

Introduction

The manner in which products are developed, the design philosophies used, and the manner in which feedback systems are employed to alter products can all have a profound impact on the amount and types of inventory that must be maintained. Consequently, we review in this chapter several key elements of product development that impact inventory from several directions – the number of raw material parts and finished goods that are held in stock, the level of parts rejection, the cost of purchased inventory and manufacturing processes, and the time required to bring new products to market.

Minimize the Number of Parts Used

Product designers can develop products that share many of the same component parts. This is particularly likely across product families, where the same basic design is being used as the foundation for a cluster of products. By doing so, a business can eliminate a number of parts from raw materials inventory. This concept also tends to result in less obsolete inventory, since so few parts are solely linked to a single product. However, it typically requires at least one product cycle to build the parts minimization concept into the product design philosophy, so it can take years to implement this approach.

Eliminate Identical Parts

It is entirely possible that a company will assign multiple part numbers to the same part. This situation arises under two circumstances:

- There are multiple design teams at work, and engineers on each team independently decide to use the same part. Each person assigns a new part number to "their" part.
- Engineers are not asked to create new products using existing parts, and so have little knowledge of the part designations that are already in place.

The trouble with this situation is that the purchasing staff is then asked to order goods for products, each of which contains "different" components that are actually the same. The result may be too much inventory on hand. Also, the department may order individually in smaller quantities, resulting in lost volume purchase discounts. Further, extra storage bins may be used to store identical items that are identified differently, which is a waste of warehouse space.

This situation can be mitigated by conducting a search for identical parts. There are several methods that can yield results:

- *Purchasing analysis.* Include the supplier part number in the item master file for every part ordered. Then create a report that searches for matching supplier part numbers in the file. This indicates that the company is ordering the identical part from a supplier under different in-house identification numbers. This approach works best when only a small number of suppliers are used, since this increases the odds that the same supplier will be tapped to provide a multitude of parts.
- *Warehouse analysis.* Those employees most familiar with the on-hand inventory are the cycle counters. They may be able to identify parts that are clearly identical. However, if random parts storage is used, items may be located so far apart that this is a difficult task. If parts are grouped by product family, it is easier to locate identical parts.

If identical parts are found under different identifying numbers, follow these steps to consolidate the part numbers:

1. Determine which part number will become the default number to be used.
2. Deactivate the part number(s) that will no longer be used.
3. Notify the warehouse staff to shift the on-hand quantities for the deactivated part numbers to the default part number in the inventory records, and to relabel these parts.
4. Adjust all outstanding purchase orders for the deactivated parts to reflect the default part number, so that these items will be properly identified upon receipt.
5. Adjust all bills of material that included the deactivated part numbers to now use the default part number.
6. Adjust all engineering drawings and supporting materials to only show usage of the default part number.

Given the number of steps involved to eliminate identical parts, it is useful to adopt a formal written procedure, and to require sign-offs on each step as part of the elimination process.

Design for Broad Tolerance

Some products are designed to work only with parts whose dimensions are very precisely defined. If a part does not exactly match the planned characteristics, it is designated as scrap and thrown away. This scrap cost can be reduced by designing products to operate with components whose characteristics can vary somewhat from specifications. A side benefit of this approach is that it may be less expensive to construct or purchase parts that have a broader tolerance range, since manufacturing costs tend to decline as tolerances are loosened. For example, a supplier may be delivering parts within a tight tolerance range, but is having to throw out a number of non-conforming parts in order to do so – which results in the cost of the rejected parts being passed through to the company. When the tolerance range is broader, the supplier throws out fewer parts, which reduces the rejection cost being passed through to the company.

It is especially useful to design for broad tolerance when the rework department has previously dispositioned parts with a "use as is" designation. In effect, this means that the practical use of nonconforming parts has not resulted in problems with the parts.

Match Materials Quality to Design Specifications

A company may obtain raw materials that are of too high a quality level in comparison to the design specifications of a product. Doing so means that customers may not even notice the difference, while the company incurs a higher cost than it should. For example, a part may be built from titanium to save a small amount of weight, while less-expensive stainless steel would be suitable from the perspective of the customer. Ideally, the purchasing staff should only buy raw materials and components that meet the expectations of customers. Doing so reduces the cost of inventory.

The same concept applies to the packaging of a product. Some products are designed with excessively robust packaging or simply too much packaging. Since packaging is to be thrown away once a product is opened, there is no point in designing an excessive amount of packaging to contain the product.

Design for Assembly

When the product development staff designs a product, it should ensure that the parts can only be assembled one way; that is, the parts will not fit together properly if anyone attempts to assemble them in a different way. By paying attention to this issue, the risk of improper unit assembly is eliminated, which in turn reduces product defect rates and warranty costs. When warranty claims are minimized, this means that less inventory must be kept in stock as reserve replacement parts for customer claims.

Design around Limited Availability Components

There may be cases where the components designed into a product are only available from a single supplier, or are heavily in demand. A possible outcome of this situation is that a company is put on allocation when it orders goods. If so, this limits the ability of the company to generate products, which constrains its profitability. Another possibility is that suppliers react to high demand by massively increasing their prices. If the cost of such a component comprises a large proportion of the total cost of a product, this can severely impact its profitability.

To avoid the limited sourcing issue, the product development staff can work with the purchasing department during the design phase of a new product to identify components that may not be readily available. It is much less expensive to design replacement parts into a product during the initial design phase, rather than in a later engineering change order, after the product has already been released.

Design around Lifetime Buy Decisions

A lifetime buy is when a needed part is no longer going to be provided by a supplier, so a company is forced to buy a large quantity of the part right now, to ensure that the part is in stock for what may continue to be a lengthy usage period. A lifetime buy is not a good decision to make, since it ties up working capital in inventory for an extended period, and eventually puts a company at risk of an obsolete inventory writedown. There are a number of ways to reduce the frequency with which lifetime buys must be made. Possible alternatives include the following:

- *Increased communications.* When a part is first designed into a product, communicate with the supplier the expected volume to be purchased per year, and for how long the purchasing is expected to continue. If substantial, this information may persuade the supplier to put off its product termination.
- *Design for common parts.* When there is a choice between designing a standard or non-standard part into a product, always go with the standard version. By doing so, the company can buy the part from multiple suppliers.
- *Design for new parts.* If a part is extremely new, then a supplier is likely to let it run for a reasonably long life cycle. Conversely, designing in an old product, such as an older model computer chip, puts a business at risk of having a supplier eliminate the part quite soon.
- *Shorten the product life cycle.* If a part used in a product is to be shut down soon, use this as a trigger to shut down the product in which the part is used, in favor of a replacement product. If there is a history of part life cycles that are quite short, this may be the best option – the company designs all of its products to have roughly the same product life cycles as the parts that go into them.

Advance Material Purchase Issues

A company may focus on rapid product releases, so that it can beat its competitors to market with new designs. Sometimes, the products they are designing include components that have unusually long lead times. In order to compress their product launch dates, a design team may authorize the purchase of these components before the final designs are completed. This approach is possible when a sub-assembly is considered to be final, even though the remainder of the product design is still being tweaked.

While an advance material purchase may appear to be a clever way to compress product design time, it can run into trouble if there is a subsequent product alteration that does impact the material. If so, a large and expensive materials purchase will later arrive, and will not fit into the final product design. The following techniques can reduce the risk of this situation occurring:

- *Manual solution – purchasing review.* The product development team should include someone from the purchasing department who is specifically assigned to monitor any changes to items requiring advance material purchases. This is the easiest monitoring solution, but runs the risk of a prospective change getting past the attention of the designated person.

- *Manual solution – drawing updates review.* If there is a change to an item requiring an advance material purchase, the change will be reflected in an altered engineering drawing, which should contain the date of the revision. Have someone periodically compare the drawing dates to the dates on which advance material purchases were made. If the drawing date is later than the purchase date, there may be a problem.

- *Automated solution - tag advance items.* The design team should maintain an ongoing series of preliminary bills of material, one for each version of a prospective product. Always tag those items in the bill that require advance purchases, and require password access to the system to alter these items. If a change is subsequently made, have the computer system issue a notification message to the team leader. However, few bill of materials systems contain this feature. Also, a bill may not be changed, even though an underlying engineering drawing is changed. Consequently, the preceding drawing updates review is the better control.

Expand the Design Team

The traditional product design team is comprised entirely of engineers, who construct theoretically perfect products, and then hand off their creations to the rest of the company. The inevitable result is a bounce-back from the purchasing department, with complaints that the required components must be custom-ordered, or from the industrial engineering and production departments, with claims that the product cannot be efficiently manufactured. Eventually, the product design bounces back and forth for a protracted period before the warring camps grudgingly agree on a revised design.

A better approach that vastly reduces design time is to add people from the purchasing, industrial engineering, and production departments to the initial design team. Doing so allows for the following benefits:

- The integration of stock parts into new products
- Product designs that yield less scrap
- Product designs that are easier to manufacture
- A reduced need for extra service parts, since the original design is so robust
- A reduced need for entirely new components in the warehouse, due to parts sharing
- A reduced need to have engineering change order modifications to existing products

The main downside to the use of expanded design teams is the time spent away from the purchasing, industrial engineering, and production departments. It may be necessary to hire extra staff to backfill the time of the people from these areas that are assigned to product development.

Include Suppliers in the Design Process

The product design team usually works in splendid isolation, developing products only in conjunction with a few people within the company. This group develops products that are both sellable and profitable, from the limited perspective of the information available to the company. In reality, this design approach is not taking advantage of information further back in the supply chain regarding the materials incorporated into its product designs. This may result in the company not using the lowest-cost components, not being aware of a new component that has just come onto the market, or not knowing about an impending supply shortage. This type of additional information is only available from suppliers, to whom the information may be common knowledge.

To access this additional information, invite key suppliers to participate in the company's design process. This approach works best when the company has already built up strong relations with its suppliers, and especially when the company already purchases in large quantities from them. If so, suppliers will be more likely to become fully-integrated members of product design teams, participating in every phase of the design process. The implied payback for assisting in creating product designs is that the company directs its purchases toward those suppliers that have rendered assistance.

The primary downside to including suppliers in product designs is that confidential information about the designs is now floating around outside of the company. This risk can be mitigated by requiring robust non-confidentiality agreements. If it turns out that a supplier breached the company's trust and released product information to third parties, the company can always exclude them from further design work and from the company's future purchases.

Review the Bill of Materials

The product development staff delivers a bill of materials (BOM) along with each new product design. The BOM precisely defines the parts and unit quantities that go into the construction of a product, and is an essential tool used for ordering raw materials. If the BOM is incorrect, a business may use it to buy the wrong quantities of certain parts, or perhaps the wrong parts. In addition, the accounting department uses BOMs to estimate the cost of goods in inventory, so an incorrect BOM can impact the financial statements. To avoid these issues, have a second person review each BOM before it is released for general use, and lock down access to the BOM file in the computer system. It may also be necessary to monitor changes to the BOM file over time, since engineering change orders may require that the file be altered.

> **Tip:** A key engineering metric is the accuracy of the bills of material. Review a sample of the bills on a periodic basis, and publish an accuracy report. BOM accuracy should be at least 98% at all times.

The accuracy of the BOM is of such concern in highly-planned environments that it may be necessary to schedule an ongoing accuracy review for all of them. The accuracy review should encompass the following points:

- Is the quantity of each item stated in the BOM correct?
- Are there any parts used in the product that are not listed in the BOM?
- Are the identification numbers stated in the BOM actually used in the product?

> **Tip:** It is allowable to not include incidental items in a BOM, such as fittings and fasteners, especially if stocks of these items are maintained by means other than BOM-based reordering systems. However, doing so means that the standard cost of a product will be slightly too low.

This review should be conducted by someone who is very familiar with the components being used, and how they are assembled into a finished product. The review may require the disassembly of finished goods, so that the broken-down version can be compared to the associated bill of materials. If errors are found, BOM records are updated as soon as possible, so that the errors no longer impact the organization. Here are several additional points to consider when reviewing BOM records:

- *Frequency.* Review those goods most frequently that are produced in the highest volume, since an error in one of these records has the greatest negative impact.
- *ECO-based.* Whenever an engineering change order (ECO) goes into effect, pull a product from the production line and compare it to the revised bill of materials that encompasses the ECO. This is a likely place in which to find a mistake, since the production work instructions may not yet reflect the impact of the change. Issues found here can indicate a larger problem with the inability of the organization to completely roll out all of the documentation related to an ECO.
- *Scrap levels.* A BOM includes the average amount of direct materials scrap that is associated with the manufacture of a product. However, the quality of raw materials and production processes will change over time, resulting in differing scrap usage rates. Thus, when there is a BOM review, also match actual scrap usage to the planned amount stated in the BOM, and revise the BOM amount as necessary. Otherwise, the standard cost of a product will be wrong, as will the planned usage level of those materials experiencing scrap usage.

> **Tip:** In order to set scrap rates in a BOM, there must first be an excellent scrap-tracking system in the production area, so that scrap usage can be tied to specific products, and the variability of scrap rates can be tracked over time.

BOM accuracy is especially important when a company uses backflushing. Back-flushing is the concept of entering the amount of finished goods manufactured into the materials management system, which then multiplies the completed unit total by the related bill of materials to calculate the amount of raw materials that must have been used. This amount is then removed from the raw material records. Consequently, if a BOM is incorrect, then so too will be the raw material records.

Use a BOM Temporary Substitution Procedure

There may be cases where there are similar raw materials or components in stock that can be swapped into a product. This situation usually arises when there are some residual quantities in stock of parts whose specifications are somewhat different from a product's requirements, but still within the allowable tolerance range for the product. In this situation, management may decide to temporarily alter the bill of materials for a product, shifting usage requirements from the normal part to the replacement part. Once the replacement item is used up, the BOM is altered back to the original part.

The temporary substitution concept may appear attractive, especially if an obsolete inventory write-off can be avoided. However, the temporary substitution process is rather complex, which may render the concept untenable for small amounts of residual inventory. Consider the amount of effort required to effect a substitution:

1. Document the item to be substituted, the quantity to be used, and the expected dates during which the substitution will be in use.
2. Obtain the approval of the product development manager and materials manager for the substitution.
3. Swap in the temporary part in the bill of materials.
4. Schedule a production run whose size is sufficiently large to use up the residual parts.
5. Reset the reorder flag for the temporary part, so that the system does not reorder it once the production run has been completed.
6. Once the production run is complete, notify the purchasing department to dispose of any remaining residual parts.
7. Reset the bill of materials back to the original part.
8. Conduct a review to ensure that the BOM has been properly reset.

Given the number of steps involved, it is probably not worthwhile to engage in smaller temporary substitutions. Consequently, it is customary to assign a dollar value to a substitution threshold for residual items held in stock, below which substitutions are not allowed. Instead, these items are scheduled for disposal (see the Obsolete Inventory chapter).

Review Inventory Returns and Shortages

When materials are picked from stock for a production job, the materials are aggregated and sent to the shop floor as a kit. The picking for this process is based upon the bill of materials that the product development staff created for the product scheduled for production. If there is an error in the bill of materials, the kitted materials will be incorrect. A BOM error triggers either a parts shortage or a parts surplus. If there is a shortage, the production staff goes to the warehouse, fills out a parts requisition form, and is issued the missing parts. If there is a surplus, any items remaining in the kitting bin after production is complete are returned to the warehouse, where they are logged back into the computer system.

In both cases, there is a computer record that indicates the presence of a kitting error. The product development staff should regularly review these records to see if the cause of a kitting error was an incorrect bill of materials. These reviews should be relatively frequent, since an incorrect bill of materials will be used again the next time the same product is scheduled for production, and the same kitting error will occur again at that time.

Tip: Kitting errors can also be caused by errors elsewhere in the company, such as mislabeled parts, incorrect picks, and parts stolen from kitting bins. Consequently, the review of inventory returns and shortages should be a joint effort between the product development, warehouse, and production staffs.

The Customer Complaint Feedback Loop

A major problem for the engineering department is product issues that appear in the field, after goods have been released. A common scenario is that the customer service department receives customer complaints and processes warranty claims, but does not notify the product development department of the issue. The feedback loop is even more prolonged when there is a distributor or retailer acting as a buffer between the company and the ultimate customer; in this case, it could be many months before the company even learns there is a problem.

Once the product development staff learns of a potential product issue, it tries to replicate the problem, and then issues an engineering change order that prevents the issue from occurring again in newer products. It may also be necessary to issue a product recall notice, so that the problem can be remedied in products that have already shipped.

If the feedback loop to the product development staff is excessively long, there may be a large amount of inventory already in the field that must be updated or replaced. If this is the case, it can make sense to work on building a fast feedback loop from customers, distributors, and retailers straight back to the product development department. By doing so, there is much less opportunity for faulty goods to be sold to customers. Examples of such a system are a formal meeting between customer service and the product development manager on a frequent basis, or giving the development staff access to the customer service database, perhaps formatted to highlight the most recent customer complaints.

Tip: The customer complaint feedback loop rarely succeeds, because it crosses over several department boundaries. To ensure greater success, appoint a manager to set up and monitor a feedback loop, thereby ensuring that information about faulty products reaches the product development department in a timely manner.

Review and Approve Engineering Change Orders

A possible result of an unusual number of customer complaints and warranty claims is that the product development team issues an engineering change order (ECO) for a product. An ECO authorizes a change to a product, such as the use of a different part that is more robust, or the replacement of a sub-assembly with a different design. While there may be a need for an ECO, it can also cause a number of problems in other departments. For example, a replacement part may be unusually difficult to obtain, or a new sub-assembly requires a change to the manufacturing process. Most commonly, those parts being replaced are now marooned in the warehouse with no planned usage, and so are eventually declared obsolete.

All of the preceding issues with ECOs can be resolved or at least mitigated by having a formal review and approval process for all ECOs. This process includes an examination of the proposed change by every department that may be impacted. The result may be a flurry of activities in these other departments to prepare for the change, or else pushback that the ECO is not possible. In either case, there is a healthy debate that should yield the best possible way to handle a customer complaint or warranty issue.

Tip: To reduce the time required for an ECO review and approval, bring together all affected departments in a formal meeting to discuss the change, allow a certain time period for additional follow-up work (such as a week), and then schedule a final meeting to conclude the review and bring the proposal to a vote.

Reduce the Number of Products

When a company manufactures a massive number of products, it is difficult to optimize the production process, and employees will have a difficult time learning about ways to improve the production process for each one. The result will likely be an ongoing low level of manufacturing efficiency. To improve the situation, consider dropping those outlier products that earn minimal profits, and yet tend to clutter up the production process. This concept will require the cooperation of the marketing manager, who is usually trying to expand sales by offering a broader range of products to customers.

A side benefit of reducing the number of products is that the company will no longer have to maintain raw material inventories to produce these goods, and can eliminate the related investment in finished goods. Since the items being eliminated are likely to have low turnover rates, this means that an inordinately large investment in inventory can be eliminated, in proportion to the sales being lost. In addition, since finished goods inventories are being eliminated for goods that only sell sporadically, the company incurs a lower risk of having obsolete finished goods inventory.

> **Tip**: If some products are to be eliminated, work with the marketing manager to create a special discount deal on the targeted goods, so that they can be eliminated within the shortest possible period of time. Doing so reduces the risk of incurring losses from obsolete inventory.

Customer Termination Considerations

Some organizations routinely review their customers to see which ones are generating the largest profits, based on the margins of the goods and services they purchase, and the direct costs of doing business with them. The result may be an ongoing pruning of a company's customer base to eliminate the least profitable customers.

This practice can be used to back into the termination of selected inventory items. If a customer is being considered for termination, also look at the mix of products that they are purchasing. If there is a preponderance of low-profit products in their purchases, this could be a good time to not only terminate the customer, but also a selection of the products that the customer was buying.

Reduce Product Options

The marketing department wants to offer as many variations on a product to customers as possible, in order to fill every conceivable product niche and thereby increase sales. Unfortunately, doing so requires that a large number of components and finished goods be kept in stock, so that the company will have each product option readily available for sale. Further, some product options will be ordered so rarely that a company finds itself sitting on the related inventory items for long periods of time. If so, the company may find itself investing in too much inventory, while also being at high risk of having to write off inventory as being obsolete.

To reduce the chance of these problems occurring, reduce the number of product options being offered for sale. Doing so shrinks the amount of components and finished goods kept in stock. This approach does not mean that the business will offer only the most rudimentary product configurations; a feature-rich product may be offered, but with only a modest number of variations on the basic design. In essence, management wants to strike a balance between having a moderate investment in inventory and giving customers a sufficient range of choices to keep them from buying alternative products from competitors.

> **Tip:** A variation on the concept is to still offer a full range of product options, but to increase the prices of those options that require an additional inventory investment by the company. Doing so at least pays for the extra inventory. Also, if demand remains strong despite the higher price, this may convince management to add a few options to products. Conversely, if an option is rarely purchased, it can be entirely eliminated from the firm's offerings.

Summary

This chapter should make it clear that the manner in which products are designed and later altered has a profound impact on a company's inventory investment. Ideally, the development process should be a broad-based one that includes many departments and suppliers, thereby aggregating knowledge about every aspect of the business that could impact a product. Once a product has been released, there must be a comprehensive system in place for collecting information about possible product flaws, as well as procedures for promptly researching and correcting any indicated problems. Finally, the design of a product must incorporate a debate about the number of products and features that will be offered, including a discussion of the amount of inventory required to support different ranges of product offerings. In short, the inventory investment is closely tied to the product development process.

Chapter 12
Inventory Record Accuracy

Introduction

It is impossible to properly manage inventory without first having highly accurate inventory records. The purchasing staff does not know which inventory items to purchase unless it has confidence in the quantities stated in the inventory database. Similarly, the picking staff cannot locate inventory items unless the database can reliably tell them where the inventory is located. The accounting staff cannot create a proper inventory valuation unless it has reliable inventory information. Thus, inventory record accuracy is the fundamental starting point of a system of inventory management. In this chapter, we describe the nature of inventory errors, factors that cause the errors, data entry methods that mitigate errors, and similar issues.

> **Related Podcast Episode:** Episode 56 of the Accounting Best Practices Podcast discusses inventory record accuracy. It is available at: **accountingtools.com/podcasts** or **iTunes**

Inventory Record Errors

Many of the techniques available for reducing the inventory investment are predicated on the existence of highly accurate inventory records, so that inventory levels can be precisely monitored. Unfortunately, there are an extraordinary number of ways in which inventory transactions can be incorrectly recorded. Here are a number of examples:

Receiving and putaways

- Received goods are not recorded at all
- A receipt is recorded against the wrong item, or in the wrong quantity
- Goods are putaway and the location is not recorded
- Goods are putaway and the location is incorrectly recorded

Picking activities

- The wrong quantity or the wrong product is picked
- A picker correctly picks an item, but scans the wrong bar code
- A picking transaction is not recorded, or recorded twice
- Picked goods are assigned to the wrong customer order
- A counting scale is incorrectly used, resulting in the wrong pick quantity

Data entry

- The quantity picked is transposed when entering the information
- Data entry does not occur until the following day

Cycle and physical counting

- A counting error is discovered that is actually caused by late data entry of a prior transaction, resulting in a correcting entry that compounds the problem
- An inexperienced person incorrectly counts inventory during a physical count, resulting in the "correction" of an on-hand balance
- A data entry person assumes the wrong unit of measure, such as rolls instead of inches

Another major factor that impacts record accuracy is, curiously, the capacity level at which a facility is operating. If there is little storage space left in the warehouse, the number of transactions increases in proportion to the amount of inventory, as goods are constantly shuffled in and out of temporary storage. Similarly, if the receiving and shipping areas do not have sufficient space for staging operations, more transactions are needed to move inventory in and out of temporary storage locations. Error rates are closely tied to the volume of transactions, so the error rate will increase as capacity levels approach their maximum theoretical limits. Consequently, a sudden spike in error rates can signal an immediate need for more storage space.

Another factor that impacts record accuracy is the speed of operations. If goods are picked from stock and immediately sent to customers, transactions are only needed to record the pick and the shipment. Similarly, if items are picked for inclusion in the production process, a rapid manufacturing flow may require only transactions for the picking of raw materials and the putaway of finished goods. However, if these processes are slowed down, inventory must also be recorded in the temporary storage locations where it may reside. Each of these additional transactions increases the risk of recording a transaction error. For example:

- Goods are picked from stock early, and are not expected to be delivered to the customer until the next day. This requires that the goods be recorded in a staging area prior to shipment the following day.
- Goods are taken from one customer order to satisfy another order. This means that the first order is shunted aside to temporary storage until the goods can be replaced. The remaining goods must be recorded in temporary storage until shipped. Alternatively, the goods may be returned to stock until the order can be fulfilled, which requires an extra putaway transaction.
- The production process requires that many subassemblies be delivered from suppliers before final assembly can be completed. The process allows for partially-completed assemblies to be held in temporary storage until subassemblies arrive. Each instance of temporary storage requires a transaction to track the location of the goods.

In short, there are a multitude of areas in which inventory record errors can arise. In the next few sections, we note how a variety of factors can have a negative impact on record accuracy.

Environmental Factors Impacting Record Accuracy

A number of issues involving the warehouse environment can impact inventory record accuracy. Environmental factors to be aware of include the following:

- *Floor and aisle lighting.* Information can be misread or incorrectly entered if there is poor lighting in the warehouse. Poor lighting can refer to both dim lighting and excessively bright lighting. For example, a fork lift driver may have to squint up into the overhead lights in an aisle to putaway a pallet, and puts it in the wrong location. Or, the lighting is so dim in an aisle that workers cannot see location tags or identification numbers. There are many ways to improve or compensate for lighting, including localized spot lights on fork-lifts, backlit displays on portable computers, and using much larger fonts on inventory tags.
- *Direct sunlight.* If scanners are being used to read bar code labels, direct sunlight on the labels can make it impossible for the scanners to see any information. In addition, direct sunlight can rapidly fade labels, making them impossible to read. The fading problem can be mitigated by using more robust labels. Items stored in direct sunlight may have to be moved elsewhere if scanners are to be used.
- *Temperature.* Computer equipment is only designed to work within certain temperature ranges, outside of which they may not be usable. Colder temperatures make it difficult for employees to write legibly or keypunch information into a computer. If pick and pack to voice systems are available for cold weather applications, they can overcome the low-temperature problem. If temperature ranges are extreme, it may be necessary to only use computer equipment within temperature-controlled parts of the warehouse.
- *Housekeeping.* When there is little attention to how goods are stored, they may routinely be placed in the wrong locations or span several locations, or be tucked away into corners and not recognized in the computer system at all. Poor housekeeping in staging areas can lead to the mixing of inventory among different customer orders or production kits. Poor housekeeping also applies to computer workstations, where paper-based transactions can easily be mixed up or lost. The only solution is an ongoing emphasis on housekeeping within the warehouse area.

While each of these items can cause record accuracy to decline, an ongoing remediation program that targets each issue can yield excellent results.

Employee Factors Impacting Record Accuracy

There are major differences in the ability of certain individuals to correctly record transactions. These differences are not immediately apparent when someone is hired, but will become apparent over a relatively short period of time. The following factors all contribute to an employee causing inventory record inaccuracies:

- *Attachment to work.* Those employees that truly care about what they do have a much higher level of record accuracy than those who are disinterested.
- *Feedback acceptance.* When employees receive feedback about an incorrect inventory transaction, some immediately accept the feedback and others become defensive.
- *Experience.* A person with minimal experience will inevitably make more mistakes than someone with years of experience in the same environment.

Only the last of the preceding factors (experience) will improve record accuracy over time. The other factors are ones that an employee must make the decision to correct.

Ultimately, everyone who is involved with inventory is responsible for the accuracy of the associated records. This means that there is no place in a company where minimally-accurate employees can be parked. Unfortunately, some employee turnover will likely be required before a company arrives at the point where inventory record inaccuracies are no longer associated with the incompetence of employees.

Labeling Issues Impacting Record Accuracy

The types and durability of the labels used to identify inventory and storage locations can have a profound impact on inventory record accuracy. Labels can easily be ripped or destroyed in the high-impact environment of a warehouse, making it much more difficult for the warehouse staff to record transactions. To mitigate problems with labels, follow these practices:

- *Label adhesion.* Buying inventory labels is a serious business, since the wrong ones may not adhere to cardboard or shrink wrap, or fall off after minimal impact, or due to high humidity levels. Consequently, obtain a sample of the labels to be used, and subject them to the full range of adhesion scenarios that are likely to be encountered. The testing may last for several months, to see if adhesion wears off over time.
- *Label durability.* Subject a set of test labels to rigorous inventory handling practices, and determine the extent to which they are damaged. This can be impacted by the thickness and fiber content of the labels.
- *Scanability.* Packing tape is frequently run over labels, especially location labels in the storage racks. If so, and bar codes are used, determine how many layers of packing tape (if any) can be used without interfering with the ability of a bar code scanner to access bar code information.
- *Label placement.* Develop standards for where labels are to be placed on inventory items, so that they are easily accessible by the staff. For example,

placing a label on the backside of a pallet does little good if it cannot be seen from the front of a storage rack.

- *Font size.* There is no such thing as an excessively large font, especially in a low-light or dirty environment. If there is excess space on a label, use it to more prominently display information with a larger font.

Proper attention to these issues can largely eliminate labeling issues as a source of inventory record accuracy problems.

Inventory Naming Conventions Impacting Record Accuracy

A key element in the record accuracy problem is the complexity of the information being entered. If inventory identification numbers, units of measure, and location codes are excessively complex, there is an increased chance that they will be entered incorrectly. For example:

- *Inventory names.* Instead of using random digits to identify an SKU, consider the inclusion of at least some meaning in the name, so that a data entry person will understand what they are entering. For example, a large blue widget could be identified as Widget-Blue-L instead of 123ABC04#. However, the result can be extremely long part numbers. Also, a numbering scheme that made sense several years ago may no longer be practical, as a business transitions to new product lines and configurations.

- *Location codes.* A typical location code describes the aisle, rack, and bin in which inventory is located. For example, location 04-M-03 signifies aisle four, rack M, bin three. Or, if goods are to be located in a bulk storage area, use just an aisle address to denote a lane in which all pallets containing a specific item are to be stored. These approaches are simple and widely-used naming conventions. Trouble can arise when the coding system varies by section of the warehouse, or for different warehouses using the same computer system. Instead, do everything possible to require the same coding convention for all storage areas.

- *Units of measure.* It may seem simple enough to record a unit of measure, such as EA for each. However, some companies obfuscate the obvious by including too much information. For example, a label stating "8/20 LB" might be intended to convey that there are eight units in a box, each of which weighs 20 pounds. This label can be misinterpreted, such as 8/20ths of a pound, or 20 units weighing eight pounds. Consequently, do not include too much information in the unit of measure.

> **Tip:** Exclude all special characters, such as hyphens, from inventory records. These characters are especially difficult to access on a portable keyboard. Instead, have the data entry software automatically insert these characters in a specific position in a data entry sequence. For example, the entry of location code B-04-T only requires a person to enter B04T, with the computer entering the applicable hyphens automatically.

There are other benefits of having simplified naming conventions. Stock pickers will have a much easier time finding and picking the correct goods from stock. It is also less likely that incorrect pack sizes will be sent to the production area or to customers.

One might believe that the issues raised in this section do not apply when the entire data collection system is automated. For example, if scanners are used to extract information from bar code labels, who cares about the complexity of the labels? This is an incorrect assumption, for information must at some point be encoded into the labels, and this can be done incorrectly. If a bar code label is incorrect, then all subsequent scans of that label will also be incorrect. Thus, the use of automated data collection simply makes errors more widespread.

> **Tip:** There is no such thing as an excessively large label that identifies an inventory item. Use the largest possible font sizes and the cleanest information layout, so the warehouse staff has a better chance of reading the label information from a distance.

Excessive Data Recordation

The typical inventory management system requires that a standard set of information be entered for each new inventory item. This can involve dozens of data fields, especially in more complex systems that seek to provide every conceivable feature to users. The result is that users must tab their way through a massive number of fields to enter the information that is actually needed. It is quite easy for a user to inadvertently tab through to the wrong field to enter information, or to skip entering needed information.

To avoid this data entry problem, configure all data entry screens to contain only those fields for which information must be entered. Also, set the system to require information to be entered in each of these required fields, thereby sidestepping the problem of missing information. Depending on the capabilities of the software, it may also be possible to reconfigure the layout of the fields on the screen, to cluster together groups of similar information and to generally speed up the data entry process.

Inventory Data Collection Methods

The method chosen to collect information about inventory transactions can have a profound impact on the accuracy of inventory records. In the following table, we note the issues and benefits associated with the most common inventory data collection methods.

Inventory Data Collection Methods

Data Collection Method	Description, Issues and Benefits
Paper-based	Description: All transactions are recorded on paper and forwarded to a warehouse clerk for entry in a manual ledger. Advantage: Can be maintained under primitive conditions and high-stress environments where computer systems are not available or usable. Disadvantages: Subject to data entry error at the point of origin as well as by the warehouse clerk. Notification documents may also be lost or seriously delayed before they reach the clerk. These delays can interfere with cycle counting.
Bar code scanning	Description: Bar codes are assigned to all bin locations and inventory items. The bar codes for other commonly-used information, such as employee identification numbers, quantities, and activity descriptions can be included on bar code scan boards that employees carry with them. The warehouse staff scans bar codes to initiate a transaction, and then uploads the information to the computer system. No manual entries are required. Advantages: Eliminates data entry errors, reduces the time of the warehouse staff in recording transactions, and eliminates the data entry work of the warehouse clerk. Disadvantages: Scanners are moderately expensive and can be broken. There is a risk of data loss if the memory component of a scanner is broken before scanned transactions can be uploaded. Does not work if there is no direct line of sight access to a label. Labels are subject to tearing, which can make them unreadable. If a label is encoded incorrectly, this will result in the recordation of incorrect information for as long as the label is used.
Radio frequency terminals	Description: This is a portable scanning unit that also accepts instructions by wireless communication from the warehouse management system. Scanned transactions are uploaded in real time. Advantages: An excellent technique for maintaining a mobile workforce in the warehouse that sends back and receives transactional information from anywhere in the facility. Disadvantages: Terminals are expensive and can be broken. Transmissions do not always work in hostile environments where there are stray radio signals.

Data Collection Method	Description, Issues and Benefits
Radio frequency identification	Description: Transponder tags are attached to inventory items, which emit an encoded set of information to a receiver when inventory items pass a receiving station. These tags are usually passive, which means they only transmit information when impacted by a transmission signal. Active tags contain their own power source, and so can transmit at any time. Advantages: Can automatically receive information from passing inventory, so that inventory movements are tracked in real time without operator intervention. Can operate even if there is no direct line of sight communication with the receiver. Receivers can accept high volumes of information within a short period of time, and can collect information from tags located relatively far away. Disadvantages: Relies upon the ability of transponder tags to properly transmit information and of receiving units to receive the information, which does not always happen. The result is incomplete transactions from data dropout. Tags are not individually expensive, but so many are needed to track all inventory items that the total tag cost can be prohibitive; the cost currently limits their use to unit-loads.
Voice	Description: The warehouse management system (WMS) sends wireless instructions to an employee, who is wearing a headset and microphone attached to a small portable computer. The computer converts the instructions to voice commands. The employee can respond with a specific set of words that the WMS can understand. Advantages: Useful in environments where hands-free communication is necessary, such as cold storage. Increases record keeping accuracy and employee productivity, while eliminating rekeying errors. Has a lower error rate than bar code scanning. A minimal training period is required. Disadvantages: Can be difficult to communicate with the WMS if there are stray signals in the warehouse environment. Not usable if the WMS must capture long strings of random numbers.

Data Collection Method	Description, Issues and Benefits
Pick to light	Description: A picking person receives a tray that contains a bar coded order number. After the order number is scanned, a display panel mounted above each storage bin flashes a light, indicating that a pick should be made; a display shows the number of units to pick, and a button is pressed when the pick is complete. The tray containing all picked items then moves to the next picking zone, where the order bar code is scanned again and all items to be picked from that area are lit up. Thus, pick to light only works in a zone picking configuration (see the Putaways and Picking chapter). The system can also be used to make on-the-spot cycle counting adjustments.
	Advantages: Can be retrofitted onto existing rack space. Works well for high-speed picking operations, and eliminates any need for the manual entry of transactions. There is also no need for a pick list. Requires minimal training.
	Disadvantages: Requires a linkage to the WMS, which controls the operation in real time. Can be expensive when large numbers of bins must be outfitted with display panels. The cost tends to limit its use to higher-volume picking operations.

The bar code scanning approach noted above can be expanded upon by requiring suppliers to label all goods shipped to the company with designated bar codes that identify the part number and quantity shipped. Then, when the goods are received, their attached bar codes are immediately scanned, and the stored information is loaded into the company's WMS. This approach is more accurate than having the receiving staff attempt to decipher the contents of each incoming load and create bar code labels on site.

The Data Entry Backlog Problem

Much of the last section contained descriptions of high-speed, automated data entry systems. What if a company cannot afford these systems, and continues to use a manual record keeping system? This is quite likely in smaller organizations with lower inventory turnover levels. In this situation, the single most important issue impacting inventory record accuracy is the data entry backlog problem.

In a manual system, paper-based transaction documents are continually arriving from all over the warehouse, documenting receipts, putaways, picks, restocking transactions, scrapped items, kitting activity, shipments, and so forth. If the warehouse data entry staff cannot keep up with this incoming flood, here are some of the resulting anomalies:

- Cycle counters routinely find that the recorded amount for an inventory location diverges from the on-hand count, since any transactions impacting that bin from the previous day(s) have not yet been recorded. Cycle counters then make adjustments to the inventory records based on what they have counted, which further reduces the accuracy of the records.

- Customers place orders based on the availability of inventory. However, the customer service staff is basing their promises on inventory records that are out of date, so that inventory may not actually be on the shelf. The result is either cancelled orders or expedited production activities to create replacement goods.
- Production is planned based on recorded parts availability. When the parts are not actually in stock, production must be rescheduled on a rush basis or overnight air freight used to obtain replacement parts from suppliers.

Given the significance of these issues, a great deal of effort should be put into erasing any data entry backlog. This can be done by overstaffing the data entry function, so that any backlog is eliminated in short order, and there is sufficient staff on hand to deal with a sudden surge in transaction volume. In addition, consider having data entry staff in any shift during which there is warehouse activity, so that the records are always up-to-date by the start of the next shift's work.

The best solution to the data entry backlog problem is to not use paper-based transactions at all. If the warehouse is a small one and transaction volumes are low, the automated systems required to avoid data entry issues will appear to be too expensive. However, if the cost of data entry staff and the time required to correct errors are included in the analysis, the cost-benefit of implementing a non-paper system may become more apparent. If not, then continue to examine the situation if warehouse transaction volume grows over time, to see if paper-based transactions can be eliminated at a later date.

Backflushing

Backflushing is the concept of waiting until the manufacture of a product has been completed, and then recording all of the related issuances of inventory from stock that were required to create the product. This approach has the advantage of avoiding all manual assignments of costs to products during the various production stages, thereby eliminating a large number of transactions and the associated labor. It also eliminates the need to manually record production picks, which is an area in which errors are particularly difficult to eradicate.

Backflushing is entirely automated, with a computer handling all transactions. The backflushing formula is:

Number of units produced × Unit count listed in the bill of materials for each component
= Pick total

Backflushing is a theoretically elegant solution to the complexities of assigning costs to products and relieving inventory, but it is difficult to implement. Backflushing is subject to the following problems:

- *Accurate production count.* The number of finished goods produced is the multiplier in the back flush equation, so an incorrect count will relieve an incorrect amount of components and raw materials from stock.
- *Accurate bill of materials.* The bill of materials contains a complete itemization of the components and raw materials used to construct a product. If the items in the bill are inaccurate, the back flush equation will relieve an incorrect amount of components and raw materials from stock.
- *Accurate scrap reporting.* There will inevitably be unusual amounts of scrap or rework in a production process that are not anticipated in a bill of materials. If these items are not separately deleted from inventory, they will remain in the inventory records, since the back flush equation does not account for them.
- *Rapid production.* Backflushing does not remove items from inventory until after a product has been completed, so the inventory records will remain incomplete until such time as the backflushing occurs. Thus, a very rapid production cycle time is the best way to keep this interval as short as possible. Under a backflushing system, there is no recorded amount of work-in-process inventory.

Backflushing is not suitable for long production processes, since it takes too long for the inventory records to be reduced after the eventual completion of products. It is also not suitable for the production of customized products, since this would require the creation of a unique bill of materials for each item produced.

We make note of the backflushing topic in this chapter in order to emphasize how easily it can be incorrectly implemented to spawn a large number of inventory record errors. However, the cautions raised here do not mean that it is impossible to use backflushing. Usually, a manufacturing planning system allows for the use of backflushing for just certain products, so that it can be run on a compartmentalized basis. This is useful not just to pilot test the concept, but also to use it only under those circumstances where it is most likely to succeed. Thus, backflushing can be incorporated into a hybrid system in which multiple methods of transaction recordation may be used.

Controls over Record Accuracy

Ideally, it should only be necessary to record an inventory-related transaction once, and then assume that the entry was made correctly. Doing so achieves a massive decline in data entry labor. However, the amount of errors actually experienced is likely to drive an additional need for controls that examine whether transactions were initially handled correctly. The following table shows the nature of a potential record accuracy problem, and the related controls that can mitigate the error rate.

Controls over Record Accuracy

Potential Error	Offsetting Control
Suppliers send incorrect quantities	• Count all pallets, cases, or units as received, or a selection of these items • Weigh pallets, cases or units as received • Visual inspection of received goods for obvious errors
Shipping department sends incorrect quantities	• Clearly delineate staging areas for each truckload, so that orders are not mixed • Second person independently counts pallets, cases, or units prior to delivery • Weight pallets, cases, or units prior to delivery • Visual inspection of goods to be shipped for obvious errors • Count the number of pallets or cases shipped and match to customer order • Do not load a truck until the entire shipment has been staged; otherwise, it is difficult to ascertain what has already been loaded
Putaway errors	• Match recorded putaways to actual locations from the prior day • Run report showing locations with zero inventory, and match to actual locations to see if they contain inventory
New employee errors	• Sort transaction logs by employee number and verify all transactions associated with new employees
General transaction errors	• Conduct cycle counts to look for general errors • Match what is on the shelf back to inventory report

Other controls than the ones noted here may be of more use, depending on the structure of the process flow and the types of inventory being handled.

When deciding upon a set of controls to install, always consider their impact on the process flow. A number of labor-intensive controls may indeed improve record accuracy, but at the price of slowing down the record-keeping process. Ideally, there should be a balance between adding additional controls and losing process efficiency.

Inventory Review Reports

There are a small number of reports that can be used to track down possible inventory record errors. The reports themselves will not pinpoint exactly why an error is occurring, but can at least indicate the right direction. The reports are:

- *Empty location report.* Run a report that shows all locations in the warehouse in which there should be no inventory. Then check each of these locations. If inventory is located in one of these bins, there is a guaranteed record accuracy problem.
- *Multi-location report.* Run a report that shows all pallet-storage locations for which more than one item is supposedly being stored. The chances are good

that one of the items is not really in storage, since there is no room for it. This report does not work in locations where cases and broken cases are stored, since many items could actually be kept in these areas.

- *Negative balance report.* Run a report that shows negative inventory unit quantities. An investigation can reveal that a key transaction has not yet been entered that will correct the balance, but this report will likely also reveal several situations where transactions have not been recorded at all. This report is described in more detail in the next section.
- *Sorted valuation report.* Calculate the total valuation of each inventory item, and sort the report in descending order of total valuation. The first page of the report can reveal situations where unit counts are grossly too high. A likely cause is that the incorrect unit of measure is being used.

Inventory review reports are detective controls, and so are only useful for locating errors after they have already occurred. These reports do not prevent errors from occurring in the first place.

The Negative Inventory Balance

An unfortunately common occurrence is that the inventory records indicate a negative on-hand balance. This situation always arises from either a delay or an error in data entry. Here are several situations that can cause a negative inventory balance:

- Goods are cross-docked from the receiving area, straight through to a truck for delivery to a customer. The shipment transaction is entered but not the receipt, resulting in a negative balance.
- Goods are replenished from reserve storage and then picked. The pick transaction is recorded but not the replenishment move, resulting in a negative balance.
- A receipt is incorrectly recorded with too small a quantity or with the wrong unit of measure, and then picked from stock. The receipt amount is too low, resulting in a negative balance.
- Goods are removed from stock, and the forklift operator accidentally records the transaction twice. With a double pick recorded, the on-hand balance appears to be negative.

A negative balance is sometimes a case of transaction documentation being delayed. If so, waiting a short period of time for the transaction to be recorded will yield a corrected inventory balance. However, other negative balances are indicative of more serious problems where transactions are lost or entered incorrectly. Since it is impossible to tell which scenario applies to a negative balance, it is best to immediately investigate every negative balance as soon as it is detected.

> **Tip:** Create an inventory report that only lists negative inventory balances, have the warehouse manager run it every day, and follow up on any negative items found.

Inventory Auditing

Given the massive number of transactions involved in the receipt, handling, and shipment of inventory, it may be useful to schedule a periodic audit by the internal audit department. These audits are usually highly targeted, so that specific activities are reviewed in detail. For example, the warehouse manager might be concerned about record accuracy related to picking activities, and so requests an audit to investigate these transactions. Even more specifically, the manager may ask for an audit of picking within a certain aisle, where error rates are unusually high.

Inventory audits are particularly useful when there is a suspicion that some employees in the warehouse area are stealing inventory. In this situation, cycle counting may not work, since the people counting goods may also be engaged in theft. By using the audit staff instead, there is a higher probability of locating specific fraudulent activity.

A variation on the auditing concept is self-auditing. Essentially, self-auditing means that employees review the transactions recorded by each other, either through the review of a small inventory count or a full-blown transaction reconstruction. This approach is only feasible if there is a sufficient amount of excess staff time available for self-auditing. Possible self-auditing methods include:

- *Cycle counting.* Have the warehouse staff review any exceptions found by their fellow cycle counters. This can also include a mutual review of any changes made to the inventory database for location or unit count alterations.
- *Picking.* Have inventory pickers compare what they picked to what is stated on their pick tickets.
- *Transaction entry.* The data entry staff can compare the paper transactions from which information was entered to a log of entered information from the computer system.

While useful, it is difficult to enforce the use of self-auditing, for several reasons. First, it is difficult to monitor auditing activities. Also, employees may pressure each other to not report any errors found. These issues can be reduced by paying a bonus to the warehouse staff that is based on the accuracy of inventory records.

The Corrective Action System

Any error found in the production and materials handling functions will likely have a negative impact on inventory. Either inventory must be scrapped, or more must be ordered, or a customer must be informed that an order cannot be shipped. In all three cases, the company loses – either because it must invest in more inventory or forego a sale. The best way to deal with these situations is to install a corrective action system.

A corrective action system is essentially a database of logged errors that are examined for corrective solutions. Every error is entered into this system, and is then assigned to an investigative team, with the goal of deriving a solution that will either eliminate or mitigate the incidence of the error. At a minimum, the database should contain the following information:

- Unique case identification number
- Complete description of the problem
- Identification information for the impacted inventory
- The area of the business in which the error occurred
- Person responsible for investigating the error
- Results of the investigation
- Actions taken to correct the error
- Scheduled date of follow-up review

In addition, someone should be responsible for reviewing the status of all open corrective action events. If an examination appears to be languishing, this fact can then be boosted to a higher level of management for more aggressive follow-up.

If an error is causing unusually significant problems, the presence of a follow-up review may be particularly important. In this case, management wants to ascertain whether the corrective action is sufficient, or if additional steps must be taken. In addition, the type of corrective action taken may itself be causing additional problems, which the follow-up review can spotlight. The trouble with corrective actions is that they represent a patch to the existing system, and so may not have been designed to fit seamlessly into the existing systems. If so, the follow-up review is intended to note any issues requiring additional examination. In short, the follow-up review is not intended to be a cursory review – instead, it can be a major re-examination of the changes made.

The end result of a corrective action system should be an ongoing reduction in the number of issues impacting inventory. However, this does not mean that all errors will eventually vanish. The introduction of new products, product lines, and processes will always trigger new error types. Also, there will be occasional outlier events that cause less-common errors. Consequently, there will always be a need for a corrective action system, even in the finest production and materials handling environment.

Summary

The inventory record accuracy issue is not an insignificant one. It is entirely possible that a mix of many environmental, technology, and employee issues all contribute to different types of errors. It may take a notable amount of investigation to discern the base-level reason for a particular issue, and even more time to determine a reasonable correction that will eliminate the problem. In one case, the author worked with a food processing company that estimated there were 65 ways to cause inventory record errors! When there are so many possible ways to cause errors and so much time is required to correct them, it is essential to focus on the largest classifications of errors first, and gradually work through to those problems causing the fewest errors. Doing so generates the most immediate return on investment, and also provides an immediate improvement to the many activities that depend on record accuracy in order to function properly, such as purchasing, production, and shipping.

Chapter 13
Inventory Counting and Reconciliation

Introduction

Inventory is a crucial company asset, since it ensures the proper flow of goods into the production process, as well as to customers. Consequently, the amount of inventory on hand must be as accurately tracked as possible at all times. Doing so calls for the use of either physical counts or cycle counting. In this chapter, we address the types of inventory tracking systems and how they relate to physical counts and cycle counting. We also note a variety of techniques for improving the efficiency of both counting systems. We finish with a discussion of the inventory reconciliation, where we investigate the underlying causes of transactional errors that were discovered during inventory counts.

The Periodic Inventory System

The periodic inventory system only updates the ending inventory balance when a physical inventory count is conducted. Since physical inventory counts are time-consuming, few companies do them more than once a quarter or year. In the meantime, the inventory account continues to show the cost of the inventory that was recorded as of the last physical inventory count.

Under the periodic inventory system, all purchases made between physical inventory counts are recorded in a purchases account. When a physical inventory count is completed, shift the balance in the purchases account into the inventory account, which in turn is adjusted to match the cost of the ending inventory.

The calculation of the cost of goods sold under the periodic inventory system is as follows:

Beginning inventory + Purchases = Cost of goods available for sale

Cost of goods available for sale − Ending inventory = Cost of goods sold

---

EXAMPLE

Milagro Corporation has beginning inventory of $100,000, has paid $170,000 for purchases, and its physical inventory count reveals an ending inventory cost of $80,000. The calculation of its cost of goods sold is:

$100,000 Beginning inventory + $170,000 Purchases - $80,000 Ending inventory

= $190,000 Cost of goods sold

The periodic inventory system is most useful for smaller businesses that maintain minimal amounts of inventory. For them, a physical inventory count is easy to complete, and they can estimate cost of goods sold figures for interim periods. However, there are several problems with the system:

- It does not yield any information about the cost of goods sold or ending inventory balances during interim periods when there has been no physical inventory count.
- The cost of goods sold must be estimated during interim periods, which will likely result in a significant adjustment to the actual cost of goods whenever a physical inventory count is eventually completed.
- There is no way to adjust for obsolete inventory or scrap losses during interim periods, so there tends to be a significant (and expensive) adjustment for these issues when a physical inventory count is eventually completed.

A more up-to-date and accurate alternative to the periodic inventory system is the perpetual inventory system, which is described in the next section.

The Perpetual Inventory System

Under the perpetual inventory system, an entity continually updates its inventory records to account for additions to and subtractions from inventory for such activities as received inventory items, goods sold from stock, and items picked from inventory for use in the production process. Thus, a perpetual inventory system has the advantages of both providing up-to-date inventory balance information and requiring a reduced level of physical inventory counts. However, the calculated inventory levels derived by a perpetual inventory system may gradually diverge from actual inventory levels, due to unrecorded transactions or theft, so periodically compare book balances to actual on-hand quantities with cycle counting (as explained later in the Cycle Counting section).

EXAMPLE

This example contains several journal entries used to account for transactions in a perpetual inventory system. Milagro Corporation records a purchase of $1,000 of widgets that are stored in inventory:

	Debit	Credit
Inventory	1,000	
Accounts payable		1,000

Milagro records $250 of inbound freight cost associated with the delivery of widgets:

	Debit	Credit
Inventory	250	
Accounts payable		250

Milagro records the sale of widgets from inventory for $2,000, for which the associated inventory cost is $1,200:

	Debit	Credit
Accounts receivable	2,000	
Revenue		2,000
Cost of goods sold	1,200	
Inventory		1,200

Milagro records a downward inventory adjustment of $500, caused by inventory theft, and detected during a cycle count:

	Debit	Credit
Inventory shrinkage expense	500	
Inventory		500

How to Set Up Inventory Record Keeping

If either a periodic or perpetual inventory system will be used to track inventory levels, there must be an organizational and record keeping structure in place to support it. Otherwise, the inventory records will be hopelessly inaccurate, and it will be difficult to locate inventory items for a count. The following steps are of use in setting up a warehouse structure that can support an inventory tracking and counting system:

1. *Identify inventory.* Create a part numbering system, and ensure that every item in inventory has been properly labeled with a part number. There should also be a procedure for identifying and labeling all new inventory as it is received or manufactured.
2. *Clean out miscellaneous accumulations.* Stray inventory items may accumulate in out-of-the-way locations, such as around work stations, in corners, and under conveyors. Return these items to their designated locations, and institute procedures to ensure that these stray areas are regularly swept clear of goods.
3. *Consolidate inventory.* If the same inventory items are stored in multiple locations, try to consolidate them into one place. This makes the counting process easier.

4. *Package inventory*. Where possible, put loose inventory items in boxes or bags, seal the containers, and mark the quantity on the sealing tape. Also put partial cases in front of or on top of full cases. This greatly reduces any subsequent counting effort.

5. *Create locations*. Create a system of inventory locations throughout the warehouse, which state the aisle, rack, and bin number in a logical manner. Verify that all locations in the warehouse have a prominently displayed location tag.

6. *Segregate the warehouse*. Install a fence around the warehouse, so that inventory can only pass through a central gate. Then count and record inventory as it passes through the central gate.

7. *Count inventory*. After all of the preceding steps have been completed, conduct a physical inventory count (see the Physical Inventory Count section).

8. *Record information*. Record the inventory quantities and locations in the inventory database.

Once an inventory record keeping system is in place, work on upgrading the accuracy of the inventory records. This can be done by installing a daily cycle counting program, which is discussed in the Cycle Counting section.

The Physical Inventory Count

If a company uses a periodic inventory system, or if the inventory records are inaccurate, it may be necessary to conduct a physical inventory count. This count provides the unit totals that form the basis for the ending inventory valuation, and can also be used to update inventory unit count records. Follow these steps when administering a physical inventory count:

Prior to the count:

1. *Tags*. Order a sufficient number of sequentially numbered count tags for the count. These should be two-part tags, and include line items for the product name, product identification number, quantity, and location. Also consider adding space for the counter's initials. There may be a punch hole in the top center, which can be used to tie the count tag to an inventory item. A sample count tag follows.

Sample Inventory Count Tag

2. *Part numbers.* Identify all inventory items that do not have a legible part number, and have the warehouse staff properly identify them prior to the count.

3. *Pre-counts.* Where possible, count items in advance, seal them in containers, and mark the quantities on the outside of the containers.

4. *Management area.* Set up management areas within the warehouse where counters are to assemble for instructions, as well as to collect and return all reports and forms needed for the count.

5. *Segregation.* Move all items not to be counted out of the counting area, or identify them with "Do not count" tags.

6. *Cutoff.* Segregate all received goods if they arrive after the cutoff date for the physical inventory count.

7. *Outside locations.* Notify all outside locations to count their inventory and send in their count totals.

<u>Counting activities:</u>

1. *Train teams.* Instruct the counting teams regarding counting procedures, and issue them count tags that are numerically sequential. Keep track of which team has been issued a set of tags.
2. *Count inventory.* Each counting team must count the inventory in the area assigned to it, fill out the count information on an inventory tag, and tape a tag to each inventory item, retaining the copy of each tag. One person should count inventory, while a second person writes down the information on tags. When a count team is done, it turns in its copies of the tags, as well as any unused tags.
3. *Track tags.* A person responsible for tags verifies that all used and unused tags have been received, and accounts for any missing tags.
4. *Data entry.* Enter all tags into a database or spreadsheet, and summarize the quantities by part number and location.
5. *Comparison.* If the company uses a perpetual inventory system, compare the count totals to the inventory records. Investigate any variances by recounting the inventory.
6. *Reporting.* Print a final report that summarizes the unit quantities of all counted inventory items.
7. *Review the process.* Examine the entire physical count process, identify areas in which it could be improved, and write down these issues for consideration as part of the next physical count.
8. *Subsequent counts.* Create a list of the largest variances noted during the physical inventory count, and return to these items for cycle counts. It is entirely possible that a counting error caused these variances, and will require correction.

Concerns about the Physical Inventory Count

One might think that the effort required to organize and complete a physical inventory count would at least result in accurate inventory records. This is not necessarily the case. There are several reasons why the information generated by a physical count may be incorrect. Consider the following:

- *Staff quality.* If the count process is a large one, or if management wants to complete the count as quickly as possible, staff from outside the warehouse may be brought in to count inventory. These people may not know how to properly identify or count inventory items, resulting in worse information than if the records had been left alone.
- *Data entry.* A massive amount of information from the count tags is keypunched into a database. Given the volume of information involved, it is very likely that there will be keypunching errors.
- *Duplicate and no counts.* There are many storage locations in a warehouse. Even in the best-organized physical count, some locations may be counted twice, while other locations are not counted at all.

Warehouse employees frequently look upon physical counts with dread, because the resulting information worsens inventory record accuracy to such an extent that they may spend weeks correcting records. Consequently, we strongly recommend moving away from physical inventory counts, and instead using an ongoing program of cycle counts to achieve higher levels of inventory record accuracy.

Physical Count Improvements

If a company finds that it cannot get away from the physical count process, there are some techniques available for streamlining the process flow in order to compress the counting process to the minimum possible time period, and to reduce error rates. Consider the following possibilities:

- *Counter qualifications.* Only warehouse employees are allowed to count inventory. No one else is allowed to do so, since they are unfamiliar with the inventory, and will make an unusually large number of errors. Given the time required to fix errors, using a small number of experienced counters is faster than using a large number of inexperienced counters.
- *Cycle count in advance.* A company may have already instituted cycle counting procedures, but accuracy levels are not yet sufficiently high to warrant the elimination of a physical count. If so, accuracy levels are likely much higher already than would have been the case without the cycle counting. Consequently, continue to run cycle counts right up to the start of the physical count. This should reduce the number of adjustments found during the physical count.
- *Hold receipts.* If an unusually large amount of inventory has just been delivered to the company, consider leaving it in the receiving area and not logging it into the record keeping system until the physical count is completed. This leaves less inventory to count, and reduces the chance of having a receiving error impact the counting process.
- *Inventory software interface.* Design a data entry program for the company's inventory records database, so that count tags can be entered directly into the system. Once aggregated, the program compares the balances to the on-hand amounts recorded in the system, and issues a variance report. This is a substantial improvement on entering tag information into an electronic spreadsheet, which is then compared by hand to the balances in the computer system.
- *Bar code tags.* Print a bar code on each tag issued, which contains the unique tag number. The data entry staff can then scan the bar code rather than manually entering the information, which eliminates a possible transposition error.
- *Record tag locations.* Have the count team note the exact aisle-rack-bin location of each inventory item on the related count tag. Then, if there is an issue with a tag, it is quite easy to locate where the tag was used in the warehouse, saving search time.

- *Pre-print tags with quantities*. Print a count tag in advance for each location that contains inventory, along with a bar coded tag number and the number of units stated in the inventory database. Counters then circle the stated inventory amount if it is correct, or enter a different number. A removable portion of the tag is then peeled off and stuck on the inventory to show that a count was completed. Once the entire count is done, aggregate all tags for which the stated quantity was correct. Design a data entry program for these items that only requires a scan of the bar coded tag number to enter the indicated quantity. Then use a different data entry program to enter all remaining tags for which different amounts were counted.

The last of the suggested improvements requires a considerable amount of up-front design work, but can yield the best overall improvement, since it streamlines counts and yields a massive reduction in data entry work.

Cycle Counting

Cycle counting is the process of counting a small proportion of the total inventory on a daily basis, and not only correcting any errors found, but also investigating the underlying reasons why the errors occurred. An active cycle counting program should result in a gradual increase in the level of inventory record accuracy.

> **Tip:** Only the more experienced warehouse staff should engage in cycle counting, since they have the most experience with the inventory. Anyone else would probably make so many mistakes that they would *decrease* the level of inventory record accuracy.

> **Related Podcast Episode:** Episode 192 of the Accounting Best Practices Podcast discusses cycle counting. It is available at: **accountingtools.com/podcasts** or **iTunes**

There are multiple methods used for selecting the inventory items to be counted each day for a cycle counting program. They are:

- *By location*. Simply work through the warehouse, section by section. This approach ensures that all inventory items will be counted, and is a simple way to coordinate the daily counts. Once the entire warehouse has been counted, start back at the beginning and do it again.
- *By usage*. The materials management department places a higher emphasis on the inventory record accuracy of those items used most frequently in the production process, since an unexpected shortage of one of these items could stop production. Consequently, high-usage items should be counted more frequently.
- *By criticality*. Some items must be on hand, or production cannot proceed. Also, these items may be extremely difficult to obtain, perhaps because suppliers require long lead times, or because the only supplier is selling goods on

an allocation basis. In this situation, the very small number of critical items should be continually monitored, with all other goods receiving less cycle counting attention. A variation on this concept is to give counting priority to those items scheduled to go into production in the near future; under this approach, cycle counts should be scheduled earlier than the lead time required to replace a part, in case the counts reveal missing parts, and replacements must be ordered in time to meet the production schedule.

- *By valuation.* The accounting department is most concerned with the record accuracy of those inventory items having the largest aggregate cost, since an error here would impact reported profits. Consequently, high-valuation items would be counted more frequently.

A further refinement of these concepts is to conduct cycle counts at the low point of on-hand quantity levels. Doing so reduces the amount of counting effort by the warehouse staff, thereby reducing the time required to complete a series of counts. A variation on this concept is to conduct cycle counts after a production run has been completed. Doing so catches any reporting errors associated with the last production run. Also, since production has just been completed, raw material unit counts should be at a low point, which facilitates counting.

Some inventory items may move so slowly that there is little need to subject them to cycle counts. In these situations, create a single annual cycle count for them, and exclude them from all other counts during the year.

Once a cycle counting methodology is in place, use the following steps to conduct daily cycle counts:

1. *Complete transactions.* Verify that all prior inventory transactions have been recorded in the inventory database. If you allow cycle counts when there are still some unrecorded transactions, counters will find differences between their counts and the cycle counting report and make adjustments, after which the original transactions are also recorded, resulting in reduced inventory record accuracy.

2. *Print reports.* Print cycle counting reports for the cycle counters, which itemize the counts to be made based on the cycle counting methodology (e.g., by location, usage, criticality, or valuation).

3. *Count.* Each cycle counter traces the items listed on his or her cycle counting report to their locations, counts the units in the storage bin, and marks any corrections on the report. Further, the counters trace items from the bin back to the report, to see if there are any items in stock that are not in the inventory database.

Tip: Only count a few items when the cycle counting program is just getting under way, since there will likely be a large number of problems to investigate and correct. The sample size can be increased once there are fewer errors to investigate.

> **Tip:** A good way to reduce count inaccuracies is to have counters move counted items into a separate container for the duration of a count, thereby avoiding double counts or missed counts. A variation is to dump all items out of a bin and then count them as they are replaced into the bin.

4. *Recount.* Have a second person conduct a recount of any indicated errors. Someone else's viewpoint may be needed to discover that an initial count was incorrect, perhaps due to an improper inclusion or exclusion, or the use of an incorrect unit of measure.

> **Tip:** Anyone assigned to recount possible record errors should have an excellent knowledge of the inventory and the counting process, thereby increasing the probability that an incorrect initial count is detected. This person is frequently a senior warehouse staff person.

5. *Reconcile errors.* Investigate any differences between the inventory record and the amounts counted. This process is discussed in the following Inventory Reconciliation section.
6. *Correct errors.* The warehouse staff adjusts the inventory database for any errors found. These adjustments should be clearly designated as cycle counting corrections.
7. *Take preventive action.* If certain errors are appearing on a repetitive basis, the warehouse manager should adjust the warehouse procedures to keep them from arising in the future.

> **Tip:** Reinforce the importance of cycle counting by having an accounting or internal audit person conduct a weekly audit of the inventory, and calculate an overall inventory accuracy percentage that is posted for the warehouse staff to see. In addition, consider paying bonuses to the warehouse staff for continuing improvements in inventory record accuracy.

When is the best time of day in which to conduct cycle counts? The main consideration is that they only be conducted after all inventory transactions for the day have been inputted into the inventory records. Otherwise, the amounts counted during cycle counts cannot be compared to any valid record quantity. Other than this consideration, the best time of day is at the beginning of a shift, before the warehouse staff becomes overwhelmed by the daily round of activities. Otherwise, there is a strong chance that a sudden crisis will divert the warehouse staff from their counting responsibilities until another day.

If there is an ongoing pattern of cutting cycle counts short to deal with other issues, a different approach is indicated. In this situation, assign cycle counting to a small group that does nothing but cycle counts and the associated investigation of errors found. This approach ensures that cycle counting will continue at all times. This approach also yields an extremely experienced group that develops great expertise in tracking down inventory record accuracy problems.

> **Tip:** If a permanent cycle counting group is formed, consider rotating them out to other duties from time to time. Doing so keeps the staff from becoming bored, and also spreads the importance of inventory record accuracy among the entire warehouse staff.

There may be situations in which the warehouse operates at all hours, every day of the week. If so, it can be quite difficult to ensure that all records have been entered and activity frozen long enough to engage in cycle counting at all. Under these circumstances, consider using the following techniques to squeeze in cycle counts:

- *Rely on exception reports*. Focus a large amount of attention on counting those inventory items that have been flagged by exception reports as being possibly in error. See the Inventory Review Reports section in the Inventory Record Accuracy chapter for more information.
- *Schedule counts around activity*. If there is a schedule of picks and putaways, use programming logic to assign counts to those areas that are not scheduled to be impacted during specific time periods. This approach also works for the production area; schedule count activity for those periods when machinery is scheduled to be down for preventive or other scheduled maintenance.
- *Schedule counts around shift changes*. There is usually a work stoppage that coincides with the end of one shift and the beginning of the next. Schedule the shifts of the cycle counters to overlap with the normal shift change, so they can count inventory when the warehouse is effectively shut down.
- *Use intermediate storage*. If goods are about to be picked for any reason, pick in advance to an intermediate storage location to get them out of the way, and then count the residual balance in a location.

Over time, the error correction process associated with cycle counts may eliminate so many procedural and other issues that the count teams are no longer finding any errors. If so, it is permissible to gradually scale back the amount of effort allocated to cycle counting. However, the counting effort must continue at *some* level, since new errors may arise that must be spotted and counteracted.

Control Group Analysis

Cycle counting is a never-ending process, which can be a problem. Someone assigned to always count inventory every day may eventually adopt slipshod habits while trying to rush through this task. Likely results are inattention to minor differences in account balances, and not bothering to follow up on errors found. A way to break through this malaise is to use control groups, either as a supplement to or in place of cycle counting.

Under the control group concept, a small group of inventory items are blocked out for study. These items typically have high transaction volumes, and are subject to a particular error that requires detailed investigation. A team of those employees most knowledgeable in inventory record accuracy issues monitors this control group, waiting for an error to appear. The group then reviews the situation, locates the problem, derives a solution, implements it, and follows up to ensure that the error has been eliminated. In short, this process is targeted at locating specific problems, rather than the cycle counting approach of scanning the entire inventory for any types of errors at all.

The control group concept works well when record accuracy is being notably impacted by a particular problem. However, it has no effect on incidental problems, unless the review team decides to specifically target them.

The control group concept can also be pursued prior to laying out a large cycle counting program. By doing so, management can see if the cycle counters have sufficient knowledge to identify and correct record accuracy problems. If not, a complete rollout of the system can be delayed while the issues are addressed within the control group. Otherwise, cycle counters might make a number of improper correction entries across the entire inventory that end up reducing total record accuracy.

EXAMPLE

Entwhistle Electric is having trouble with the record keeping associated with its inventory putaway operations. It appears that some of the putaways are not being recorded. Currently, putaways are conducted using any available storage location in the facility outside of the main picking area. To concentrate attention on the problem, putaways for the next week are only allowed in Aisle A, with putaways in the following week restricted to Aisle B, and so on. By using this approach, location audits can be concentrated in a small area, and errors traced back to putaway operations that span a relatively brief period of time.

100% Count Analysis

In some inventories, there are a very small number of extremely high-value items. These items typically have quite small cubic volumes, and yet comprise a significant part of the value of the entire inventory. If this is the case, it is not sufficient to review count balances with cycle counting, since reviews may only take place at long intervals. Instead, consider engaging in a 100% count of these items on a very frequent basis, perhaps daily.

By engaging in such an oppressively frequent review, any transaction errors or fraudulent withdrawals will be spotted immediately, thereby allowing for prompt corrective action. This approach is not cost-effective for less-valuable items, and so should be confined to considerably less than one percent of the items listed in inventory.

Inventory Reconciliation

Inventory is reconciled when you compare the inventory counts in the company's records to the actual amounts on the warehouse shelves, figure out why there are differences between the two amounts, and make adjustments to the inventory records to reflect this analysis.

Inventory reconciliation is an important part of cycle counting, since the warehouse staff uses it to continually update the accuracy of its inventory records. Inventory reconciliation is not as simple as adjusting the book balance to match the physical count. There may be other reasons why there is a difference between the two numbers that cannot be corrected with such an adjustment. In particular, consider following any or all of these steps:

- *Recount the inventory*. It is entirely possible that someone incorrectly counted the inventory. If so, have a different person count it again (since the first counter could make the same counting mistake a second time). Further, if the physical count appears to be significantly lower than the book balance, it is quite possible that there is more inventory in a second location - so look around for a second cache of inventory. Recounting is the most likely reason for a variance, so consider this step first. Also, it can make sense to wait a day or two to see if a missing transaction turns up that can explain the difference.

- *Match the units of measure*. Are the units of measure used for the count and the book balance the same? One might be in individual units (known as "eaches"), while the other might be in dozens, or boxes, or pounds, or kilograms. If a recount has already been conducted and there is still a difference that is orders of magnitude apart, it is quite likely that the units of measure are the problem. This is especially likely if goods are recorded using an unusual unit of measure.

- *Verify the part number*. It is possible that you are misreading the part number of the item on the shelf, or guessing at its identification because there is no part number at all. If so, get a second opinion from an experienced warehouse staff person, or compare the item to the descriptions in the item master records. Another option is to look for some other item for which there is a unit count variance in the opposite direction - that could be the part number that you are looking for.

- *Look for missing paperwork*. This is an unfortunately large source of inventory reconciliation issues. The unit count in the inventory records may be incorrect because a transaction has occurred, but no one has yet logged it. This is a massive issue for cycle counters, who may have to root around for unentered paperwork of this sort before they feel comfortable in making an adjusting entry to the inventory records. Other examples of this problem are receipts that have not yet been entered (so the inventory record is too low) or issuances from the warehouse to the production area that have not been entered (so the inventory record is too high).

- *Investigate backflushing records*. If the company uses backflushing to alter inventory records (where inventory is relieved based on the number of finished goods produced), then the bill of materials and the finished goods production numbers had better both be in excellent condition, or the reconciliation process will be painful. Backflushing is not recommended unless manufacturing record keeping is superb.

The preceding points cover the most obvious issues that can impact inventory record accuracy. In addition, there are many transaction-specific issues that can cause an error. Consider the following additional investigation steps:

- *Examine transaction history.* Review the flow of transactions that were recorded since the last cycle count. There may be an obvious change in the number of units used somewhere in the flow. For example, 100 units are received, but only 50 are put away. Also, there may be a transfer between locations, with the unit count changing as part of the transfer.
- *Examine scrap.* Scrap can arise anywhere in a company (especially production), and the staff may easily overlook its proper recordation in the accounting records. If there is a modest variance where the inventory records are always just a small amount higher than the physical count, this is a likely cause.
- *Investigate possible customer ownership.* If there is no record of an inventory item at all in the accounting records, there may be a very good reason for it, which is that the company does not own it – a customer does. This is especially common when the company remodels or enhances products for its customers.
- *Investigate possible supplier ownership.* To follow up on the last item, it is also possible that there are items in stock that are on consignment from a supplier, and which are therefore owned by the supplier. This is most common in a retail environment and highly unlikely anywhere else.
- *Investigate data entry person.* There may be a high incidence of errors associated with the person recording transactions. This could be an actual error, or could be indicative of a fraudulent transaction where goods are being removed from the warehouse.
- *Investigate variance trends.* If a series of variances are always negative, this is a strong indicator of either incorrect bill of material records or fraud. If there is no trend, with an equal number of positive and negative variances, look for variances that offset each other. This can indicate that inventory items are being misidentified, such as through picking errors.
- *Investigate canceled actions.* There may be a record of a cancelled purchase order, shipment, or production job. If the amount of the variance matches this cancelled activity, it is possible that the action actually occurred, and the cancellation was never reversed.
- *Investigate production errors.* If a shortage of raw materials coincides with the production of an excess amount of finished goods, it is possible that a withdrawal of raw materials from stock for the production process was not recorded. This investigation requires detailed matching of bills of material to the missing amount of raw materials.
- *Investigate quality withdrawals.* If a product has a history of significant quality rejections and finished goods are missing from stock, it is entirely possible

that the quality assurance staff rejected some finished goods and never recorded the withdrawal. This is an especially likely scenario, since the quality staff is unaccustomed to the detailed level of transaction recording that other employees consider to be routine.

- *Investigate payables*. A supplier may have invoiced the company for substantially more than the receiving department says was received. If so, the supplier may be correct, and the amount that should have been recorded as received is substantially higher. This is a rare case where an issue raised in the accounting department can point toward a record accuracy issue.
- *Investigate temporary storage*. There may be a record of goods that have been received, but which never appeared in a normal storage location. These items were likely recorded correctly, but no putaway transaction was ever recorded. A search of supposedly empty bins may find the missing goods.
- *Investigate prior cycle counting adjustments*. If the amount of a detected error approximately offsets a previous cycle counting adjustment, the error may be due to incorrect cycle counting procedures. This is a particularly pernicious error, since just one inexperienced cycle counting person can cause a large number of record errors.

If all forms of investigation fail, then there is no choice but to alter the inventory record to match the physical count. It is possible that some other error will eventually be found that explains the discrepancy, but for now you cannot leave a variance; when in doubt, the physical count is correct. A variation under which the variance should also be accepted is when count scales are used to count goods, and the amount of the variance is within the accuracy tolerance of the counting scales.

Tip: Do not ignore a small variance. Even a variance that is immaterial on a percentage basis may be the first indicator of what may grow into a large accuracy problem.

The preceding points give a solid grounding in the reasons why there are errors in inventory records, but they are not the only reasons; other errors may be caused by unique record keeping systems or in particular industries, so compile a list of errors that have been discovered in the past, and use it when conducting an inventory reconciliation.

Summary

We cannot emphasize enough that some form of inventory counting will always be necessary – it is not sufficient to rely upon a perpetual inventory system, no matter how perfect the underlying inventory procedures may be. It takes very little to reduce inventory record accuracy, perhaps just a lack of training of a new employee in one type of transaction. Inventory counting is the last line of defense in ensuring that accuracy problems are detected in a timely manner. For more information about the causes of inventory record inaccuracy, see the Inventory Record Accuracy chapter.

Chapter 14
The Supply Chain

Introduction

A company that has a serious interest in managing its inventory levels realizes that it must interact with the chain of suppliers that provide it with goods. If there is a delivery problem or quality issue anywhere in this chain, the issue will impact the company, and therefore its performance with customers. Consequently, the best approach to managing the supply chain is to think of it as an interlinked set of companies that will compete as a group to secure sales. With this viewpoint in mind, we have structured the following sections to focus on how to identify the best suppliers, construct a supply chain, and manage suppliers, as well as what to do when there are disruptions in the chain. The ideal result is a cluster of organizations that can operate with a minimum of inventory, and which can deliver goods right through the chain in the most efficient manner.

Sole Source Inventory Purchases

A traditional method for reducing the cost of purchased parts is to put them out to bid, thereby forcing suppliers to bid against each other to offer the lowest price. This also gives a company a designated backup supplier, in case there are problems dealing with the primary supplier. However, the primary focus on obtaining the lowest prices also has the following negative effects:

- Products may be of lower quality
- Deliveries may be delayed
- Extra time is needed by the purchasing staff to monitor bidding situations
- There may be lower-volume purchases from each supplier, which tends to drive costs higher

Given the number of problems with having multiple suppliers, it may be better to instead sole source purchases with a smaller number of core suppliers. Doing so has the following advantages:

- Suppliers can be screened in advance to ensure high product quality
- Suppliers will be more amenable to requests for custom packaging and unique order sizes
- Deliveries are more reliable, since suppliers want to preserve a long-term relationship
- There is minimal purchasing paperwork required to place orders, since there are no bids

- Since the same order volume is spread among fewer suppliers, the result should be volume discounts
- Less time is required to monitor suppliers, since there are fewer suppliers
- A supplier may give the company preference when it does not have enough goods to fill all customer orders
- Long-term suppliers are more likely to agree to just-in-time deliveries
- In order to make just-in-time deliveries, the company can set up electronic notifications with its suppliers
- Long-term suppliers are more inclined to participate in joint product development teams

In cases where key components are involved, it may still be necessary to designate a backup supplier, but in most cases the advantages of sole sourcing far outweigh the use of multiple suppliers.

Supplier Assessment

If the decision is made to sole source, there should be an evaluation process for determining which suppliers to use. The evaluation does not have to be a rigid one, with point scoring for various criteria. It may be better to evaluate based on a range of issues, and then settle upon the best supplier based on the overall mix of results. The following points are worth investigating as part of the evaluation:

High priority items

- *Financial condition*. The supplier must be in good financial condition, based on a review of its financial statements for the past few years. This point should only be overridden when materials cannot be obtained from any other supplier.
- *Capacity*. The supplier must have enough capacity to service the needs of the company on a timely basis. Otherwise, late or partial deliveries could become a serious hindrance.
- *Quality*. The supplier must be able to produce goods to the company's specifications with such reliability that there is no need to inspect the goods upon receipt.
- *Just-in-time capabilities*. If the company demands just-in-time deliveries, then the supplier must be able to deliver on a very frequent basis. This usually calls for a local production facility or distribution warehouse.
- *Number of facilities*. If there is a concern that a production facility could be shut down for any reason, evaluate whether a supplier can also produce needed goods from another facility. The second facility should not be subject to the same risk as the first facility. For example, if one facility is located in a flood plain, the backup facility should not also be in the same flood plain.

Lesser priority items

- *Engineering capabilities*. Many components are commoditized, so no special supplier engineering capabilities are needed. In other cases, a supplier can provide significant service to a company by assisting in joint development efforts. If the latter is the case, engineering capability becomes a high priority item.
- *Health and safety compliance*. This issue is generally left to suppliers to handle on their own. However, if a company (usually in the consumer goods field) is subject to review by watchdog organizations, it may be necessary to ensure that certain minimum standards are maintained by suppliers. Otherwise, the company may find that its suppliers are a public relations problem.
- *Legal system*. If there is an expectation that the company may have to pursue legal remedies against a supplier, is the legal system where the supplier is located sufficiently developed to allow the company to gain satisfaction? Realistically, if the company must consider this option, it should not be dealing with a prospective supplier at all.

When engaging in sole sourcing, be sure to devise a reporting system for evaluating the quality, prices, delivery times, and other factors for each *existing* supplier, to see if the company is obtaining sufficient service from each one.

Enhanced Supplier Relations

It is useful to examine the suppliers that a company uses, to determine which ones provide unique and particularly valuable goods and services, and which ones provide more pedestrian products to the company. If a supplier falls into the first category, it behooves the company to go to some lengths to establish deep and long-term relations with it. By doing so, the company may be able to obtain preferred customer status, which gives it delivery priority, best pricing, and cooperation in the development of new products.

However, the establishment of deep relations with a supplier does not mean an occasional lunch between the owners. Instead, all of the following may be needed:

- *Long-term purchase orders*. The company should show its commitment to long-term purchases by negotiating long-term master purchase orders that commit it to make significant purchases over a long period of time.
- *Information sharing*. Allow the supplier to have direct access to the company's production planning system, so the supplier can properly schedule deliveries.
- *Product planning*. Invite the supplier to participate in the company's new product development process, in exchange for sole sourcing the components built into these products.

- *Partnerships.* Create joint product development projects, in which each party has an equity stake.
- *Ownership.* Consider offering to buy a minority stake in the supplier, or even swapping shares in each other for a cross-ownership arrangement.

It is quite difficult to maintain the level of interaction with a supplier that is recommended here. Consequently, it can make sense to limit the number of these close relationships to only those suppliers considered most crucial to the competitive stance and long-term viability of the company.

Foreign Sourcing Considerations

Much of the sourcing discussion in this book comes down in favor of using suppliers located as close as possible to the company. Doing so presents advantages in terms of responsiveness and short delivery times. Nonetheless, some organizations find the low costs of some foreign suppliers to be an overwhelming argument in favor of foreign sourcing. However, before being swept away by the attractiveness of low prices, consider the following issues:

- *Exchange rate risk.* The company will likely have to pay its foreign suppliers in their home currencies, which presents the risk that the exchange rate will have trended in an unfavorable direction by the time the payment is due. Also, the company may engage in hedging transactions to offset this risk, which presents an additional cost.
- *Intellectual property.* A less-ethical supplier may sell cut-rate knock-offs of the company's products in the local market, which are then spread world-wide and compete with the company's products everywhere.
- *Management.* The company will probably need to maintain a local management presence at the site of each supplier, to make decisions on behalf of the company. This can be expensive, since the local representatives must be housed and provided with an adequate level of security.
- *Shipping distance.* If goods must be shipped a long distance from a foreign supplier, this not only increases the freight cost of deliveries, but also decreases the responsiveness of the supplier. The company must place orders far in advance of when the goods are needed, and will continually have to sell off a large amount of in-transit inventory from the supplier before it can launch new products.
- *Trends in labor costs.* If a country has unusually low labor costs, many other companies will also buy from suppliers in that country. The resulting increased demand for labor will drive up wage rates, especially if there is not an especially large pool of laborers in the country. The result is a relatively short period of time during which labor rates are unusually low, after which a cost spike can be expected.

Given the concerns noted here, a reasonable position to take is that foreign sourcing is a more attractive option over the short term. As the time line extends, it becomes more apparent that the cost advantages of foreign labor markets will decline.

A better reason to use foreign sourcing is when the supplier in question has such superior products and services that it would be foolish to use any other supplier. In this case, the *supplier* is more likely to be choosy about selecting its customers, in which case the company may not be able to obtain the services of the supplier that it wants.

The Lead Supplier

A company may have a difficult time coordinating the deliveries of a large number of suppliers. This can be a particular problem when the company's purchasing department is understaffed or does not share its production schedule with suppliers. The result is a continuing series of missed production runs, since manufacturing must be halted when parts do not arrive on time. Or, to counteract late or missing deliveries, the purchasing staff elects to keep much more reserve inventory on hand than would normally be the case.

This state of affairs can be improved upon by designating a small number of suppliers as lead suppliers. These suppliers are responsible for delivering major sub-assemblies to the company, and do so by coordinating the activities of all the suppliers who deliver components for a particular subassembly. The result is a much smaller group of suppliers for the company to deal with on a direct basis.

The lead supplier role is relished by many suppliers, since it gives them a larger share of the company's purchasing dollars. In addition, such a supplier is in an excellent position to increase its profits, either in exchange for the greater administrative task it has taken on, or by controlling the prices charged by the sub-contractors for which it is now responsible.

There are some downsides to the lead supplier concept, which are:

- The company is now sole-sourcing a larger part of its business to a potentially powerful supplier, which could use this position to demand higher prices.
- If a lead supplier gets into financial difficulties or goes bankrupt, this can cause considerable disruption among the sub-contractors for which it was responsible.

Despite these disadvantages, many organizations can profit from the use of lead suppliers, if only to streamline the structure of their supply chains.

The Stable Production Schedule

Once materials have been sole sourced, the next step in managing the supply chain is to provide suppliers with a stable production schedule. This means that the company commits to locking down its production schedule for a certain period of time. By doing so and providing the production schedule to suppliers, they can reliably determine the amount of goods that must be shipped to the company, and so can use this information to create their own production estimates. Otherwise, if the production schedule is constantly being changed, suppliers will be unable to plan their own production, resulting in a gyrating series of inventory shortages and overages.

For what period of time should the production schedule be locked down? This interval should equate to the amount of lead time that suppliers need in order to deliver goods to the company. Thus, if the supplier with the longest lead time requires at least two weeks of advance notice before it can make a delivery to the company, then the company should freeze its production schedule for the final two weeks before products will enter the manufacturing process.

> **Tip:** If customers demand shorter lead times than the company can give, the solution may be to eliminate those suppliers that demand the longest lead times. Doing so compresses the time period over which the production schedule must be frozen, which in turn allows for shorter quoted lead times to customers.

The stable production schedule concept is less applicable in a pull production environment, where the company is only producing to the orders of its customers. In this situation, the production schedule that forms the core of a push production environment does not exist, so suppliers are forced to either maintain significant inventory buffers to deal with the short-term orders of the company, or to shift to their own pull production environments.

Automatic Supplier Replenishment

What about a situation where a customer is a retailer, and is selling a supplier's goods straight to the end customer? In this case, the purchasing department of the retailer examines the sales data from its point-of-sale terminals and issues a replenishment purchase order to the vendor supplying the goods. The retailer's purchasing department represents a delay in the fulfillment chain, since it may require several days for this group to spot an upcoming shortage and issue a purchase order to correct the issue. A possible solution is to give the supplier direct access to the retailer's point-of-sale information, and allow it to refill stock positions automatically.

Automatic supplier replenishment eliminates the retailer's purchasing department from ongoing reordering activities, possibly cutting several days from the interval normally needed to refill a stockout condition. With a shorter lead time requirement for replenishments, this means it is possible for the retailer to reduce the amount of stock it maintains at its stores. However, the following conditions must be present for automatic supplier replenishment to work:

- *Steady demand.* There should be a reasonable history of consistent customer demand, so the supplier can send a consistent stream of goods to the retailer.
- *Replenishment level.* The retailer will not want to run the risk of being responsible for paying for large amounts of additional inventory that are jammed into its stores by suppliers, and so will put a cap on the amount of goods

automatically replenished. This will likely be close to the amount by which customers draw down stocks at retailer locations.

- *Review intervals.* The retailer is relying on the supplier to ascertain when inventory should be replenished, so the supplier must commit to detailed monitoring of the point-of-sale information it is given.

The Total Inventory Concept

Many of the changes that a company makes to reduce inventory do not actually eliminate inventory – they just move inventory back to a supplier. The supplier is supposed to hold a larger amount of inventory off-site, and deliver it only when called upon. This approach increases the amount of working capital that the supplier must invest, and also shifts all the usual inventory holding costs onto the supplier. The result is a weakening of the finances of a company's supplier base. When suppliers earn a lower profit, they are less interested in working with the company, are at increased risk of bankruptcy, and cannot reinvest in their own operations to improve efficiencies. In short, shifting inventory back onto suppliers is a short-term proposition that does not help a company in the long run.

The only way to maintain a healthy group of suppliers is to strip inventory out of the *entire* supply chain. This approach requires a large amount of effort, working with primary suppliers to improve their systems and practices. One way to detect which suppliers to approach with this assistance is to measure total inventory. Total inventory is the sum of all inventories in all locations, as stated in the following exhibit.

Total Inventory Calculation

+	Inventory already located at the company
+	Inventory already produced for the company by suppliers
=	Total inventory

This calculation requires that the company ascertain the amount of company-specific inventory at suppliers, which can be difficult to obtain. Consequently, this may be a measurement that is only compiled once every quarter or year. However, the calculation effort can highlight the largest pockets of inventory, which are then targeted for reduction.

Tip: The total inventory concept works best when inventory items are sole sourced. In this case, a company's engineers and procurement specialists only have to work with a single supplier to create reductions in total inventory. This work is multiplied if the company must work with several suppliers to reduce the same inventory item.

EXAMPLE

Mole Industries manufactures a variety of trench-digging machines. The company assembles components produced by five primary suppliers. The president of Mole is deeply interested in reducing the total inventory of the company, and so commissions the following total inventory measurement:

Inventory Specific to:	Inventory at Mole Industries	Inventory at Supplier	Total Inventory
Supplier A	$2,500,000	$1,250,000	$3,750,000
Supplier B	150,000	1,000,000	1,150,000
Supplier C	10,000	3,000,000	3,010,000
Supplier D	1,700,000	250,000	1,950,000
Supplier E	450,000	250,000	700,000
Totals	$4,810,000	$5,750,000	$10,560,000

The initial calculation reveals that there may be significant opportunities for inventory reduction by working with Suppliers A, B, and C. The most egregious case of excessive inventory appears to be related to Supplier C, where the company maintains essentially no inventory on site, having shifted a large inventory burden back onto Supplier C.

The concept of total inventory can be applied to several of the following sections, which advocate stripping inventory out of the entire supply chain.

Downstream Postponement

The postponement concept is that a company should store goods one level below their final configured form. The reason is that a far smaller number of stock keeping units (SKUs) can be maintained. For example, if a widget can be sold with five different attachments, maintain just the widget in stock, and add whichever of the five attachments are ordered just prior to shipment. By doing so, the company can maintain a single stock of base-level widgets, rather than its best guess as to the final configurations that customers may order.

The postponement concept can be encouraged among suppliers. By doing so, suppliers also have to maintain less inventory, which reduces their working capital requirements. A smaller amount of cash needed to run the business improves the financial prospects of a supplier, which in turn yields a stronger supply chain. The only downside for the company is that it may have to accept slightly longer supplier lead times, which they need to make final configuration adjustments to the goods to be shipped.

Supply Chain Buffer Stock Reduction

When a supplier does not have much visibility into the ordering patterns of a major customer, the supplier is much more likely to create a large buffer stock of finished goods to protect it from excessively large orders placed by the customer. Meanwhile, the customer may also be maintaining a safety stock buffer to protect it from shortages if the supplier cannot fulfill an order in a timely manner. If this sort of duplicate inventory buffering is occurring throughout several levels of a supply chain, there can be an inordinate amount of excess inventory. If the level of ordering information can be enhanced down the supply chain, the various members of the chain can agree to reduce some of this inventory.

An improved level of communication can be achieved by sending real time customer sales information as far down the supply chain as possible, along with constant updates to orders being prepared for delivery to the various suppliers. There must also be a formal discussion of the amount of inventory buffers actually needed in the supply chain, with the intent of sparing as many companies as possible from the burden of maintaining an excess investment. This is a difficult process to achieve, and is only a realistic option when the ultimate customer is a large one that places significant orders back through the supply chain. A minor customer will not attract the interest of its suppliers in regard to a joint inventory reduction.

The main concern of customers in reducing supply chain buffers is that a supplier may go out of business or decide to stop selling to the customer. If so, and the customer had already reduced its safety stock, the customer will be faced with immediate stockout conditions while it searches for a replacement supplier, which can cripple its sales. Consequently, this approach should only be followed when there is a healthy operating relationship with a set of financially robust suppliers.

Reduce Supplier Delivery Times

Suppliers may require a fairly long lead time on orders placed by their customers. If so, customers must estimate the amount of usage they will actually need during the lead time interval, and maintain that amount of inventory on hand to ensure that they do not run out. Further, if there is a sudden spike in usage, customers must maintain additional safety stock to prevent a stock out condition. This issue can be mitigated by switching to suppliers that offer shorter lead times. A shorter lead time allows customers to maintain less inventory on hand, which reduces their working capital investment.

The ideal supplier is one that can deliver goods on a same-day or next-day basis. In this case, the reduced working capital investment can offset any increased price that such a supplier may charge. This type of extremely fast delivery period also means that customers only have to forecast their usage for a few hours or a day, resulting in extremely accurate orders that will closely match actual requirements.

Tip: A supplier may require that a certain quantity be ordered at one time in order to take advantage of a specific pricing deal. However, despite the need for a single order, it may still be possible to split the order into multiple deliveries, so that some items are delivered later. Doing so reduces the overall investment in inventory at one time.

The type of supplier that can be so responsive to customer orders is almost certainly located near its customers, or maintains warehouses near them, thereby reducing delivery times. This has the additional benefit of reducing the risk of interrupted deliveries due to weather events, such as icy roads and traffic accidents that plague longer-distance deliveries. Unfortunately, it can be difficult for a smaller business to persuade a high-grade supplier to relocate to a nearby facility. In this case, a company may be forced to continue using a distant supplier. If so, a possible option is to work with a local supplier to upgrade the quality of its goods and services, and then shift all purchases to it.

A variation on the local supplier concept is to deliberately use local suppliers, even if they are more expensive, for the delivery of goods that have higher usage variability. The company is essentially paying more for the ability to order more frequently and in lesser volumes. By doing so, it can maintain relatively low inventory levels for items that have uncertain demand. For all other goods that have more consistent and predictable demand levels, it is probably still possible to use more distant and lower-cost suppliers that demand larger order sizes.

The most advanced solution for obtaining rapid delivery times is when a supplier can be convinced to set up its operations either immediately adjacent to or actually within the company's facilities. If this can be achieved, then parts can be delivered to the company's production processes by conveyor belt, with no lag time at all. This option is a rare one that requires the presence of the following factors:

- The company is willing to sole source goods from a specific supplier for an extended period of time
- The company is large enough to provide a major amount of business to its suppliers
- The company is willing to let suppliers tap directly into its computer systems for production demand information

Aggregate Deliveries with Freight Forwarders

What if a business has a number of suppliers within a geographic region? Should they be allowed to individually deliver their own goods to the company? Doing so can result in an unreliable mix of delivery times, and many suppliers may not issue advance notice of their deliveries with electronic advance shipping notices (ASNs). An alternative that organizes these deliveries is to use a freight forwarding company.

A freight forwarder sends trucks to each supplier in turn to pick up goods intended for the company, aggregates these goods in a consolidation warehouse, sends a single ASN to the company for each truckload to be delivered, and then ships the goods. This approach is especially valuable if a number of suppliers are located in a foreign country, since a freight forwarder can be responsible for getting all of the goods from that country through customs. Forwarders are especially adept at working with customs officials, and so can eliminate valuable time from the customs clearing process.

Ideally, a freight forwarder can also maintain goods in a nearby warehouse and only ship them to the company's facility when they are needed for a production run.

Though freight forwarders are not inexpensive, they provide a number of valuable services that can improve the reliability of deliveries, speed customs approvals, and improve the flow of information regarding goods in transit. They are particularly useful when a company works with a mix of smaller suppliers located well away from the company's facilities.

Suppliers Own On-Site Inventory

Have suppliers own their inventory in your warehouse until the moment when it is used or sold. This eliminates the holding period for inventory, thereby shifting the cost of the inventory to suppliers until the inventory is needed. Also, the company incurs no risk of inventory obsolescence, since suppliers will take back any unused inventory.

This approach is usually only possible if inventory is sole sourced to certain suppliers, so that they can be assured of more sales in exchange for taking on the inventory holding cost. Also, the goods cannot be customized, so that suppliers can take back their goods if not used by the company and sell them elsewhere.

This approach works best if the company tracks the on-hand unit levels for supplier-owned inventory, and suppliers are given access to this information. Better yet, give suppliers direct access to the company's production schedule, so they can plan for the exact amount of upcoming demand for the SKUs for which they are responsible. Another possible trigger is to send kanban notifications to the supplier when inventory levels reach a predetermined reorder point, which places responsibility for triggering replenishment activities on the company, not the supplier.

While this approach will reduce a company's investment in inventory, there may be an offsetting increase in the prices charged by suppliers. They are taking on an increased funding cost, and may also need to send their staff on-site to review inventory levels. However, a price increase may be avoided if a supplier can be the sole source of an increased number of SKUs. Another concern with supplier-owned inventory is that suppliers may want to overstock goods, in order to keep from making too many replenishment trips to the warehouse. If so, the company may find that it is allocating an excessive amount of warehouse space to the supplier's goods.

Suppliers Pre-Configure Goods

Some goods are ordered from suppliers that will then be sold straight to customers without modification. If so, request that suppliers deliver the goods in the same unit quantities in which they are ordered by customers. For example, if customers tend to order in quantities of 25, then have the supplier deliver the goods prepackaged in this size. If customers tend to order in several quantities, then order a mix of prepackaged sizes from the supplier. Doing so shifts the order preparation task back onto the supplier, while also allowing the company to pick and pack customer orders within the minimum possible period of time.

> **Tip:** Set price points to encourage customers to order in the quantities in which goods are prepackaged for delivery. For example, a sharp discount for orders of five units will likely yield a preponderance of orders for this unit size.

Reserve Supplier Capacity

There may be situations where a company must obtain a certain quantity of parts for its production process, but supplies are constrained. In this case, the company could pay a fee to a supplier to reserve capacity in its production system for a certain number of units. The company then has the choice of activating the option or electing to not have the extra units manufactured. If activated, the company then pays the supplier the usual price for any delivered goods, which is in addition to the fee already paid to reserve capacity. If no additional units are needed, then the supplier retains the fee.

This approach is more likely to be accepted by suppliers when they can activate extra reserve capacity by opening up another production shift. It is not a viable option when there is no reserve capacity available, and the supplier will have to delay deliveries to another customer in exchange for giving priority to the customer paying the fee. Earning a reputation for accepting payments from customers to jump the priority queue is a good way to lose customers.

Vertical Integration

There may be situations where certain suppliers provide such a valuable service to a company that it makes sense to buy them outright. By engaging in vertical integration, the company is assured of the entire output of the supplier. This can be of critical importance if there are few other suppliers available, and especially if the company has been experiencing restrictions on the amounts of raw materials that it can obtain. Vertical integration is a particularly choice alternative when the purchase of a supplier can be used to prevent raw materials from being sent to a competitor. Another good reason for an acquisition is when a supplier owns intellectual property that keeps other suppliers from providing goods of the same level of quality, price, or innovation.

Despite the advantages of vertical integration, this concept should only be employed at rare intervals. There are several reasons for minimizing its use, including the following:

- *Reduced competitive pressure*. When a supplier is purchased, the sale of its entire output may essentially be guaranteed to the buyer. When this happens, there is less pressure within the supplier to improve its competitive posture, eventually resulting in reduced efficiency and a stale product line.
- *Integration risk*. If there is an intent to combine operations with the supplier, there will likely be disaffection among employees at some of the changes, resulting in the departure of key employees.

- *Cost*. The cost of an acquisition is high, since the owners of a valuable supplier are unlikely to part with their shares unless a stout premium is offered. Consequently, there must be a real need for an acquisition before a company decides to part with a large pile of cash.

Supply Chain Cooperation

Inventory problems can begin deep in the supply chain, resulting in pockets of unnecessary inventory piling up that a company may not even be aware of. However, suppliers are aware of these issues, and will charge the company for the holding cost of this inventory. Consequently, it makes sense to improve the level of cooperation between suppliers and the company. Here are several ways to do so:

- *Sponsor workshops*. The company can have on-site or off-site meetings with its suppliers, where the company pays for industry experts (or its own engineers) to speak on various subjects. This can spread knowledge down through the primary suppliers, but only if they choose to attend, and implement what they learn.
- *Create joint ventures*. Rather than using entirely new suppliers for certain parts, establish joint ventures with existing suppliers. Doing so provides them with more revenue, builds their expertise, and gives the company more experience in dealing with them.
- *Work together on improvements*. There may be any number of projects that the company and its suppliers can jointly work on to improve processes and/or reduce the amount of inventory in the system. These projects are especially useful for building trust over time.
- *Work together on new products*. Suppliers can provide a considerable amount of input into the components used for new product designs. In exchange, the company provides suppliers with orders for their parts, to be used in new product designs. The outcome should be more robust and lower-cost products that are better able to attain targeted margins.

Supply Chain Configuration Issues

Theoretically, it should be possible to minimize inventory throughout the supply chain by ordering parts from suppliers only when a customer order is received. In this scenario, the receipt of an order triggers notifications to all primary and secondary suppliers to produce and forward the requisite materials to the company for final assembly. Ideally, such a fully-synchronized supply chain would operate with minimal inventory, while still providing a reasonably high order fill rate. In reality, a fully synchronized supply chain is quite difficult to achieve. Consider the following issues that can interfere with the concept:

- *Deep bill of materials*. The bill of materials for a complex product may require the use of multiple levels of subassemblies, each of which is created by a secondary or primary supplier, and each of which requires a certain amount of lead time.

- *Number of suppliers*. A complex bill of materials may contain hundreds or even thousands of parts, involving a large number of suppliers whose activities must be synchronized.
- *Sole sourcing*. Some parts are only available through one supplier, who may not be amenable to any synchronization efforts.
- *International*. Additional delays are built into shipments coming from international suppliers, where logistical costs are commonly reduced by waiting for several less-than-container load shipments to aggregate into a full container load.

These issues are less severe when products have few components and are produced in high volume, since there are only a few suppliers, and demand is reasonably predictable. Conversely, synchronization is an increasingly elusive target when customer demand is low and products are highly complex.

No matter what the level of product complexity may be, there is still some opportunity for supply chain synchronization. There should be a core group of primary suppliers for which customer orders will trigger inventory deliveries to the company. For these suppliers, goods are produced to order, with no replenishment. The rate and mix of production will match actual customer orders. Kanbans are used here to trigger orders for specific parts and subassemblies.

However, the use of customer orders to trigger production will break down at the point where additional delays in the supply chain will extend the production time period beyond the time that a customer is willing to wait for an order to be fulfilled. Beyond this point, the supply chain must rely upon forecasts of expected demand, and produce in expectation of customer orders.

At the point in the supply chain where the production triggering mechanism changes from a pull system to a push system (see the Impact of Production on Inventory chapter), there should be an inventory buffer. This buffer should be of sufficient size to ensure that kanban notifications can be fulfilled. It is quite likely that the number of items subject to kanban notifications will be substantially smaller than the number of items further down the supply chain that are controlled by a push system.

Tip: The synchronization concept breaks down in the supply chain wherever the maximum output of a bottleneck is less than a spike in customer demand. These hitches will become apparent when there are spikes in demand, or anticipate them by making inquiries of suppliers regarding their bottleneck issues.

A key point in developing a system of supply chain synchronization is to have the company issue a notification as deep in the supply chain as possible, as soon as a customer order is received. Otherwise, it may take days for a primary supplier to issue a notification to a secondary supplier, and so forth down the supply chain. In the latter case, there may be weeks of notification delays built into the supply chain.

In summary, there are limits to the effectiveness of the supply chain synchronization concept, which are set by the nature of the product and the volume of customer demand. The concept is still tenable, but only for a certain distance back into the supply chain, after which a variety of factors water down its effect. If a company wants to synchronize as much of its supply chain as possible, it must weigh the benefits against the cost of creating a customer order notification system, as well as of increasing bottleneck capacities and buffer stocks at key points in the supply chain.

> **Tip:** If the company anticipates considerable sales growth, it should communicate this concern back down the supply chain, so that bottleneck capacities and buffer stocks can be increased well in advance of the projected sales increase.

Supply Chain Disruption

Some of the techniques used to reduce the inventory investment involve just-in-time concepts, such as having raw materials delivered just as they are needed to supply a company's production lines. These methods certainly will reduce the overall inventory investment, but what happens if there is an unexpected disruption in the supply chain? Perhaps a supplier's production facility was flooded or damaged by a hailstorm. Or, the eruption of a volcano shuts down international air traffic. Or perhaps an earthquake damages the roads so severely that no deliveries can reach the company. There are many ways in which the supply chain can be disrupted, and some are extremely difficult to predict.

The usual approach for dealing with supply chain disruptions is to reevaluate the entire system of supply immediately following the occurrence of a major disruption. This is a reactive approach, and the outcome is typically an adjustment to the supply chain that is intended to keep that specific event from having a negative impact again. For example, if the government is overthrown in a country where a supplier is located, the buyer may choose to shift all parts orders away from that country for a period of time. The trouble with this approach is the highly reactive nature of the response.

A better approach to supply chain disruptions is to monitor disruptions throughout the world, and extrapolate these events to the company's own supply chain. For example, if a tsunami inundates a coastal region, a follow-up discussion should address the existence of flood plains for all major supplier facilities throughout the world. Similarly, if a major hailstorm causes massive damage somewhere, this could trigger an analysis of whether goods intended for shipment to the buyer are stored anywhere in transit where hail damage might occur. Thus, the occurrence of a general risk type is used as the basis for an analysis of what such an event could do to the company.

There are a number of specific actions that may be taken to mitigate supply chain disruption. Consider the following situations:

- *Weather related.* A company's main assembly plant is located in a region that is subject to severe winter storms. Its main supplier for a key part is located 200 miles away. If a storm blows through, deliveries may be delayed by several days, until the roads are safe to navigate. The company has a choice of either building a buffer of extra parts on-site, or of sourcing the part with a supplier located a short distance away from the assembly plant. Factors to consider are the total cost of sourcing from the local supplier, the quality and reliability of the local supplier, and the cost of the buffer stock.

- *Flood plain.* A company's main assembly plant is located in a flood plain that is projected to flood once every 100 years. However, upstream levies are being built that will increase the level of floodwaters in the area adjacent to the assembly plant. The result is likely to be a flood once every 10 years. The company not only needs to move its facility to higher ground, but must also ensure that the surrounding access roads are not subject to flooding. If a road floods, it will be impossible to bring in raw materials, which effectively shuts down the facility, no matter where it is located. It may still be necessary to increase the amount of inventory stored on-site, to avoid supply disruptions.

- *Pirates.* A company buys a large proportion of its coffee crop from an African country. The coastline of this country is infested with pirates, which routinely make off with shipments being sent by boat. The coffee from this country is highly prized, so sourcing elsewhere is not an option. Instead, the buyer can either contract with a shipper that uses armed freighters, or arrange to have coffee shipped by airplane instead. In either case, transportation costs will increase.

- *Derailment.* A company ships large quantities of plastic pellets to its facility, where the pellets are used to create injection molded products. The company requires one rail car delivery of plastic pellets every three days to ensure that its injection molding equipment is fully operational. There is only one rail line that services the company's general area. The rail line is not being properly maintained, increasing the risk of a derailment that could block access to the facility. In this case, the company could arrange for alternative transport by truck to circumvent a derailment. However, it must also construct a separate storage tank for the pellets that is loaded by truck, as well as a feeder line that shifts the pellets from this location to the injection molding equipment. Thus, some internal construction is needed to mitigate the risk.

The result of taking (for example) any of the preceding actions should be a more robust supply chain that can weather the more likely disruptions. However, taking these steps may not result in the lowest possible investment in inventory. Instead, the inventory investment may very well increase, as a trade-off to reduce the impact of a perceived risk. If a substantial increase in inventory is projected, management should weigh the increased cost of inventory against the reduced risk of a supply chain disruption, and decide which alternative is better for the company. In many cases, the benefits of a strong, well-considered supply chain will easily outweigh the increased amount of inventory.

Summary

The main concept to take away from this chapter is that the level of information sharing that an effective supply chain engages in should be extremely high. Only by constant discussions of current and prospective ordering needs can a group of suppliers be converted into an effective tool that provides a business with a strong competitive advantage. In addition, a company should engage in a detailed evaluation of its suppliers, to see if there are weaknesses in the supply chain that can be mitigated or eliminated. Finally, it is helpful to periodically examine potential events that could disrupt the supply chain, and to take mitigation steps in advance to reduce their effects. By addressing all of these areas, a company can nurture a robust supply chain that provides it with just enough of the highest-quality inventory to meet the needs of its customers.

Chapter 15
Warehousing Efficiencies

Introduction

Modern inventory management concepts place a premium on the reduction of inventory. However, doing so means that there is little margin for error in a supply chain. Even the slightest hiccup in the timely delivery of goods will impact a company's production process, as well as its own deliveries to customers. Consequently, there is usually some need for an inventory buffer, which takes the form of a warehouse. For this reason, there is little expectation that the typical company will eliminate its warehouse. Instead, there is a focus on administering the warehouse in the most efficient manner possible.

The traditional emphasis in the warehouse has been on storage – that is, a massive facility with endless aisles and bins that ascend to the roof. However, stored goods cost money, in terms of interest cost, product obsolescence, insurance, and so forth. Consequently, a better view of the warehouse is one in which inventory resides for the minimum possible amount of time (if at all). In this chapter, we explore a multitude of concepts that can lead to a greatly reduced warehouse investment. We begin with an analysis of the cost of inventory, which is the driving reason for the efficiencies noted in the remainder of this chapter.

The Cost of Inventory Storage

Before we embark on an exploration of warehouse efficiencies, it is useful to first ascertain the cost of storing inventory. Once it becomes apparent just how expensive it is to store inventory, the drive to produce warehouse efficiencies may accelerate. Consider the following costs:

- *Facility cost.* This is the cost of the warehouse, which includes depreciation on the building and interior racks, heating and electricity, building insurance, and warehouse staff. This is largely a fixed cost; it does not vary if there are small changes in the amount of inventory stored in the facility.
- *Cost of funds.* This is the interest cost of any funds that a company borrows in order to purchase inventory (or, conversely, the foregone interest income). This can be tied to a specific unit of inventory, since selling a single unit immediately frees up funds which can then be used to pay down debt. This cost of funds varies with the market interest rate.
- *Risk mitigation.* This is not only the cost of insuring inventory, but also of installing any risk management items needed to protect the inventory, such as fire suppression systems, burglar alarms, and security guards. As was the case with facility costs, this is largely a fixed cost.

- *Taxes*. The business district in which the inventory is stored may charge some form of property tax on the inventory. This cost can be reduced by selling off inventory just prior to the date on which inventory is measured for tax purposes.
- *Obsolescence and damage*. Inventory may become unusable over time (especially for perishable items), or it may be superseded by technological advances. In either case, it may only be disposed of at a large discount, or have no value at all. This tends to be an incremental cost that is more likely to be associated with low-turnover goods.

As noted in several of these points, a large proportion of inventory storage costs are fixed; thus, a company with an empty warehouse will find that the incremental cost associated with one extra unit of inventory is quite small. However, a company operating a filled warehouse must deal with large step costs to accommodate additional units of inventory. To reduce these costs to any great extent requires that a business eliminate a large proportion of its inventory.

EXAMPLE

Tsunami Products manufactures and sells a number of plumbing products targeted at the residential bathroom, including shower heads, faucets, and toilet fixtures. Tsunami maintains a large warehouse, in which are stored several thousand stock keeping units for all possible configurations and colors of the company's products. There is pressure from the president to reduce the company's product offerings, due to the high cost of storage. Before responding to the president's request, the materials manager decides to quantify the cost of inventory storage. She derives the following information:

Expense Item	Last Year Cost
Facility Cost	
Warehouse rent	$180,000
Depreciation on storage racks	80,000
Depreciation on fork lifts	50,000
Warehouse utilities	40,000
Staff compensation	600,000
Building insurance	25,000
Cost of funds (6% interest cost on $30,000,000 of inventory)	1,800,000
Risk Mitigation	
Inventory insurance	60,000
Depreciation on fire suppression system	15,000
Burglar alarm annual fee	4,000
Taxes (property taxes)	80,000
Damage (Inventory rendered unusable and scrapped)	25,000
Total cost	$2,959,000
As percent of $30,000,000 inventory investment	10%

The cost of inventory storage turns out to be 10% of the cost of the stored goods. The materials manager is particularly startled by the cost of funds, which comprises more than 60% of the total cost. The president points out that this cost of funds is unusually low, and will likely increase in a tighter credit market. Consequently, just to mitigate changes in the cost of funds, it is imperative that Tsunami reduce the cost of its inventory storage.

The Cost of Travel Time

Most warehouse tasks involve large amounts of travel time, as the staff is engaged in putting away goods, replenishing bins, picking goods, or cross-docking received goods to shipping docks. Consequently, many of the warehouse efficiencies described in this chapter are designed to reduce travel time. To what extent can travel time reduction impact costs? Since warehouse activities are highly repetitive, a modest reduction in travel time translates into massive labor cost reductions. Consider the following example.

EXAMPLE

The warehouse manager of Entwhistle Electric has been told by senior management that he must find a way to cut back on total departmental expenses by $50,000. This seems impossible, since the department is running flat out each day to complete its assigned tasks. The manager brings in a consultant, who suggests that a reconfiguration of the warehouse to reduce travel times could be a good source of cost savings.

The warehouse is currently configured for random putaways, so that any item may be stored in any part of the warehouse. The consultant monitors the staff, and concludes that the average travel time for any warehouse transaction is 60 seconds. He notes that a properly configured warehouse with high-usage items stored near the front of the warehouse should yield a 20% travel time reduction. If a 20% reduction can be achieved, the resulting savings would be:

2,080	Work hours per year
× 0.85	Work hours reduced for vacation and inefficiencies
× 60	Minutes per hour
= 106,080	Net available minutes
× 0.20	Assumed efficiency improvement
= 21,216	Reduction per person in minutes required
÷ 60	Conversion back to hours
= 354	Hours saved per year
× $25	Fully burdened hourly labor rate
$8,850	Savings per employee

Since the warehouse employs ten people who are engaged in inventory move activities, the prospective savings from a reduction in travel times is almost $89,000, making the $50,000 target look quite easy.

We now turn to an examination of ways to improve warehouse efficiencies, which can mitigate the costs described in this and the preceding section.

Cross Docking

Cross docking involves receiving goods from suppliers, breaking down the inbound pallets into the quantities wanted by customers, merging them with other inbound goods also required for customer orders, and shipping them out on a different vehicle. This approach requires a large number of shipping docks for inbound and outbound trucks, as well as a well-organized order consolidation area and a sufficient level of technology to track the flow of goods.

At the lowest level of sophistication, a company is not entirely sure of the exact dates and times when supplier deliveries will arrive. The result is a continuing need for storage, since some items must be parked off to one side in order to keep from interfering with the flow of goods between trucks. At the highest level of sophistication, suppliers are required to deliver within precise time slots on certain days. At this high level of precision, inventory flows into one side of a facility, remains on-site for a few hours, and flows out the other side. However, attaining this level of sophistication calls for in-depth interaction with suppliers, as well as tight meshing with the delivery schedule for outbound customer orders.

> **Tip:** Backordered goods represent an excellent opportunity for cross docking, since customers are awaiting the immediate delivery of these items. Consequently, consider implementing advance shipping notices (ASNs) with all suppliers, in order to be forewarned when backordered items are about to arrive.

Cross docking works especially well when all incoming goods have an identifying bar code label already attached to them by the supplier. In this case, a bar code scanner can scan each container as it leaves the trailer, which loads the information into the warehouse management system (WMS). The WMS then compares the receiving information to any open customer orders. If there is such a match, a fork lift operator is notified via a radio frequency terminal to transport the received goods to the appropriate shipping door. This record matching function can be completed in moments, making the use of bar codes a boon to cross docking activities.

Flow-Through Warehousing

Flow-through is a variation on cross docking. Under flow-through warehousing, received goods are broken down from their shipment quantities and moved to a processing area, where the company provides some sort of value-added service to the received goods. The goods are then moved to an order fulfillment area, where they are assembled along with other ordered goods and shipped to a customer. Under this concept, inventory is never stored in a fixed bin – instead, it moves quickly from one step to another, and departs the company facility as soon as possible. Another way of looking at flow-through is that the receiving function is merged with the production and order fulfillment functions; all other static warehouse functions are eliminated.

A flow-through system is technology intensive. It requires precise tracking of incoming goods, their movement through the company facility, their routing through any value-added processes, and subsequent assembly into customer orders. This calls for real-time tracking at the unit level, typically using either bar coding or radio frequency identification tags. Consequently, the flow-through concept is a valid choice only for the more sophisticated businesses.

Flow-Through Warehouse Designs

A traditional warehouse maximizes the amount of space devoted to the storage of inventory. In a flow-through system, a highly-efficient storage space is less important than having a large amount of space assigned to staging activities. Also, the distance between the shipping and receiving docks should be minimized, to reduce travel times within the facility. Another issue is a large yard, so that trailers whose contents are not immediately needed can be parked nearby for easy access. Finally, the ideal flow-through warehouse contains a large number of access doors, so that many inbound and outbound deliveries can be processed at the same time.

Flow-Through Warehouse Equipment

The equipment requirements of a flow-through warehouse are substantially different from those of a traditional warehouse. There is much less need for the highly automated systems used to extract goods from fixed bin locations. Instead, a company can eliminate or at least reduce its investment in automated storage and retrieval systems, and shift funding instead to the purchase of conveyors, gravity-flow racks, and pallet-flow racks.

Tip: Conveyors are designed to handle only certain sizes and weights of containers, so be fairly sure that the same general items will be transferred within a facility for the next few years before investing in these systems. If there is a reasonable probability that requirements will change in the near term, consider shifting to less-efficient but more flexible racking systems.

When to Use Flow-Through

The flow-through concepts embodied by cross docking and the flow-through warehouse work best only under certain circumstances. Ideally, the level of demand should not fluctuate much from a standard level. The materials planning staff should have a good idea of how many units of which products will be required on an ongoing basis.

For example, a company distribution center may service a large number of retail stores within a region. The amount of sales from this group of stores is well known, and variations in sales are both seasonal and predictable. In this case, the materials planning staff can reliably plan for customer demand, and schedule a matching amount of supplier deliveries. Conversely, if customer demand fluctuates wildly, it is much more difficult to match up inbound supplier deliveries with customer orders. Instead, a significant amount of inventory must be maintained on-site to act as a buffer.

The flow-through concept also works well when customers can easily select from alternative products. For example, a company that maintains a number of retail stores can offer several variations on the same general shirt design, so that a stockout condition on one shirt does not necessarily mean that a customer will make no purchase at all. In this case, flow-through can still be achieved, because there is some degree of allowable variability in the types of goods shipped to customers. Conversely, flow-through does not work in the warranty and replacement parts business, because customers need *specific* parts; something similar is not good enough. In this business, it is necessary to maintain substantial amounts of inventory at all times.

The ability to employ flow-through also depends upon the amount of additional work that is applied to goods between the receiving and shipping docks. As the amount and complexity of work increases, the likelihood of using flow-through declines. For example, swapping out the packaging on a product in order to rebrand it is relatively simple in most cases, and can be inserted into a flow-through system. However, re-painting a product in a different color is much more complex and time-consuming, and will likely require a more extended stay on the company premises.

Yet another issue impacting the use of flow-through is the reliability of suppliers. A supplier must be able to deliver the correct goods within the correct time slot, every time. A delivery made too early must be stored on-site, while one that is delivered too late will delay a delivery to a customer. It can take time to build up enough experience with a supplier to decide whether they can be included in a flow-through system. The result can be a traditional warehousing arrangement for newer or less-reliable suppliers, and a separate flow-through system for those suppliers that have proven their reliability.

A final concern is that the information technology environment must be in real time. It is no longer possible to batch-process transactions overnight, resulting in inventory movement orders that are enacted the following morning. Instead, inbound deliveries must be immediately logged into the system (perhaps with an advance shipping notice, where the supplier describes the contents of an incoming delivery) with perfect accuracy and routed through to a processing step or an outbound queue. If a company cannot operate such a system, it should not attempt a flow-through solution.

The one business model in which most of these issues are workable is the retail environment. A company has a good idea of customer demand, customers are willing to buy similar goods, there is no valued added to in-transit deliveries, and suppliers are generally reliable. Other business models may include some of these features, but rarely all of them, and so are less amenable to the use of flow-through warehousing.

Storage by Fixed Location

In the following sections, we will discuss different ways in which inventory can be configured within the warehouse to yield the highest possible efficiencies. However, before proceeding with these concepts, it is useful to address a fairly common and traditional storage system, which is storing goods by fixed location code; in other words, permanently assigning inventory to a fixed spot in the warehouse.

Storage by fixed locations is not very space-efficient, since some locations may be overloaded with stock, while other locations are reserved for inventory that is not currently on hand at all. A likely outcome is that a significant proportion of the warehouse space will go unused. Nonetheless, there are circumstances where this concept can make sense. Consider the following:

- *Primitive systems.* A warehouse is largely governed by paper-based transactions, to the extent that inventory records tend to lag well behind the locations of actual on-hand inventory. In this case, the warehouse staff cannot trust the record-keeping system, and so instead must resort to a close knowledge of where inventory is supposed to be stored. Accordingly, they memorize all inventory locations, so they know where to locate and putaway inventory.
- *High frequency items.* There may be such demand for certain inventory items that they are constantly flowing through the warehouse in large volumes. If so, it can make sense to permanently assign them a forward location in the warehouse, where they are easily accessible. If this approach is used, limit the amount of space permanently reserved, and shift all excess quantities to reserve storage. By doing so, the amount of reserved space is likely to be filled most of the time, so there is no problem with unused storage locations.

The real issue is the first of the two points. Many organizations that have low inventory usage levels and excess warehouse space may be entirely comfortable with maintaining permanent storage locations. If so, there is no issue unless inventory levels increase to such an extent that there is no warehouse space left for new inventory items. If this point is reached, then the use of fixed storage locations should be revisited.

Warehouse within a Warehouse

A warehouse is not necessarily at its most efficient when the entire space is used for the same functional activities. Instead, there are a number of ways in which the space can be subdivided, resulting in a more efficient overall operation. The concept is addressed through the remainder of this section, as we cover a number of ways in which the warehouse environment can be broken down.

Warehouse by Customer

A customer does not care how a seller configures its warehouse – the customer only wants to receive ordered items in a timely manner. When a customer orders a sufficiently large quantity of goods from a seller, it is deserving of special treatment, rather than having its orders picked alongside those of all other customers, and sharing in the pain of waiting for backlogged goods. In this situation, it can make sense to create a warehouse within a warehouse, where goods ordered by a specific customer are segregated. There are several reasons for taking this approach:

- *Faster picking.* The seller can overstaff the customer-specific warehouse with extra order handling personnel, so that these orders are fulfilled in the shortest possible amount of time.
- *Reserved inventory.* Inventory levels are deliberately set higher for a key customer. The seller overstocks in order to reduce the likelihood of a stockout condition for this customer. This means that inventory is not commingled with the rest of the warehouse area.

This concept should only be applied to the largest customers, where excellent service is crucial. Otherwise, a company will end up with a number of customer-specific areas within its warehouse, each one both overstocked and overstaffed. The result is an excessive investment in inventory and higher operating expenses.

> **Tip:** Segmenting a warehouse by customer makes it easier to conduct cost accounting analyses for these larger customers, since the exact cost of setting aside and staffing separate warehouse space can now be traced back to individual customers.

> **Note:** A warehouse by customer may include inventory items owned *by* a customer. If so, the company must have a system in place for properly tagging and segregating these items upon receipt. Otherwise, there is a risk that these items will be recorded as being owned by the company itself, valued as part of its inventory, and even sold off.

Warehouse by Distribution Channel

The warehouse within a warehouse concept can also be applied to separate distribution channels. For example, a company may distribute its goods through an Internet store, a chain of retail stores, and a group of distributors. Sales made through the Internet store are shipped individually, while deliveries made to the retail stores are in case sizes and deliveries to distributors are always made in pallet sizes. Based on these differing delivery requirements, the warehouse could be configured to commingle inventory across all three distribution channels, but to have separate order fulfillment and packing lines for each channel. By doing so, orders can be packed that meet the specific requirements of customers, while maintaining relatively low inventory levels.

Warehouse by Product Family

An examination of customer orders may reveal that the bulk of orders received relate to a specific family of products. If so, it can be most efficient to cluster inventory by product families within the warehouse, so that orders related to those families can be picked within a short travel distance. The decision to do so should be based on the percentage of customer orders calling for a mix of products taken from different product families.

This approach does not always work if a stock keeping unit (SKU) is used in multiple product families. In this situation, the goods may have to be stored in multiple locations in order to be clustered with each product family.

> **Tip:** Consider marketing different product families as though they are from different companies, so that customers place separate orders for each family of products. Doing so results in orders that can be picked entirely from a single product family, which makes for simplified warehousing by product family.

EXAMPLE

Locate Inc. produces a broad range of GPS-enabled location tracking devices. These products include GPS watches for trail runners and triathletes, GPS heads-up displays for automobiles, and GPS units for watercraft. Each of these product families is marketed and branded through different marketing teams, though they are all identified as being Locate Inc. products. An examination of customer orders reveals that only 2% of all orders received request products from a mix of product families. All other orders are specific to a single family. Based on this information, the warehouse manager elects to organize the warehouse by product family, with separate picking and packing teams assigned to each family.

Warehouse by Season

Some product sales are highly seasonal. If so, customers may order them in a frenzy during a short period of time, after which sales plummet. If a company stocks these types of items, it is useful to track the historical customer ordering patterns by time period, and rotate these items through the warehouse, depending on expected ordering volumes. For example, a company sells snow shovels, and so moves these items close to the front of the warehouse during the winter months, and then shifts them to a distant corner for the remainder of the year.

Warehouse by Pallet and Case

In many warehouses, picking is conducted from opened cases. This allows a large number of SKUs to be maintained within a relatively small forward area that is situated close to the order packing area. When all cases available for picking have been emptied, additional cases are brought forward from a reserve area in the rear of the warehouse, where full and partial pallets are stored. This common approach is essentially a warehouse within a warehouse, with high-usage cases kept in high-traffic areas and pallets in more distant locations. A variation on the concept is to store pallets in forward areas, but only for those items being shipped in high volumes.

This approach also works when there is a clear differentiation between orders that require full pallets and those orders requiring lesser quantities. In these situations, separate picking and packing operations can be set up to deal with each type of order.

Another permutation of the concept is when there is a history of customers ordering a specific number of units. For example, perhaps a large number of customers routinely order 30 units, rather than a full pallet of 100 units. If so, have the manufacturing or warehouse staffs build reduced-size pallets in advance that match these common order sizes, and store them separately. Doing so results in faster order fulfillment speeds.

Tip: Customers can be encouraged to order in those case and pallet sizes that the company stocks by setting price breaks that match these quantities. Thus, if a discount is offered for a unit count of ten (which happens to match a quantity of one case), then customers will likely buy a full case, rather than in some other partial-case quantity.

One problem with creating smaller pallet sizes is that the warehouse racking system is likely preconfigured to accept a specific pallet size. If smaller pallets are inserted into these racks, a considerable amount of cubic storage space may be wasted. This issue can be overcome by altering the racking configuration to accept smaller pallets, though doing so means that the racking system will be less amenable to storage changes intended to reshuffle higher-usage items to the front of the warehouse. Or, if the warehouse contains a moderate amount of unused storage space, not maximizing the use of a few storage areas is unlikely to be of much consequence.

Tip: When reconfiguring a pallet to include fewer units, be sure to post the total revised unit count on the pallet, which reduces the risk that cycle counters will assume a unit count for a full pallet.

Warehouse by Order Completion Zone

An examination of customers may reveal that a small subset of inventory items will complete a significant amount of customer orders. These items may not be within the same product family; instead, they are simply a cluster of inventory items that customers typically order. If the existence of these items can be teased out of the customer order data, then consider setting up an order completion zone in the warehouse for these items. The intent of such a zone is to achieve productivity levels and order processing rates that are several times higher than the average levels for the remainder of the warehouse. Also, an order completion zone is one that matches the name – all of the items needed to complete an order are included in the zone, so that no additional picking activities outside of the zone are needed.

Given the high volume of activity in an order completion zone, it can make sense to invest more heavily in fixed assets in this area. For example, carousels and gravity-flow racking can be used to increase the efficiency of the picking staff.

Storage by ABC Classification

If there is no obvious methodology for storing goods as a warehouse within a warehouse (see the preceding section), then a more basic approach is to use the ABC classification system. This system is based on the concept that a small proportion of the total number of SKUs in a facility is accessed most of the time, with the remaining SKUs being accessed at much longer intervals. In essence, inventory is divided into three classifications based on usage, which are noted in the following exhibit.

Inventory Classifications

Classification	Usage Percentage
A	The 5% of inventory responsible for 75% of all transactions
B	The 10% of inventory responsible for 15% of all transactions
C	The 85% of inventory responsible for 10% of all transactions

The proportions indicated in the table are approximate, and will vary somewhat based on actual experience. Nonetheless, it is clear that quite a small proportion of the total inventory experiences a massive amount of the total transaction volume.

It is fairly easy to assign an ABC code to each SKU, and then derive storage locations within the warehouse based on that designation. In a manufacturing environment, "A" raw material items should be positioned as close to the production area as possible, to minimize travel times. In a distribution environment, "A" items should be positioned as close to the shipping area as possible, to minimize the time required to fulfill orders. Conversely, "C" items can be positioned in the nether regions of the warehouse, since they will only be accessed at long intervals. "B" items are located between the locations occupied by the "A" and "C" items.

Tip: ABC designations should be based on projected activity levels, rather than historical levels. Historical activity may not carry forward into the future, especially if some products are being discontinued or have seasonal sales.

Storage Based on the Putaway to Picking Ratio

The use of storage locations can be optimized by a close examination of the putaway to picking ratio. This ratio compares the number of trips needed to bring an SKU to a storage location (typically one trip) to the number of trips needed to move the item from the storage location to the point at which it is used. For example, a case containing 20 units is putaway in a storage location, but those 20 units are individually picked to fill various customer orders over the next few weeks. This is a putaway to picking ratio of 1:20.

When the ratio is close to 1:1, this means that a storage location has been optimized for all projected usage. Conversely, a large ratio shows that the warehouse staff is consuming a massive amount of travel time in handling goods. Since the amount of picking travel is usually much greater than putaway travel (assuming more picks than putaways), this means that storage locations should ideally be situated as close to the point of use as possible.

EXAMPLE

Entwhistle Electric receives one case that contains 50 cell phone batteries. This case will later be opened, and individual batteries will be extracted to fill customer orders at various times. The case is placed in a pre-designated bin that happens to be near the center of the warehouse. The travel time to the bin is one minute. Based on this information, the putaway to picking ratio is 1:50, and represents 51 total minutes of travel time (one minute for the putaway and 50 minutes for 50 separate picks).

After examining the inherent inefficiency of this situation, the warehouse manager re-designates the bin to be immediately adjacent to the packing area. When the next case arrives, the warehouse staff spends two minutes traveling to the new location for the putaway transaction. The travel time for pickers has now been reduced to 15 seconds, or ¼ minute. This means that the new putaway to picking ratio is 2:12.5, for a total of 14½ minutes of travel time. While there is still an imbalance in the ratio, a massive reduction in the total travel time has been achieved.

A further reduction could be achieved if the company were to set a volume discount for a two-pack of batteries, thereby cutting the number of picks in half and dropping the total travel time to 8¼ minutes.

Efficiencies within Storage Racks

So far, we have addressed restructuring the storage of goods throughout an entire warehouse. What about improving the efficiency of storage within the racking system? Enhancements to this more localized issue are noted below.

Accessibility of Storage Bins

When pickers select items from the bins in a warehouse, it is easier for them to do so when items are stored within a vertical range that does not require them to bend down or reach over their heads. Thus, the highest-volume items should be stored within this range, with lower-volume items parked in the less-accessible bins. This approach can have a significant impact on the speed with which picking can be accomplished, and also improves worker safety.

Co-Locate Correlated Items

A close examination of customer orders may reveal that customers tend to order pairs of items (or larger clusters) with great frequency. If so, consider storing these items in close proximity to each other in the warehouse. For example, customers may order an ink-jet printer and refill cartridges at the same time. Or, they may order a certain size of pants and a matching belt at the same time. Or perhaps lawn mowers are usually ordered at the same time as a gasoline container. In short, if the ordering data reveals a repetitive correlation for certain inventory items, consider storing them in adjacent bins.

Size Picking Bins to Store Sufficient Quantities

A common method for reducing clutter in the warehouse is to schedule an inventory restocking team during the third shift, which reloads designated picking bins. The restocking team then goes home and two shifts of pickers work through the remainder of the day. For this scheduling system to work, it is necessary to maintain sufficient quantities of goods in the picking bins to last for two shifts. To do so, the restocking team must restock based on the highest probable volume of picking during the two day shifts. For example, it could be determined that a quantity that matches the maximum amount picked during 95% of all picking days (two standard deviations) is sufficient. If so, the bins must be sized to accommodate this unit volume.

An alternative to this approach is to use gravity-flow racking, so that the restocking team is on one side of a rack, and pickers are on the other side (see the Warehouse Storage Systems chapter). This approach requires less inventory in the picking bins, since replenishment can occur throughout the day. However, a gravity-flow system is more expensive than a bin system, and so is usually confined to a small number of high-volume picking situations.

Aggregate Storage Locations

If a company uses a product for a significant period of time, it is likely that the goods will be stored in more than one bin. If so, it is also likely that some portion of the goods will be picked from each of these locations. The result is multiple bins that are not fully utilizing their designated storage space. The worst-case scenario is that so little is stored in each location that the picking staff must eventually visit several locations to find enough of a product to fill a customer order. If so, travel is increased and multiple pick transactions must be processed through the warehouse management system.

To avoid these issues, consider conducting a periodic review of all inventory items that are stored in more than one location. It is entirely acceptable to have a small forward location for case and broken case quantities, supported by a single reserve storage space in the rear of the warehouse. However, if an examination of storage locations indicates the presence of more than two locations, it may be time to aggregate inventory into a reduced number of locations.

The need for an aggregation review will depend on the inventory turnover level within a warehouse. A high-turnover situation is much more likely to leave several residual inventory balances spread around the warehouse than one in which inventory rarely moves.

Size Cartons to Customer Order Sizes

It is vastly more efficient for the picking staff to pull entire cartons of goods from storage for delivery to customers, rather than breaking open cartons and delivering smaller unit quantities. There are two ways to persuade customers to order in full-carton quantities. One is to set quantity price breaks to match the size of cartons. Thus, if a carton contains fifty units, there should be a price break sufficiently large to encourage customers to always order in quantities of fifty.

However, there are some customers who persistently ignore these volume purchase discounts, and only order the exact quantities they want. If so, review ordering data to determine which ordering quantity is most common. If this order quantity recurs in sufficiently large volume, consider creating a carton size for it. This approach only has limited applicability, since a business cannot afford to clutter up its warehouse with an array of different case sizes. However, it may be cost-effective to employ one or two additional carton sizes.

Use Standard Containers to Store Inventory

The preferred container size in any warehouse is always the pallet, since rack space is designed for it and unit counts are easily made based on a standard number of units per pallet. The situation is far less efficient once pallets are broken down into cases and broken cases. In this situation, it is much more difficult to count the number of units on hand, as well as the number of units replenished and picked.

In these situations, consider using standard container sizes to store similar types of inventory. There are a variety of possible container sizes. For example:

- The container size matches the most common customer order size. Thus, if customers always order in quantities of ten, repackage broken cases into that quantity.
- There is no common customer order size, but a larger container than the standard case size makes it easier to move goods between locations. This is particularly useful when the container has carry handles or slots on the sides.
- A particular container size fits into a small storage bay.
- Very small items, such as washers, are counted and sealed in a standard bag size, with the unit count written on the front. As long as the bag is sealed, counters know that the stated quantity is correct. Once the bag is opened, a more detailed count must be performed.

No matter which standard container sizes are used, prominently display the unit count on the outside of each container, so the warehouse staff can easily determine how many units they are moving.

Another variation on the concept is to use standard containers for all but a few stray units, which are stored in front of the containers. The stray units are picked first, leaving the fully-loaded containers on the shelf – which are the easiest to count.

Tip: Include a bar code of the container unit count on each container, so the warehouse staff can more easily enter the quantity into their portable data entry terminals.

There is a certain amount of effort involved in shifting goods to standard container sizes, so do not overdo this concept. Just repackage inventory when doing so makes a significant different in the tracking of inventory.

Drop Shipping

When a business sells merchandise that it has acquired from a supplier, it must deal with the following transactions, all of which can potentially involve damage to the goods:

- Receive inventory
- Move goods to quality review area
- Examine goods based on receiving criteria
- Move reviewed goods to warehouse storage area
- Pick goods and combine with other items for shipping
- Ship merchandise to customer

In situations where a business is reselling goods produced by someone else, there is an opportunity to employ drop shipping. This method involves having the supplier ship goods directly to the customer of the seller. By doing so, the seller never has to touch the inventory at all, which eliminates the long list of activities just described. In addition, the seller no longer has to invest in any inventory, since the supplier maintains it. This approach is especially useful when the goods being resold are bulky, since the seller can potentially eliminate a large amount of storage space in its warehouse facility.

Though drop shipping can be a useful alternative for a reseller, it suffers from the following issues:

- *Supplier resistance*. Suppliers may not agree with it, since doing so can involve shipping a large number of small unit-count deliveries, which are expensive to pack and ship.
- *New procedures*. The seller must institute new procedures and controls to issue shipping notifications to suppliers and ensure that the shipments are made. There must also be a system for notifying the billing department when shipments have been made, so that invoices can be issued.
- *Lost sales*. The customer will now know the name of the supplier, which could lead it to order directly from the supplier in the future.
- *Supplier reliability*. The supplier chosen for drop shipping must be absolutely reliable, since customers are under the impression that goods shipped from the supplier are actually coming from the seller. Thus, a snafu at the supplier reflects poorly on the reputation of the seller.

In short, drop shipping tends to be a limited solution, but can be quite useful in those cases where it can be applied.

Eliminate Informal Storage

Warehouse efficiencies are best pursued within the warehouse, since this is an environment that can be constantly monitored. A problem arises when inventory informally finds its way outside of the warehouse, since there is no formal management of this inventory.

Informal storage arises when excess amounts of raw materials and sub-assemblies are kitted and sent to the production floor, but are not returned to the warehouse. Instead, the production managers and machine operators realize that these items can be of use in the future to tide them over when there are parts shortages. The result is an array of inventory items that are squirreled away in a variety of informal locations.

The existence of informal inventory storage causes several problems in different parts of the organization. Consider the following issues:

- Informal inventory clutters up the production area, which is an issue when production cells are used, since there is little excess space for storage. An excessive amount of clutter also presents a safety risk for workers.
- An informal inventory item may be slipped into a production run at a later date, when part specifications may have changed or the part is too old to be used. The result can be a failed product.
- The fact that excess parts were issued is never realized by anyone, since the parts are never returned. This means that the underlying bill of materials is never corrected, so that even more extra inventory is sent to the shop floor whenever the related products are scheduled for production again.
- Since the purchasing staff is not aware of the informal inventory, it orders more replenishment stock at regular intervals, which is more inventory than the company actually needs.

Given the number of negative effects related to internal storage, an efficient warehouse practice is to routinely comb through the production area, retrieve any of these items that may be found, and log them back into the warehouse system.

Store Inventory at Production

This section is positioned after the preceding section about eliminating informal inventory in order to prove a point – the *planned* storage of goods outside of the warehouse can have beneficial effects. This is not the case when such storage is *unplanned*.

Certain types of inventory take up an inordinate amount of warehouse staff time. They are included in a high proportion of products, and so are constantly being requested by the production staff or included in kits intended for production. Given the usage level, these parts are also stored in large volumes. Further, because they are constantly being picked from stock, the pick locations contain broken cases that are difficult to count. Because of the high transaction volume, there are more likely to be inventory record inaccuracies. The result is a great deal of putaway, picking, and monitoring work by the warehouse staff. And to make matters worse, these inventory items are generally inexpensive, so all of that staff time is being spent on a very small proportion of the total inventory value.

A possible solution to this quandary (which will be heavily endorsed by the warehouse staff) is to shift all low-value, high-volume goods from the warehouse to the shop floor. These items are stored in readily-accessible bins, so the production staff can travel just a short distance to access the items. This approach also removes the shifted items from the warehouse records.

Products do not always flow seamlessly through the production facility. Instead, they may be held up for various reasons and shifted back to the warehouse until the remaining finishing steps can be completed. An alternative is to hold partially completed assemblies near the production area, so that these items can be easily accessed when production resumes. Doing so also reduces the possibility of damage that can occur when work-in-process items are shifted to and from the warehouse.

The following ramifications arise from the decision to store inventory in the production area:

- The shifted items are no longer being tracked as an asset, and so will instead be charged to expense as soon as they are purchased – not when they are used.
- Since the shifted items are not tracked in the inventory records, reordering must be by a manual inspection process, which calls for the implementation and enforcement of a separate ordering procedure.
- The shifted items are out in the open and unguarded, so there is an increased risk of theft. If there is evidence of theft, it may be necessary to shift some items back into the warehouse.
- Moving items out of stock will result in the inventory records showing zero balances, which a material requirements planning (MRP) system might interpret as a trigger to issue a purchase order for replacement parts. To keep this from happening, set a flag in the item master for each of the moved parts to no longer trigger an automatic purchase order.
- The shifted items may be listed in the bills of material for a variety of products. If the items are removed from the bills of material, this can result in a notable decline in the standard costs of these products. Since bills of material are used in a standard costing system to record the on-hand cost of inventory items, this change can reduce the recorded amount of inventory on hand.
- If a company is also pursuing the goal of reconfiguring the shop floor around production cells (see the Impact of Production on Inventory chapter), adding inventory to the shop floor could interfere with the planned flow of production. This could severely limit the extent to which inventory can be moved to the production area.

Despite the issues just noted, it is reasonable to move a modest number of lower-cost items to the production floor. The various departments involved with the decision can monitor the outcome to see if the change is beneficial, and if additional alterations should be made. Over time, it is likely that the mix of items stored in this manner will change in conjunction with the mix of goods produced.

Design Storage for Less than Peak Demand

An efficient warehouse is one that minimizes the overall cost of storing and handling inventory. A large part of this cost is related to the size of the facility, in the form of rent, utilities, and facility maintenance. Consequently, it makes sense to plan the size of the facility for an inventory amount that is somewhat less than the peak storage level. Any inventory exceeding the capacity of the facility is then shifted to temporary storage, either in adjacent trailers or in nearby short-term rental space.

This is not an easy concept to turn into actual practice, for the ideal facility size depends on two factors, both of which can only be estimated. They are:

- *Trend of total storage requirements*. The overall trend of storage requirements may be changing over time, in which case one must delve into the reasons for the change, and then estimate whether they will continue. For example, if a company is adding retail stores in the region serviced by a warehouse, it would be reasonable to estimate the future storage requirements of the warehouse based on the number of additional stores that will be added.
- *Nature of storage spikes*. If there is a short-term spike in storage that then declines rapidly back to an average level, then it makes sense to shift some inventory to short-term storage for the duration of the spike. However, if the spike is of long duration (such as a half-year), then it may be less expensive to simply design for peak-period storage in anticipation of the maximum storage requirement.

> **Tip:** If some inventory is to be moved to an off-site location, review production and sales plans to determine which items are least likely to be used during the peak storage period, and move these items to off-site storage.

If the company is using temporary storage space even during that part of the year when storage requirements are at a low point, it is clearly time to plan for an expanded warehouse facility. Otherwise, the company will be burdened with overly complex material handling situations, as it constantly moves goods to and from outside storage locations.

Predictive Storage

Once a company has dealt with a customer for a certain period of time, it can gain an understanding of the specific products that the customer orders, as well as the frequency of these purchases and the order quantities placed. Based on this information, it can preposition those inventory items most likely to be ordered by customers at the warehouse located closest to them. Doing so allows the company to minimize the need for any overnight delivery charges, since it has already stocked the necessary items in advance, using lower-cost transportation. This approach also allows the firm to achieve high fulfillment rates within a short period of time.

Predictive storage works best when the average customer orders frequently and on a repetitive basis. For example, this approach works well for a grocery supplier where orders are placed on a daily or weekly basis, and not so well when customers only place orders at long intervals, such as once a year. This approach is especially efficient when most customers are located in major metropolitan areas, since the firm can position goods in nearby warehouses from which transit times are especially short for the majority of customers.

Warehouse Management System

As the name implies, a warehouse management system (WMS) is a computerized system that essentially runs the warehouse. It is a core ingredient of a large-scale warehouse that must handle thousands of transactions on a regular basis. The main features of a typical WMS are as follows:

- Track the locations of all in-house and in-bound SKUs in real time.
- Instruct the warehouse staff where to putaway and pick goods within the warehouse's racking system. This includes replenishment activities that move goods from reserve storage to the main picking areas. The instructions should minimize the amount of travel time when no goods are being moved.
- Organize the flow of goods used in cross-docking.
- Monitor the flow of picked goods into packed customer orders, and organize their shipment through the correct shipping dock.
- Optimize the locations of SKUs based on their usage patterns and other factors.
- Track the productivity of those employees engaged in the higher-volume warehouse activities.

In addition, any number of more specialized modules can be integrated into a WMS. For example, systems from other parties may be added that allow for bar coded or RFID data entry. Conversely, information in a WMS may be used to drive other third party modules, such as pick to light solutions. Thus, a business can achieve a comprehensive, world-class system by bolting together and integrating a number of systems to manage all of its warehouse operations.

As just noted, a WMS may have the functionality to cross-dock inventory. If so, the system takes note of supplier deliveries that have just arrived, and matches them with customer orders. There are two types of cross-dock matching that a WMS could make. These are:

- *Planned matching*. The system matches receipts with existing customer orders. The WMS then directs that the goods be sent to a specific shipping dock, where an outbound truck is awaiting the goods.
- *Opportunistic matching*. The system matches receipts with expected customer orders. The WMS then directs that the goods be staged near a specific shipping dock, in the expectation that a near-term customer order will be received and then shipped from that location. This approach works well for seasonal items for which there is a high level of demand, or if a high level of demand is being triggered by a specific marketing promotion.

Another WMS feature is to offer yard management. A yard management module tracks the contents of every trailer stored in the yard. The WMS uses this information to schedule when a trailer needs to be moved to a receiving dock for offloading. Since trailers are essentially an additional set of warehouse bin locations, tracking them should be considered an essential element of a WMS.

The system must communicate with employees via wireless terminals, so that transactions can be handled "on the fly," as employees move through the warehouse. There are many ways to communicate information to employees, including a standard computer screen, a heads-up display, by synthesized voice, and pick-to-light systems.

The ideal WMS is one that seems to operate in the background, handling the bulk of all warehouse transactions via wireless terminals so smoothly that warehouse performance is vastly improved.

Tip: A WMS is so specialized and industry-specific that the standard warehouse module provided by an integrated systems supplier is probably not adequate. Instead, consider using a more specialized best-of-breed system, and integrating it into the company's other computer systems.

Distribution Requirements Planning

A company may employ a central warehouse that feeds goods to regional warehouses, which in turn send goods as needed to customers, retail stores, and distributors. This multi-layered system may result in the efficient distribution of goods, but does not give the central warehouse any visibility into the actual demand for goods in the field. If the company owns all of the various tiers in the distribution chain, or can convince them to use it, a good solution to this problem is a distribution requirements planning (DRP) system.

Under a DRP system, those distribution points closest to the end user enter their demand forecasts. The system then compares these forecasts to the inventory balances already on-hand at the regional warehouses to determine how much additional stock is needed, factors in lead times, and arrives at the amount of inventory that must be shipped from the central warehouse in order to satisfy the demands of the entire distribution system. A DRP system is also used to adjust the timing of deliveries, so that on-hand balances are kept to reasonable levels at all points in the distribution chain. The system is also used to aggregate deliveries so that transportation costs can be minimized with the use of full truck loads.

In essence, a DRP is an excellent front-end to the manufacturing resources planning system described in the Impact of Production on Inventory chapter. A DRP system provides the best possible view of actual demand for a company's products, so that manufacturing activities can be properly scheduled to meet that demand. The result is essentially just-in-time distribution, rather than the more traditional just-in-case model that requires more inventory.

The main problem with a DRP is that the resulting information is completely dependent upon the reliability of the forecast information entered into it. If someone supposedly close to the end user creates a seriously incorrect forecast, it can have a major negative effect on overall inventory levels. Consequently, it makes sense to compare the forecasts being entered into the system by adjacent regions, to see if there are any anomalies that should be examined in more detail.

Fair Shares Analysis

Unless a company's central warehouse is wildly overstocked, there will be ongoing instances where the orders placed by regional warehouses will exceed the amount of stock that is currently on hand. When orders exceed the amount on hand, the usual response from the central warehouse manager is to fill those orders that came in first, and backorder all other orders. The problem with this passive approach to incoming orders is that some of the regional warehouse orders do not have any actual customer orders behind them – instead, some of the orders are intended to sit in stock until needed. Thus, some regions will receive an overabundance of inventory, while others will have stockout conditions, and so will probably lose sales.

The solution to this distribution problem is called fair shares analysis, and involves the following logic for distributing goods to downstream warehouses:

1. Inventory is first distributed based on actual customer orders; then
2. Inventory is distributed based on forecasts indicating impending customer orders; then
3. Any remaining inventory is issued to replenish on-site safety stock levels.

The intent behind fair shares analysis is to maximize sales, since inventory is directed specifically to those locations where sales are either guaranteed or most likely to occur. Thus, in a situation where inventory levels are constrained and customers are at risk of ordering from competitors, fair shares analysis is a useful tool.

However, the system does not necessarily take into account the reduced cost of shipping in full truck loads, so a possible result is increased freight costs associated with more frequent less-than-full loads. Also, the analysis works best when there is complete visibility into on-hand inventory levels in all warehouses in the network, so all of the warehouses should be tied together with the same inventory management system.

Ship Overnight from a Single Location

A company may distribute goods to its customers from a number of regional warehouses. If so, the same parts must be stocked at each location, which can result in an excessive aggregate investment in inventory. One possibility is to ship goods only from a central location, but timed to reach customers with the same speed that they are accustomed to receive goods from a local warehouse. This may call for the use of an overnight delivery service, or perhaps a two-day delivery arrangement.

Overnight delivery from a central location can be quite an expensive proposition for all types of inventory. However, it can be a workable concept for inventory that has the following two characteristics:

- *Uncertain demand.* When demand is difficult to predict, the amount of inventory to stock in regional warehouses is also difficult to estimate. The result is usually stockouts in some locations and excess inventory in other locations. In this situation, storing all inventory in one place is the easiest way to keep control over unit levels.
- *High value items.* It is relatively easy to justify the cost of an overnight delivery for goods that are small and of high value, since the ratio of shipping cost to inventory cost is low. Conversely, shipping a large and bulky item by overnight delivery service is a losing proposition.

We are not advocating that all inventory items be shipped by overnight delivery service from a single warehouse; instead, review the inventory held at regional warehouses to see if anything meets the preceding two criteria, and shift just the qualifying items to a central location. Further, this review should be made at regular intervals, as warehouse locations and delivery costs change. Depending on the circumstances, there may be an increase or decrease in the number of qualifying inventory items over time.

Retain Low-Turnover Inventory at Warehouse Level

In a retail operation, there will always be a number of items that do not sell especially well. These low-turnover items tend to clog retail stores, leaving less room for the proper display and storage of hot-selling goods. If every retail store has an overabundance of slow-moving stock, then the company as a whole is investing an enormous amount in low-turnover inventory. There is also a heightened risk that some portion of this inventory will become obsolete, necessitating significant write-downs.

One way to manage this inventory more effectively is to retain most slow-moving items in the regional warehouses that service clusters of retail stores. By keeping this inventory in one place, the warehouse can easily apportion it out to the various stores as their goods are gradually sold off. This also means that a reduced amount of total inventory is needed, since the inventory held at the regional warehouse level takes the place of the safety stock that would normally be held at each of the retail stores. Also, if there is increased usage of these items in one sales region, it is easier to transfer excess inventory to it from the other regional warehouses than from individual retail stores.

There are several issues with this concept. First, the regional warehouses must be able to use very fast deliveries to the retail stores for which they are responsible, since these stores could be rendered out of stock on some items by just a few customer purchases. Second, the inventory tracking systems at the retail level must be excellent, so that stockout conditions are immediately obvious to the warehouse managers. Finally, analysts must continually pore over the sales data by store, to see which inventory items are experiencing declining sales; this triggers an order to pull some stock back to the warehouse level. Conversely, detecting an increasing trend in the sales data would trigger the issuance of more stock back to the retail locations. As long as these issues can be addressed, a business can do an excellent job of moderating its inventory investment while still maintaining enough on-site inventory to please customers.

> **Tip:** It is also possible to retain stocks at a regional warehouse for *all* types of inventory (including high-turnover items), rather than keeping extra inventory at the retail stores. While this approach (known as the *hold and flow* system) will reduce overall inventory levels, it presents the risk of local stockout conditions for popular items, and so requires constant replenishment runs from the regional warehouse.

Combine Warehouse Missions

There are a number of warehouse types. A company may have distribution centers that are used to consolidate products arriving from different locations, and then ship combined deliveries to customers. There may also be fulfillment warehouses, where goods are picked and consolidated for delivery to individual customers. There are also local warehouses, which focus on rapid deliveries to local customers. Further, a company may have value-added services warehouses, where minor product customizations are performed prior to shipment.

Each of these warehouse types may appear necessary when viewed by itself. However, inventory can be damaged when it is moved through several of these warehouses, since the risk of damage increases along with the number of touches. For example, a product may initially be sent to a distribution warehouse and then forwarded to a local warehouse. Also, a large number of warehouses can result in an excessively large total amount of inventory. Instead, consider combining the missions of selected warehouses, so that customers are still serviced reasonably quickly, while reducing the inventory investment and the risk of product damage.

EXAMPLE

Entwhistle Electric produces small batteries for mobile applications. One of its main customers is a cell phone manufacturer, which demands the delivery of batteries to its production line on an hourly basis. The obvious decision is to set up a battery depot not far from this customer, and stock it solely to fulfill the needs of the customer. However, a deeper analysis of the situation reveals that Entwhistle could situate the depot slightly further away from the customer, but closer to a regional airport, from which it can service a number of other customers. The end result is that Entwhistle moves a regional warehouse closer to this customer, rather than setting up an additional warehouse.

Adjust the Warehouse Network

A company may employ a large number of regional warehouses, in order to more rapidly fulfill the orders of customers located in those regions. The initial locations of these warehouses were likely based on a combination of travel times to the existing mix of customers, as well as the cost of labor and warehouse facilities. Over time, the mix of customers will change, as will the costs of maintaining the warehouses. Thus, it is possible that a warehouse network will eventually be sub-optimal; that is, the average customer delivery time will no longer be minimized, while changes in local labor rates and the vagaries of the real estate market may have altered warehousing costs. In addition, a company may buy another business that maintains its own warehouse network, in which case the combined group of warehouses probably service overlapping regions.

This state of affairs calls for a periodic cost-benefit examination of the entire warehouse network, probably conducted by a consultant that specializes in this type of analysis. The consultant will attempt to optimize the customer delivery times and warehouse costs just noted. In addition, the analysis may take into consideration the following issues:

- The incremental cost of moving warehouses to a new location. This is a particular concern when an existing facility has a highly automated and integrated structure that is difficult to disassemble and reassemble in a new facility.
- If the warehouse networks of an acquirer and acquiree are to be combined, how does the increased number of SKUs impact the overall size of the warehouse? An excessively large facility is not as efficient, which may result in a recommendation to maintain a larger number of smaller facilities.
- It may be possible to configure a new warehouse facility to use a large amount of automation. If so, it may be cost-effective to locate a facility in a high labor-cost area, since the automated facility will need to employ fewer people.
- Can an existing facility be expanded, contracted, or modified in any way in order to keep it usable? This can depend on the availability of nearby land, the reasonableness of landlords, and how much the company wants to spend on materials handling and storage systems.
- If the company sells a large proportion of its goods to a small number of customers, the future prospects of those customers are of great concern to the company. This analysis includes not just a review of the viability of customers, but also of changes in their locations, and in the mix of products that they may order.

Ship from Stores

When a company has both online stores and a retail presence, it can route online orders to those stores located closest to its online customers, and then schedule deliveries to the customers from those stores. Doing so eliminates the cost of having a separate warehouse system, along with the attendant costs of facilities, staff, and inventory. There is also a cost savings in the delivery aspect of the transaction, since the company is now paying a third-party shipper for quite a short-range delivery. Further, orders can be routed to those stores that have excessive amounts of inventory, thereby reducing the risk that these goods might otherwise have to be sold later at a discount. If a business sells high-fashion goods for which selling periods are short, this also allows stores to eliminate items from stock quickly, thereby allowing for the introduction of new fashions more promptly.

Another favorable aspect of the arrangement is that the total time from placement of an order to product delivery can be quite short, which can be marketed to customers as a benefit.

The approach works well for companies that have a large number of retail outlets; otherwise, the nearest store may be a substantial distance away from a customer. However, the concept could be applied by smaller organizations that have concentrations of stores within certain regions. If so, the store density may be high enough within a specific area to allow for practical shipping from stores just within that area. The concept can then be expanded as the business gradually increases the number of stores that it operates.

Summary

One of the main themes of this chapter has been to segment the warehouse, depending on the type of demand. This means that the warehouse should not be treated as a monolithic entity that is never changed, and through which pickers roam over vast distances. Instead, customer orders must be closely analyzed to determine what types, sizes, and product families are being ordered. Based on this information, the warehouse can be segmented to optimize the fulfillment of customer orders. This is a never-ending process, since the nature of customer orders constantly change. The result is a warehouse whose layout and contents are being modified on an ongoing basis.

The same concept can be applied to a network of warehouses. The usage rates of goods from each location must be regularly reviewed, resulting in a constant rebalancing of inventory levels between warehouses. At longer intervals, the warehouses themselves can be shifted, to take advantage of changes in customer locations, ordering patterns, and storage costs.

Chapter 16
Warehouse Storage Systems

Introduction

The standard image of a warehouse is of lengthy aisles that have identical pallet storage racks extending down both sides, and off into the distance. While this is a reasonable configuration for many organizations, there are many other storage systems available. When the storage needs of a business are examined in detail, it is likely that some standard pallet storage racks will indeed be needed. However, these systems will likely be supplemented by a variety of other storage systems. In this chapter, we examine the characteristics of inventory that can trigger the use of alternative storage systems, the nature of those systems, and several related topics.

Inventory Storage Characteristics

Before deciding upon the types of storage systems that will be employed in a warehouse, it is first necessary to understand the characteristics of the inventory items that will be stored. Here are a number of issues to consider:

- *Picking activity.* A small proportion of all items in the warehouse will be picked the majority of the time. The pareto principle, which states that 20% of the items comprise 80% of the activity, reasonably represents the amount of picking activity to be expected. Those inventory items being picked the most should be compressed into the front area of the warehouse for easy access, while those picked the least are relegated to the nether regions of the available storage space. Items picked very frequently are most amenable to an automated picking solution, while rarely-picked items can probably be accessed with low-cost manual picking solutions.
- *Cubic space.* Items stored in pallet configurations are the most easily transported, and are stored in standard-sized storage racks. It is more difficult to maximize the cubic storage space when smaller, non-standard sizes are used. Thus, pallet and non-pallet storage sizes call for different storage systems, or at least different beam heights within racks.
- *Weight.* Lighter items can be stored in racks that do not have cross bracing. These racks can be accessed from both sides and are less expensive, but are subject to collapse if burdened with excessive loads.
- *Inventory life span.* Certain types of inventory have very short shelf lives, and so must be used quickly. This means that the storage system must be configured to present the oldest inventory items to pickers, which is known as a first-in, first-out (FIFO) system. These systems typically involve gravity flow, where goods are put away in the rear of a rack, and then roll forward to the

front of the rack, where they are accessed by pickers. Conversely, if life span is not an issue, then other storage systems may be used where inventory is stacked well back in a storage space (such as a double-deep rack or a stacking lane), and so is not readily accessible.

- *Fixed asset investment.* If a company is willing to invest a large amount in its warehouse operation, it can maximize the cubic volume of space used, while also using automation to reduce the travel time of those employees engaged in picking and putaway work. Conversely, a low fixed asset investment eliminates several of the more expensive storage alternatives, such as carousels, in favor of such low-cost but less-efficient solutions as stacking lanes.

- *Wage rate.* If the fully-burdened labor rate in a warehouse is quite high, it can make more sense to employ more automated (and expensive) storage solutions that minimize the need for labor. For example, carousels can be installed that bring items to pickers, rather than requiring pickers to walk to the inventory. Conversely, if wage rates are quite low, it may be possible to dispense with the more automated systems and simply hire lots of staff to manually access the inventory.

- *Cost per square foot.* Some warehouses are located in areas where the cost of land and construction is so low that it is easy to justify storage solutions that do not maximize the use of the entire cubic volume of the warehouse. On the other hand, some warehouse locations are so expensive that every last cubic inch of space should be used, rather than buying or renting additional storage space. The first situation may allow for the use of stacking lanes, while the latter situation may call for investments in double-deep racks, movable racks, and mezzanine storage.

- *Cost of capital.* When the cost of capital for a business is extremely low, it makes more sense to invest in expensive storage solutions, since funds are so cheap. In this environment, investments in highly automated solutions are more common. Conversely, if the cost of capital is high (which may relate more to a tight credit market than the financial condition of a company), it may not be economically feasible to make major investments in warehouse storage systems.

It is likely that a combination of the preceding factors will drive the decision to invest in a certain type of inventory storage system. For example, a contemplated location within a city where the costs of both real estate and labor are high will likely incline a business toward the use of mezzanine storage, vertical carousels, and automated storage and retrieval systems. Conversely, cheap land, low labor rates and a high cost of capital could drive a business in the direction of a very low-cost solution, such as standard racks, bins, and stacking lanes, with all-manual picking systems. In the next section, we give an overview of the different types of storage systems.

Storage Systems

The type of storage system installed in a warehouse depends upon a mix of the factors just noted in the preceding section. The following exhibit notes how well various racking systems match up to these criteria.

Storage System Characteristics

Criteria	Storage Type	Description
Small cubic volume	Storage drawers	Stacked drawers that can be divided into many smaller compartments. Ideal for storage of small unit quantities of small items. Can also be locked to prevent unauthorized withdrawal of expensive items. Storage drawers can be expensive, and are not especially high, so that space above them is more likely to be unused.
Moderately small cubic volume	Bin shelving	Open shelf space on a storage rack. Can be subdivided. A large part of the cubic volume may be unused. Less expensive than storage drawers. Cannot be locked, so there is a greater risk of theft than with storage drawers.
High volume picking and smaller cubic volume goods	Carousels	A powered system that moves bins to the picker, who remains in one place. This is an expensive solution, but can greatly increase picker productivity, as well as provide some security for items stored in the bins. Picker efficiency can be impacted by a slow carousel, so it pays to invest in higher-speed systems, and perhaps in several carousels per picker. Also, an excessively large carousel can require extra time for the correct bin to rotate through and be presented to the picker. The most expensive racking solution. See the following Carousels section.
Low volume picking, smaller cubic volume goods, premium on available floor space	Movable racks	Racks are mounted on wheels and compressed together, leaving one open aisle. Racks must be moved to open an aisle and create the space to access and pick an inventory item. A slow solution for pickers, but maximizes the use of storage space. Only usable space is through head height; any cubic space above that point is wasted. This is a relatively expensive storage option.
Variable storage volume and larger cubic volumes	Pallet stacking frames	Portable racks that can be easily broken down and stored. Ideal for accommodating spikes in storage volume that are not expected to last long enough to warrant the acquisition of more permanent fixtures. Especially useful when loads are not otherwise stackable, and so must be stored in a more rigid framing system.

Criteria	Storage Type	Description
High volumes of goods stored on pallets	Single-deep rack	The most common racking system, using low-cost metal uprights and cross-members, suitably braced, to hold pallet-sized loads. Each bin in a single-deep rack can accommodate pallets stacked a single layer deep, so that inventory having a short life span can be easily accessed. Racks can be many levels high, so that different stock keeping units (SKUs) can be stored in the same vertical space.
Low volume picking, smaller cubic volume goods	Mezzanine storage	Bin shelving constructed in a second story above the main storage area. Requires more time for pickers to access and is not amenable to automation, so is used primarily for smaller, low-volume items. Items stored here should be light weight, or else a robust (and expensive) support structure must be installed. Gravity-flow racks (see next) can be used to shift picked goods from the mezzanine down to the ground floor.
Higher volume picking, smaller cubic volume goods, inventory ages quickly	Gravity-flow rack	Racks are set at a slight downward angle and filled from the rear, so that the oldest items roll downhill toward the pickers. The oldest items are therefore always presented to pickers first. The weight of the next units in line push the front unit forward for presentation to pickers. Putaways and picking can be accomplished at the same time, since these functions are done at opposite ends of the rack.
High volumes of identical goods stored on pallets, inventory ages quickly	Pallet-flow racks	This is the same as the gravity-flow rack, but for pallets. The racks incorporate automatic brakes to keep pallets from accelerating as they slide toward the front of the rack. Tends to reduce pallet damage, since pallets are manually moved less frequently. This solution is expensive.
High volumes of identical goods stored on pallets, inventory does not age quickly	Double-deep rack	Racks are configured one behind the other, so that pallets can be stored two deep. This configuration eliminates the aisle that would normally be between the two sets of racks, and so conserves warehouse space. Requires a special forklift to access the rear pallet locations.
High volumes of identical goods stored on pallets, inventory does not age quickly	Push-back rack	Double-deep racks with angled load rails installed across the two sets of racks. The result is essentially a pallet-flow rack, where gravity pushes pallets to the front rack. This approach eliminates the need for a special forklift to access the rear pallet location.

Criteria	Storage Type	Description
High volumes of identical goods stored on pallets, no racking system	Stacking lanes	Pallets stored in lanes in an open area of the warehouse, with several pallets stacked on top of each other. Can only be accomplished if the pallets have sufficient structural rigidity and there is minimal humidity to avoid degrading the rigidity of the pallets. Goods are then available only on a last-in, first-out basis. This approach works well when large increments of goods are shipped out at once, such as via a full truckload of one type of inventory.
High volumes of identical goods stored on pallets, inventory does not age quickly	Drive-in rack & drive-thru rack	A drive-in rack is a system of racks that allow a forklift driver to drive several pallet positions deep into the racks to store or remove pallets. Can be used to store an even greater volume of similar goods than stacking lanes. Thus, a drive-in racking system is most applicable to very large volumes of the same SKU. A drive-thru rack is accessible from both ends, so that pallets can be stored from one end and accessed from the other end. This approach is useful for first-in, first-out inventory that has a short shelf life.

There is no single ideal storage solution for a warehouse. Instead, there should be a mix of storage systems, based on the cubic volume of goods, how frequently they are accessed, and the cost structure of the warehouse.

EXAMPLE

Country Office Supply Co. is a low-budget operation that stores large amounts of office supplies and furniture in a warehouse, and sells these goods to its largely rural customer base. The company cannot afford the more expensive storage systems, has no goods in stock with short shelf lives, and mostly deals with single unit and case sized orders. Based on this situation, Country uses bin shelving for all of its office supply products, and stores office furniture in double-deep racks in the rear of the warehouse.

Urban Supply Co. is located near the center of a major metropolitan area, and sells office supplies and furniture to inner-city customers. Warehouse space is extremely expensive, so Urban focuses on maximizing the use of space within its warehouse. Accordingly, the company invests in movable racks and push-back racks to eliminate aisle space, as well as mezzanine storage to take advantage of unused space above the warehouse floor.

Country Fresh Produce sells organically-grown produce to local grocery stores. The sole concern of Country Fresh is to supply goods within an extremely short period of time under the FIFO concept. Accordingly, Country Fresh invests in gravity-flow racks and pallet-flow racks.

Beam Height

A visually pleasing warehouse is one in which all racks have the same beam height. For example, an entire warehouse may be configured to have every location in a storage rack with beams set five feet apart. The level of consistency is beautiful to behold, but unfortunately does little to properly utilize storage space. If there are a number of off-sized storage items, such as half-pallet loads and individual cases, then a large amount of cubic volume above these items in a rack will be unused.

A more effective use of rack space is to set a variety of beam heights, based on a survey of the cubic volume taken up by a company's current on-hand inventory. A likely result will be a range of beam heights in different parts of the warehouse, into which inventory can be slotted with little excess room.

Tip: When a company is storing its own products, an alternative to adjusting the beam height to maximize space usage is to alter the height of the cases stored on a pallet. Usually, a height reduction of less than an inch can yield an extra stacking layer that takes up any remaining storage space.

Honeycombing Effects

Among of the last items noted in the preceding table were stacking lanes and drive-in racks, which are a particularly effective solution when there are large numbers of the same stock keeping unit (SKU), and large amounts of available floor space for storage. However, this method suffers from *honeycombing*, which is empty spaces in the stacking lanes or drive-in racks. Honeycombing occurs because only one SKU can be stored in each lane or rack, and each location cannot be used for an alternative purpose until all of the inventory in it has been moved out. Thus, if a small residual unit volume of an SKU is sitting in a lane, the remainder of that lane is effectively unusable. The negative effects of honeycombing can be mitigated in two ways:

- *Move to racks.* If there is a small unit quantity remaining in a lane, shift it to nearby rack space.
- *Shorten lanes.* Configure the stacking lanes to have different lengths. Some lanes can be quite long, and are designed to accommodate large unit volumes. Other lanes are much shorter, and are intended for SKUs stored in smaller quantities. This solution is not as applicable to drive-in racks, which are more difficult to reconfigure.

As SKU unit quantities change over time, so too can the lengths of the assigned stacking lanes, simply by altering the taped lane lengths.

Honeycombing can also occur in a double-deep racking configuration, since there may only be one pallet in a space designed for two pallets. This issue can be resolved by only storing pallets in double-deep racks for which there is an expectation that both pallets will be picked at the same time, thereby leaving the entire space open again for storage.

Yet another honeycombing situation is when the size or other characteristics of a product reduce the amount by which other products can be stacked on top of or adjacent to it. For example, a product whose packaging has weak construction will collapse if additional weight is placed on it. The result is unused space above the stored product. This issue can be resolved either by altering the packaging or reconfiguring rack space to introduce more racks into the same vertical space.

A final cause of honeycombing is when products are putaway in a sloppy manner, so that there is excess space around them. This can cause a surprising amount of honeycombing in all directions – there may be excess space in front of, behind, above, and on either side of stored goods. This cause of honeycombing requires the most labor to correct, especially if the problem is widespread. If sloppy putaways are a significant problem, it could take weeks of effort to achieve a reduced level of honeycombing.

In short, honeycombing can lead to the non-use of a significant amount of a warehouse's excess storage space. Only careful planning of space usage and proper putaway techniques will mitigate its presence.

Automated Dispensing Units

Some types of inventory are both small and expensive, and so require a higher level of control than other types of inventory. This can be a particular concern when the items are consumer products, and so are more likely to be stolen. In these situations, a possible storage option is the automated dispensing unit. This is essentially a locked storage bin that only allows access to someone with the correct identification number, access card, or fingerprint. The person removing goods must also enter the number of units taken. By doing so, specific usage levels can be tracked by employee.

A higher level of security can be achieved with dispensing units that require the user to punch in the identification number of a specific item. Once selected, only the bin containing that item will open, thereby ensuring tighter control over all other items stored in the unit. This type of unit can be configured by employee, so that a certain employee is only allowed access to those inventory items that he needs in his position.

An automated dispensing unit will track remaining quantities on hand, and can even be configured to notify suppliers with replenishment orders. The information from these units can also be aggregated, making it possible to review usage levels by person, inventory item, project number, and storage cabinet. The units can be interfaced with an enterprise resource planning system, so the information is widely accessible throughout a company.

While the main emphasis of an automated dispensing unit is on control, it is also an excellent solution for employees who do not want to travel to the warehouse, fill out a requisition form, and wait for inventory to be delivered to them. Instead, they can walk to a nearby cabinet, enter an access code, remove what they need, and close the door. Also, the use of automated dispensing units can be expanded to include maintenance, repair, and operations (MRO) items, which tend to be expensive and are therefore in need of tracking.

Carousels

There are situations where it is more cost-effective to bring inventory to the picker than it is for the picker to travel to the inventory. This situation applies when the travel time of pickers would be inordinately high, and/or when the employee labor cost is high. If so, a carousel storage system may be the answer.

A carousel stores inventory in bins, and uses a motor to rotate the bins for presentation to a picker. A picker stands in front of the carousel and picks items from bins as they rotate forward and are presented to him. The picker enters locations into a computer to access the next item required, or the computer does so automatically. A carousel comes in two varieties:

- *Horizontal carousel.* Rotation of the unit is around an axis that is perpendicular to the floor. Thus, rotation is parallel to the floor. A horizontal carousel can be quite long, but this may make the rotation interval to the next target bin excessively long. The carousel may also be up to 20 feet high, but the extra height requires that the picker access higher items on a ladder or lift platform, which reduces picking speed.

- *Vertical carousel.* Rotation of the unit is around an axis that is parallel to the floor. Thus, rotation is parallel to the wall. A vertical carousel occupies little floor space, but can use all of the available vertical space, right up to the ceiling. A tall unit requires a longer rotation interval to the next target bin. These units are considered to be more efficient than horizontal carousels, since target bins are always presented to pickers at waist height, which eliminates stooping and reaching. An additional benefit of the vertical carousel is security, for the unit is sheathed in sheet metal, and is also high enough to deter most thieves. These units are more expensive than horizontal carousels, due to the need for more powerful motors to drive the unit against the force of gravity, as well as the added metal sheathing.

There is a certain amount of wait time for a picker while a carousel is rotating to the next bin from which goods are to be picked. The picker can be made more productive during this down time by positioning him or her between two or more carousels. The person can then pick from one carousel while the other unit is rotating to the next target bin.

> **Tip:** The carousel speed should be sufficiently high to eliminate any wait time by a stock picker. Otherwise, any labor savings associated with the carousel investment will be reduced or eliminated.

If a warehouse manager has been having trouble with inefficient pickers, carousels provide an excellent supervisory solution. Pickers using carousels are located in a fixed position at the end of an aisle, and so are easily monitored.

> **Tip:** If the elimination of picker travel time is the main justification for the purchase of carousels, consider the lower-cost alternative of shifting those goods with high-volume picks to the front of the warehouse. Doing so greatly reduces the amount of picker travel time.

The Pallet

Some mention must be made of the platform on which the bulk of all inventory items are stored and shipped – the pallet. This basic wooden platform is intended to provide a common storage dimension, as well as an easy way for the tines on a forklift to slip under a load for easy pickup. The pallet is easy to construct, is moderately durable, and is widely accepted. When loads are properly configured on a pallet, there is also less risk of loss or damage during handling, since there is no need to touch the items on the pallet. In short, the pallet is the overwhelming favorite worldwide storage platform.

> **Tip:** Some pallets can be purchased that have embedded RFID tags, which can be a useful feature if a company is tracking unit-loads with an RFID system.

Despite its popularity, the presence of a pallet reduces the amount of cubic volume that can be stored during transport, since the typical pallet is six inches high. Depending on the number of pallets and the height of pallet loads, this can represent as much as a 10% reduction in trailer space, which is not trivial. There is also a risk that a pallet will be damaged, which can result in a load slipping off the pallet and damaging inventory.

The volume and damage problems with pallets can be avoided by replacing pallets with slip sheets. A slip sheet is a thick piece of plastic or fiberboard that has the same width and length as a pallet, but which is much thinner and lighter. Slip sheets are more difficult to destroy and eliminate most of the excess volume of pallets. Their reduced weight also results in lower transport costs. However, once a load is removed from a trailer, the load with its integrated slip sheet must then be put right back on a pallet for warehouse storage. Also, slip sheet loads can only be picked up when a forklift has a special attachment. Consequently, the slip sheet option is only a viable alternative when storage space on a trailer is at a premium, or when shaving transport costs is a major goal.

> **Tip:** The standard pallet size is different in many countries. Consequently, if a company plans to accept loads originating in another country, it is useful to plan for the expected volume of these different pallet loads, which may call for adjustments to the rack space.

Pallet Loading

A key concern when using pallets is that loads are properly configured for storage, and that the structural integrity of stored items allow for the stacking of pallet loads. If not, storage space may not be properly utilized, and stored items could be damaged. In particular, be aware of the following issues:

- *Case overhang.* Cases may be improperly stacked on a pallet, so that some boxes are hanging over the edge of the pallet. If so, these cases can bang against the rack walls, causing damage to inventory. In addition, the overhanging walls of these cases are not supported by the pallet, and so have reduced structural integrity. If pallets are to be stacked, the weakened case walls can lead to the collapse of a stack. Finally, the edge of the forklift may collide with the sidewalls of the lowest level of overhanging cases, damaging their contents.
- *Side storage.* Cases may be stacked on their sides on a pallet. This may be a problem in a humid environment, where cardboard cases are weakened by the humidity. In this situation, goods only intended for vertical storage can be crushed or damaged as the cases compress.

Software is available that accepts the dimensions of the cases to be loaded on a pallet, and returns a visual representation of how the cases should be stacked on the pallet. The suggested configuration can be adjusted to match the cubic volume of the rack space in which a pallet is to be stored. This inexpensive system is extremely useful for ensuring that the cubic volume of storage space is maximized.

A less-efficient alternative to pallet loading is simply to undersize the load. Doing so eliminates the risk of case overhang and side storage issues, but at the cost of a potentially drastic reduction in the amount of cubic storage space used.

Liquid Storage

The storage situation can be approached in an entirely different manner for liquids. The traditional approach has been to treat liquids like solids; liquids are packaged in containers that can be stored on a pallet. Doing so increases the cost of packaging, and takes up space within the warehouse storage system. Further, bottles stored on pallets take up about half the space on a pallet – the remaining space is the air between the bottles. For a more space-effective solution, consider setting up storage tanks on site, to which liquids are transported by suppliers, and then piping the liquids to dispensers as needed. This approach eliminates the storage of all packaging, and also allows liquids to be stored in out-of-the-way locations. Further, the use of tanks and piping means there is no picking function. Instead, liquids are dispensed from a pipe that is routed to wherever the liquids are needed.

Liquids stored in tanks can also be excluded from routine inventory counts. Instead, install liquid-level sensors in each tank and route this information to monitors that reveal the exact quantity on hand. When this information is tied to the inventory record keeping system, the on-hand balance is always correct, without the need to create inventory transactions for inputs to and exports from the tanks.

In short, if a business stores a substantial amount of liquids, consider putting the special properties of liquids to good use and eliminating traditional packaging in favor of tank storage.

Summary

The main focus of this chapter has been to describe the many options available for storing inventory, rather than to recommend any particular type. The type of storage that should be used will become obvious after you have reviewed the types of inventory being stored, the frequency with which items are picked, the life span of the inventory, and numerous other factors. The likely conclusion is that a warehouse must be configured with a variety of storage systems, each one designed to address the unique storage issues presented by a company's inventory investment. Over time, the characteristics of this inventory investment will change, possibly requiring incremental changes in the types and layouts of storage systems. In rare cases, a radical shift in inventory characteristics will call for a massive replacement of storage systems.

Chapter 17
The Warehouse Layout

Introduction

The warehouse is not just a cavernous facility in which inventory is stored. Instead, it is a major cost center whose efficiencies are massively impacted by the manner in which storage space, work areas, and aisles are laid out. In this chapter, we explore the sequence of activities used to design an efficient warehouse layout, as well as numerous other considerations that must be addressed to ensure that the proper configuration is installed.

Planning the Warehouse Layout

There is no ideal warehouse layout that applies perfectly to the needs of every company. Instead, the layout must be adapted to the nature of the goods being stored in it, the volume of putaway and picking activities, the types of storage and materials handling systems to be used, and the intentions of management regarding the flow-through characteristics of the operation. Working through these issues involves the following steps:

1. *Calculate space requirements.* Estimate the amount of square footage needed for each of the activity and storage areas of the warehouse. This estimate should include consideration of future changes in inventory usage levels, as well as whether inventory storage is modeled based on maximum scenarios. A lower level of usage can be assumed if some inventory is parked in off-site storage. The portions of the warehouse for which space requirements should be calculated include:

    - Receiving (depends on the planned number of dock doors, and usually assumes the presence of enough room in front of each door to accommodate the contents of an entire trailer load; also depends on the need for travel lanes through the goods taken from or intended for trailers)
    - Pallet storage
    - Case and broken case picking
    - Sortation (can be extensive if a zone picking system is planned)
    - Packing (depends on the use of automated packing systems)
    - Shipping (same considerations as just noted for receiving)
    - Cross-docking
    - Forklift storage and battery charging area
    - Storage for unused pallets and packaging
    - Administrative

- Aisles (depends on the types of storage systems and material handling equipment to be used. In general, aisle width is based on the turning radius of the fork lifts to be used in a particular aisle.)

2. *Incorporate flow pattern.* The next step is to build into the warehouse design the anticipated flow of materials through the facility. There are four possible layouts that can be used, which are as follows:

    - *Front to back.* Goods are received at one side of the facility, are stored in the middle, and shipped from the opposite side. This layout works well when the peak receiving and shipping times are the same, since the two dock locations are far apart. However, separate materials handling equipment must be used in the receiving and shipping areas, since they are not adjacent.
    - *Modular.* The warehouse is split into modules, with each one designed to yield the optimum materials flow for a specific type of inventory. For example, refrigerated goods might be in one area, with a high-speed cross-docking layout in the next warehouse module over, followed by a module that emphasizes zone picking for small goods from broken cases. Thus, the modular approach is a hybrid design.
    - *Multi-level.* When the cost of land is very high, a storage facility may make use of additional stories. This is the least effective configuration, due to the costs and poor workflows associated with moving goods up and down through multiple levels.
    - *U-shape.* Materials enter at one corner of the warehouse, and then follow a clockwise or counterclockwise flow, passing through areas designated for storage, picking, sortation, and shipping. This is the most common configuration, for the receiving and shipping docks are adjacent to each other, making it easier to cross-dock goods and employ the same materials handling equipment in both areas.

3. *Assign general areas.* Within the designated flow pattern, pair each area of the warehouse with another area for which there should be a considerable amount of materials cross-over. The following are all reasonable pairings:

    - Pair receiving with a cross-docking area, since materials will logically flow from receiving into cross-docking.
    - Pair cross-docking with shipping, since materials will be aggregated in cross-docking just prior to shipment.
    - Pair case picking with broken-case picking, since pickers need access to both locations during their picking tours.
    - Pair receiving with reserve storage, since many received items are sent straight to long-term storage.

4. *Assign high or low storage.* If items will be stored for long periods, assign them to higher storage locations, while such labor-intensive activities as

picking and packing are assigned floor-level locations. This step can highlight the need for changes in the cubic volume of space needed, and may result in the use of additional mezzanine-level storage. Another likely result is bin shelving and storage drawers at floor height, with pallet rack space constructed above them.

Tip: If storage requirements are expected to peak sharply from the average storage level, then it makes economic sense to plan for a smaller warehouse to accommodate average storage levels, and plan to use off-site storage for peak periods. Otherwise, much of the warehouse space will be unused for protracted periods.

The end result of this examination should be a warehouse configuration that fits the *estimated* warehousing requirements of a business. These requirements can change suddenly, so it also helps to design a configuration that is not especially difficult to reconfigure.

Tip: If warehouse space is leased, consider negotiating for a shorter leasing period, coupled with the right to extend the lease. Doing so gives the company the flexibility to terminate its warehouse operations if the requirements of the business change drastically.

An additional consideration is that putaway and picking efficiencies will drop dramatically as the number of filled storage spaces approaches 100%. At this capacity level, putaways may be to locations that are inconvenient for picking purposes. Also, there is more reshuffling of inventory to forward picking locations, which increases the likelihood that inventory will be damaged in transit. Consequently, it can make sense to plan for a maximum usable warehouse capacity level of about 85%.

Yet another consideration is the size of the adjacent yard in which trailers are to be parked. If it is the intent of management to store goods in trailers during peak storage periods, then the number of trailers required for this function should be modeled, and the yard configured to be of sufficient size to contain the necessary number of trailers.

Tip: If storage trailers are to be used, consider the level of security required to ensure that goods stored in these trailers are not pilfered.

There are also a number of lesser considerations that must still be configured into the warehouse plan, and which can have a notable impact on the final warehouse layout. Consider the following issues:

- *Employee parking.* Keep the employee parking area well away from the loading bays, so that employees cannot fraudulently move items directly from trailers to their cars.
- *Exits.* There must be adequate access to emergency exits from the building.

214

- *Fire suppression.* If there is a fire suppression system in the building, the related cluster of overhead pipes will limit the height of storage racks.
- *Forklift height.* If the company already plans to use a certain type of forklift, the maximum reachable height of that forklift will establish the maximum height of storage racks.

The myriad of factors noted in this section will likely result in several possible warehouse configurations that yield approximately the same operating characteristics. If so, select the version that is most easily reconfigured. Doing so makes it easier to respond to future changes in the types of inventory to be stored, and to changes in any corporate policies relating to inventory.

Sizing the Receiving Area

The receiving area is one of the more difficult parts of a warehouse to size correctly, since it is subject to issues that are, to some extent, outside of the control of the warehouse. For example, the purchasing department may not specify the exact time slot during which a supplier is allowed to deliver goods. If so, there can be a pile-up of deliveries that are hastily unloaded and not put away or forwarded at once, resulting in large stacks of inventory remaining in the receiving area. Similarly, the production department might decide that it is more efficient to conduct product repackaging in the receiving area in a cross-docking arrangement where goods are sent from the receiving area straight to trailers designated for delivery to customers. If so, space must be found for the repackaging work. Consequently, proper sizing of the receiving area is highly dependent upon decisions made in other departments. This calls for joint planning to ensure that the correct activities are implemented as part of a warehouse design project.

> **Tip:** When new projects must be implemented to justify a reduction in the size of the receiving area, it is best to plan for excess receiving space. Then, if the supporting projects are not entirely successful, the receiving area will not be an excessive bottleneck on other warehouse activities.

Sizing the Inspection Area

The typical receiving area of a warehouse includes a section that is set aside for the storage of goods that have yet to undergo an inspection. The inspection can require a substantial amount of time, especially when some suppliers have a reputation for delivering goods of inferior quality. If there are many deliveries undergoing these detailed reviews, the inspection area can be quite large.

When planning warehouse space, there may be a temptation to simply carry forward the existing inspection area, with adjustments based on expected changes in receiving volume. However, this is one area of the warehouse that could undergo significant shrinkage, depending upon activities elsewhere in the company. For instance, if the purchasing department elects to concentrate its purchasing with a smaller number of suppliers, it will presumably eliminate many of the lower-quality suppliers whose goods were undergoing detailed inspections. Also, if the purchasing staff also elects to certify the quality of suppliers, then the deliveries of these suppliers will be routed around the inspection area, and may even be delivered straight to the production area, if needed for the manufacture of goods.

Given the possibility of these actions by other departments, the inspection area may be radically downsized in warehouse planning. However, it is unlikely that the area can be entirely eliminated, unless a comprehensive campaign is followed to certify the goods of 100% of all suppliers.

Sizing and Locating Dock Doors

The traditional dock door configuration is one with a width of nine feet (in the United States), which accommodates the standard tractor-trailer delivery with rear access. The preceding warehouse layout discussion was predicated on the use of this dock size, usually clustered together for the receiving area and the shipping area. However, what if the bulk of all deliveries are on a just-in-time basis? If so, deliveries may be made from a side-load trailer, or a rear access trailer that is narrower and lower than the standard trailer dimensions. Also, if deliveries are made straight to the production area, they may bypass the warehouse entirely.

In the just-in-time scenario just described, it is still useful to maintain dock doors of the normal configuration, since some suppliers will continue to use standard-size trailers, and the facility may eventually be sold to a company that does not use just-in-time deliveries. To accommodate smaller vehicles, consider including a moderate number of alternative loading docks into the facility, as well as ramps that can be used to access goods being delivered at a height lower than the standard dock door height.

In addition, it is wise to configure the warehouse to have somewhat more than the standard number of dock doors, in case just-in-time deliveries to the production area are abandoned, and deliveries are instead re-routed back through the warehouse.

Treatment of Aisles

A large part of the warehouse space is taken up by the aisles that traverse its storage areas. Aisles are typically laid out in the same width everywhere, on the false assumption that a standard width must be used to accommodate the turning radius of the largest materials handling vehicles employed within the warehouse. In reality, aisles can be configured in three widths. The scenarios under which each width can be used are as follows:

- *Pallet storage area.* When a storage area is configured for pallets, the aisles must be wide enough to accommodate the turning radius of the lift trucks used to store pallets. The aisles should have sufficient buffer width to minimize the risk of damage to equipment and pallets during putaway and picking operations.
- *Broken case area.* High-volume manual picking is most commonly employed in broken case storage areas, which means that heavy materials handling

equipment will never enter these aisles. Instead, configure aisles to accommodate manual pickers and their picking carts.

- *ASRS*. If there is an automated storage and retrieval (ASRS) system in place, set the aisle width to accommodate the ASRS system. This typically results in a much narrower aisle than is employed for a pallet storage area.

An aisle is essentially wasted space, since inventory cannot be stored in it. Consequently, the effectiveness of every aisle should be maximized by ensuring that it provides access to stored goods on *both* sides of the aisle. If there is no storage on one side, then an aisle is only half as effective as it should be. This situation arises when aisles are situated along the periphery of a warehouse, adjacent to the walls. To improve the utility of these aisles, always position storage racks along the walls, with aisle space inside of these racks. This issue must be addressed during the initial planning for warehouse layout, since it is much too difficult to reconfigure the layout at a later date to add storage along the walls.

> **Tip:** If there is only a single rack that is accessible from aisles on either side, see if cross-bracing can be safely eliminated from this rack. Doing so allows for access into the rack space from the aisles on both the front and back sides of the rack. This can yield more efficient picking, and allows for putaways from one aisle while picking is being conducted from the other aisle.

Treatment of Building Supports

The layout of storage systems within a warehouse should take into account the positioning of building columns. They should not intrude into the aisles, since this can make it extremely difficult to establish proper flow patterns for materials handling equipment. For example, a column in the middle of an aisle will force a forklift operator to circle around to the back end of the aisle via an adjacent aisle in order to access rack space on the far side of the aisle. Consequently, always configure the rack layout to incorporate all columns that will otherwise interfere with travel lanes.

Warehouse Security

Inventory is an asset, and so is subject to theft. In addition, a non-warehouse person walking through the warehouse might inadvertently move goods from one location to another, thereby reducing inventory record accuracy. To reduce the risks of theft and inventory inaccuracy, the warehouse should be cordoned off from casual access. In particular, if the warehouse is within the same building as other company operations, there is a good chance that non-warehouse personnel will have easy access to the inventory. If this is the case, consider constructing a fence that blocks access to the inventory, and route all traffic through a warehouse gate. The presence of a gate allows the warehouse manager to more easily control access to stored inventory. For example, if an unauthorized person needs access to the warehouse, they can be met at the warehouse gate and assigned one of the warehouse staff as a guide.

If the warehouse is not operating on a 24 × 7 basis, it may be necessary to extend the protective fence all the way to the ceiling, so that no one can climb over the fence while the warehouse is unoccupied. Depending on the history of unauthorized warehouse access and the value of the inventory, it may also be necessary to add other security measures, such as a security guard and video monitors.

Warehouse Sizing Considerations

Most of the discussion in this chapter has addressed the configuration of the warehouse. In addition, the overall size of the facility could be detrimental to its efficiency. A large warehouse can suffer from long travel times for the putaway and picking employees. In addition, it is more difficult to supervise across longer distances, or at least an additional layer of managers may be needed in order to do so. Further, it may be necessary to invest more heavily in automated storage and retrieval systems in a large facility in order to minimize labor costs.

To see if there is a problem, consider tracking the aggregate cost of employee travel and materials handling equipment depreciation for the facility, and benchmark it against the same costs incurred by smaller facilities that operate in roughly the same manner. If the size of the facility appears to be a liability, consider implementing the warehouse within a warehouse concept discussed in the Warehousing Efficiencies chapter; this concept involves the compartmentalization of the warehouse in order to improve operating efficiencies. A more elaborate alternative is to shut down a large warehouse and shift goods into smaller facilities that can each be operated more efficiently. However, the latter approach means that management staff will be duplicated across the smaller warehouses, which will increase costs.

Considerations for Acquiring Warehouse Space

Many of the preceding discussion items relate to a situation where a business plans for the ideal warehouse configuration, and then constructs a warehouse to match its requirements. But what if the company instead elects to buy or lease an existing warehouse? Such a facility is highly unlikely to possess the exact characteristics stated in the warehouse plan. If so, be sure to consider the following issues before obtaining the facility:

- *Dead space*. A warehouse may have been constructed to have a footprint that does not match the ideal storage configuration, resulting in space that is not usable.
- *Dock doors*. The facility may not have the number of receiving and shipping doors demanded by the warehouse plan, or they are located in areas of the facility that will require a reconfiguration of the ideal warehouse layout. For example, a U-shaped facility might be contemplated where the receiving and shipping doors are adjacent, while the facility being reviewed is designed for a flow-through configuration, with receiving doors on one side and shipping doors on the other.

- *Floor support weight*. A key consideration is the amount of weight that the floor can support. If the company wants to install a substantial multi-level racking system in which heavy loads will be stored, the floor must be thick enough to support the planned weight.
- *Height*. There should be sufficient cubic volume in the warehouse to support the planned height of the ideal warehouse configuration. If the unobstructed height is too low, more square feet of storage space must be obtained, which drives up the cost of the warehouse.
- *Support columns*. The columns used to support the roof should be laid out in such a manner that they do not impede the flow of travel through warehouse aisles.
- *Wire guided vehicles*. If the company plans to use wire guided vehicles in the facility, this may require that wires be embedded in the floor, which the facility landlord may not accept.

From a financial perspective, acquiring an existing warehouse might appear to be the ideal solution, especially if the real estate market is at a low point. However, finances should be a secondary consideration if there is simply no way to rejigger the company's ideal warehouse configuration into an existing space. If management were to insist on buying or leasing such a property, it would likely find that the reduced ownership or leasing costs are eventually offset by the increased cost of operating in a fundamentally inefficient facility.

Summary

One might construe from this chapter that a warehouse should be designed with great precision, to arrive at the perfect layout that will yield exceptional efficiencies. While that is certainly an excellent goal, the reality may not be quite so perfect. In many cases, a company must rent or purchase existing space that is already configured in a certain way, and which does not precisely meet its requirements. Also, the operations of a business may change radically within the planned usage interval of a warehouse, rendering an originally "perfect" configuration much less efficient. For these reasons, warehouse planning tends to be an ongoing process where configurations are modified with some regularity, with the intent of working within existing constraints to achieve better performance.

Chapter 18
Inventory Measurements

Introduction

The inventory asset can represent a company's largest investment. As such, management should be well aware of how this investment is being used through the examination of a variety of measurements. In this chapter, we address the general concepts of inventory turnover and obsolete inventory, along with several ancillary measurements that are designed to focus attention on whether the amount of inventory on hand is the correct amount, and what to do with any excess inventory.

Related Podcast Episode: Episode 27 of the Accounting Best Practices Podcast discusses inventory measurements. It is available at: **accountingtools.com/podcasts** or **iTunes**

Overview of Inventory Measurements

Inventory is technically considered an asset – at least, it is categorized as such on a company's balance sheet. However, it can be considered a liability, since inventory is not easily liquidated, can become obsolete in short order, and can physically clog a facility to such an extent that it interferes with operations. Because of the liability aspects of inventory, all of the measurements in this chapter are intended to spotlight when a business has too much inventory – not when it has too little.

The traditional measurement of inventory is turnover, which is a comparison of the amount of inventory to sales, to see if the proportion is reasonable. We also subdivide this measurement into turnover for raw materials, work-in-process, and finished goods – each of which can be applicable under certain circumstances. When using inventory turnover measurements, keep in mind that the results will be largely based on the manufacturing system in place, as well as purchasing practices. For example, a practice of buying in bulk and using a "push" production system will inevitably lead to lower inventory turnover, while just-in-time purchasing and a "pull" production system will be associated with much higher turnover results.

We also discuss inventory accuracy, which is an enormously important concept. Inventory records must be as close to 100% accurate as possible, or else there will be major issues with the ability to meet scheduled production targets and fulfill customer orders in a timely manner.

Our last remaining major area addresses the concept of excess inventory. There should be measurements for detecting any inventory that is either clearly obsolete or which has aged past a certain number of days. These items will likely require disposition at a reduced price, so we also address the amount of returnable inventory and the rate at which its value is likely to decline over time. These concepts should be built into an ongoing process of identifying and selling off inventory at a rapid clip, so that no excess funds are stored in inventory that is unlikely to provide an adequate return on investment.

Average Inventory Calculation

Average inventory is used to estimate the amount of inventory that a business typically has on hand over a longer time period than just the last month. Since the inventory balance is calculated as of the end of the last business day of a month, it may vary considerably from the average amount over a longer time period, depending upon whether there was a sudden draw-down of inventory or perhaps a large supplier delivery at the end of the month.

Average inventory is also useful for comparison to revenues. Since revenues are typically presented in the income statement not only for the most recent month, but also for the year-to-date, it is useful to calculate the average inventory for the year-to-date, and then match the average inventory balance to year-to-date revenues, to see how much inventory investment was needed to support a given level of sales.

In the first case, where you are simply trying to avoid using a sudden spike or drop in the month-end inventory number, the average inventory calculation is to add together the beginning and ending inventory balances for a single month, and divide by two. The formula is:

$$(\text{Beginning inventory} + \text{Ending inventory}) \div 2$$

In the second case, where you want to obtain an average inventory figure that is representative of the period covered by year-to-date sales, add together the ending inventory balances for all of the months included in the year-to-date, and divide by the number of months in the year-to-date. For example, if it is now March 31 and you want to determine the average inventory to match against sales for the January through March period, then the calculation would be as calculated in the following exhibit.

Average Inventory Calculation

January ending inventory	$185,000
February ending inventory	213,000
March ending inventory	142,000
Total	$540,000
Average inventory = Total ÷ 3	$180,000

A variation on the average inventory concept is to calculate the exact number of days of inventory on hand, based on the amount of time it has historically taken to sell the inventory. The calculation is:

$$365 \div (\text{Annualized cost of goods sold} \div \text{Inventory})$$

Thus, if a company has annualized cost of goods sold of $1,000,000 and an ending inventory balance of $200,000, its days of inventory on hand is calculated as:

$$365 \div (\$1,000,000 \div \$200,000) = 73 \text{ Days of inventory}$$

Though useful, the average inventory concept has some problems, which are as follows:

- *Month-end basis.* The calculation is based on the month-end inventory balance, which may not be representative of the average inventory balance on a daily basis. For example, a company may traditionally have a huge sales push at the end of each month in order to meet its sales forecasts, which may artificially drop month-end inventory levels to well below their usual daily amounts.
- *Seasonal sales.* Month-end results can be skewed if a company's sales are seasonal. This can cause abnormally low inventory balances at the end of the main selling season, as well as a major ramp-up in inventory balances just before the start of the main selling season.
- *Estimated balance.* Sometimes the month-end inventory balance is estimated, rather than being based on a physical inventory count. This means that a portion of the averaging calculation may itself be based on an estimate, which in turn makes the average inventory figure less valid.

Inventory Turnover Measurements

The turnover of inventory is the rate at which inventory is used over a measurement period. This is an important measurement, for many businesses are burdened by an excessively large investment in inventory, which can consume the bulk of available cash. When there is a low rate of inventory turnover, this implies that a business may have a flawed purchasing system that bought too many goods, or that stocks were increased in anticipation of sales that did not occur. In both cases, there is a high risk of inventory aging, in which case it becomes obsolete and has reduced resale value.

When there is a high rate of inventory turnover, this implies that the purchasing function is tightly managed. However, it may also mean that a business does not have the cash reserves to maintain normal inventory levels, and so is turning away prospective sales. The latter scenario is most likely when the amount of debt is high and there are minimal cash reserves.

In this section, we address the classic inventory measurement, which is inventory turnover, followed by the calculations for each component of inventory – raw materials, work-in-process, and finished goods.

Inventory Turnover Ratio

To calculate inventory turnover, divide the ending inventory figure into the annualized cost of sales. If the ending inventory figure is not a representative number, then use an average figure instead. The formula is:

$$\frac{\text{Annual cost of goods sold}}{\text{Inventory}}$$

You can also divide the result of this calculation into 365 days to arrive at days of inventory on hand. Thus, a turnover rate of 4.0 becomes 91 days of inventory.

EXAMPLE

An analyst is reviewing the inventory situation of the Hegemony Toy Company. The business incurred $8,150,000 of cost of goods sold in the past year, and has ending inventory of $1,630,000. Total inventory turnover is calculated as:

$$\frac{\$8,150,000 \text{ Cost of goods sold}}{\$1,630,000 \text{ Inventory}}$$

$$= 5 \text{ Turns per year}$$

The five turns figure is then divided into 365 days to arrive at 73 days of inventory on hand.

Raw Materials Turnover

If a large part of a company's total inventory investment is in raw materials, it may be useful to focus attention specifically on this area with the raw materials turnover measurement. This measurement is of interest to the purchasing manager, who is responsible for maintaining the flow of goods into the production area. This measurement can also be used by the engineering manager, who can focus on designing products that use common parts already found in stock. Raw material turnover is of particular interest in just-in-time environments where the intent is to drive the investment in raw materials down to a level very close to zero.

To calculate raw materials turnover, divide the dollar value of raw materials consumed in the period by the average amount of raw materials on hand through the period, and then annualize the result. For example, if the measurement is for a one-month period, multiply the result by 12. The calculation is:

$$\frac{\text{Dollar value of raw materials consumed in period}}{\text{Average dollar value of raw materials inventory}} \times 12 \quad = \text{Raw materials turnover}$$

223

There are a few situations in which raw materials turnover can be further refined. Consider the following possibilities:

- *Obsolete inventory.* A high proportion of obsolete raw materials may be keeping the turnover figure from being improved. If so, run a calculation of which items have not been used recently, and forward this list to the purchasing staff to see if the indicated items can be sold off. Then run the turnover measurement without the obsolete items.
- *Overnight delivery costs.* The turnover figure can be artificially reduced by paying extra to have raw materials delivered through an overnight delivery service. If this is happening, track the cost of incoming freight in conjunction with the raw materials turnover measurement.

EXAMPLE

Aberdeen Arquebus sells its old gun replicas in a highly seasonal business, where most purchases are made in the spring, in anticipation of the summer battle re-enactment season. Accordingly, the owner exerts pressure on the purchasing staff to minimize raw material levels, so that there are few raw materials left in stock after the selling season is complete. The following table shows the results of this effort by quarter, where production ramps up in the fourth and first quarters, followed by a rapid decline in the second quarter.

	Quarter 1	Quarter 2	Quarter 3	Quarter 4
Raw materials consumed	$380,000	$210,000	$85,000	$420,000
Raw materials inventory	$254,000	$93,000	$28,000	$335,000
Raw materials turnover	6x	9x	12x	5x

Note: The results of each calculation are multiplied by four to annualize results.

Work-in-Process Turnover

An excessive amount of work-in-process inventory is a strong indicator of an inefficient production process. When production is not well-organized, clumps of inventory will pile up throughout the production area. Conversely, a just-in-time system can operate with very small amounts of work-in-process inventory.

To measure work-in-process turnover, divide the annual cost of goods sold by the average cost of work-in-process inventory. The calculation is:

$$\frac{\text{Annualized cost of goods sold}}{\text{Average work-in-process inventory}}$$

This is the most difficult inventory turnover figure to compile, for there is usually no formal system for tracking specific units of inventory through the production process, as well as the state of completion of each unit. If so, compiling this measurement is nearly impossible. However, if there is a formal tracking system in place, then the average work-in-process figure may be available through a standard report.

Another issue with work-in-process inventory is its extreme variability. The amount in process may vary to a noticeable extent on a daily or even hourly basis, so the use of an average inventory level is advisable.

EXAMPLE

Creekside Industrial is in the throes of a manufacturing system changeover, from a manufacturing resources planning (MRP II) system to a just-in-time system. The production manager wants to be sure that the company is realizing the full benefits of the transition, and so authorizes the compilation of before-and-after work-in-process turnover measurements. The results are:

(results are annualized)	MRP II Turnover	Just-in-Time Turnover
Cost of goods sold	$16,500,000	$15,900,000
Average work-in-process inventory	$1,375,000	$795,000
	12x	20x

The measurement comparison reveals that Creekside has experienced a notable drop in its work-in-process investment as a result of the switch to a just-in-time system.

Finished Goods Turnover

There are situations where a company may have quite a large investment in finished goods inventory in comparison to its sales level. This situation most commonly arises for one of the following reasons:

- *Fulfillment policy.* Senior management wants to differentiate the company from its competitors by offering a fast fulfillment rate for all customer orders, which can only be achieved with a large amount of finished goods on hand.
- *Seasonality.* Sales are highly seasonal, so the seller increases its finished goods during the months prior to the selling season, in order to meet demand.
- *Obsolescence.* Some portion of the finished goods inventory is obsolete, and so is selling at a very low rate.

To calculate finished goods turnover, divide the dollar value of finished goods consumed in the period by the average amount of finished goods on hand through the period, and then annualize the result. For example, if the measurement is for a one-month period, multiply the result by 12. The calculation is:

$$\frac{\text{Dollar value of finished goods consumed in period}}{\text{Average dollar value of finished goods inventory}} \times 12 = \text{Finished goods turnover}$$

One issue with finished goods turnover is how costing information is compiled. The cost of finished goods is comprised of the costs of direct materials, direct labor, and

225

overhead. These amounts can vary if there are changes in the standard costing methodology that a company employs. Also, these costs can be fraudulently altered in order to increase the amount of ending inventory, thereby reducing the cost of goods sold and increasing profits. Thus, the costing methodology can have an impact on finished goods turnover.

EXAMPLE

The senior managers of Billabong Machining want to ensure the highest level of customer satisfaction by promising order fulfillment on 99% of all orders placed within one day of order receipt. Given the large array of widgets that Billabong offers for sale, this pledge requires the company to maintain an inordinately large investment in finished goods. The following table reveals the finished goods turnover rate before and after the fulfillment policy was begun.

(results are annualized)	Before Fulfillment Policy	After Fulfillment Policy
Finished goods consumed	$4,800,000	$5,100,000
Finished goods inventory	$400,000	$1,275,000
	12x	4x

Given the massive decline in turnover, the management team might want to rethink its decision to fulfill customer orders so quickly, especially since sales have not increased much as a result of the decision.

Inventory Accuracy Percentage

A business relies upon the accuracy of its inventory records to maintain its production and customer fulfillment systems. For these records to be truly accurate, they must contain accurate information in the following areas:

- Quantity on hand
- Location of inventory
- Unit of measure
- Part number

If any one of these items within an inventory record is wrong, then the entire set of information can be considered sufficiently incorrect to render the entire record useless. For example, the inventory quantity may be completely accurate, but if the location code is wrong, the materials handling staff cannot find the item. Or, if the part number is wrong, a component cannot be used. Consequently, the inventory accuracy formula encompasses all four elements.

To calculate inventory accuracy, divide the number of *completely* accurate inventory test items sampled by the total number of all inventory items sampled. An accurate inventory test item is considered to be one for which the actual quantity, location, unit of measure, and part number matches the information stated in the inventory record. If even one of these items is found to be incorrect, then the entire item tested should be flagged as incorrect. The formula for inventory accuracy is:

$$\frac{\text{Number of completely accurate inventory test items}}{\text{Total number of inventory items sampled}}$$

EXAMPLE

An internal auditor for Radiosonde Corporation conducts an inventory accuracy review in the company's storage area. He compiles the following incorrect information for a sample test of eight items:

	Audited Description	Audited Location	Audited Quantity	Audited Unit of Measure
Alpha unit	No	No		
Beta unit	No			
Charlie unit		No		
Delta unit	No	No		
Echo unit		No		
Foxtrot unit	No			No
Golf unit				No
Hotel unit				No

The result of the test is inventory accuracy of 0%. The test score astounds the inventory manager, who has been focusing solely on quantity accuracy. Even though the quantity counts did indeed prove to be accurate, the inventory records were well below expectations for the other data items.

Excess Inventory Measurements

If a company maintains any inventory at all, it is quite likely that some portion of this investment is obsolete. A business needs to have an ongoing inventory evaluation system that highlights obsolete items, as well as a well-defined system for disposing of these items as quickly as possible, and at the highest price. In this section, we address several variations on obsolete inventory measurement, as well as how to focus attention on the opportunity cost of not disposing of inventory in a timely manner.

Obsolete Inventory Percentage

When a company has a significant investment in inventory, one of the more essential accompanying metrics is the obsolete inventory percentage. This measurement is needed to derive that portion of the inventory that is no longer usable. The percentage should be tracked on a trend line and compared to the results of similar businesses, to see if a company is experiencing an unusually large proportion of inventory problems. Actions taken that relate to this percentage can include:

- Changes in the reserve for obsolete inventory, if the percentage is varying from the long-term trend.
- Changes in the amount of activity to disposition obsolete inventory in a manner as advantageous to the company as possible.
- Actions taken to reduce the underlying causes of obsolescence, such as buying in smaller quantities, switching to a production system that is based on customer orders, and better management of engineering change orders.

To derive the obsolete inventory percentage, summarize the book value of all inventory items which have been designated as not being needed, and divide it by the book value of the entire inventory. The formula is:

$$\frac{\text{Book value of inventory items with no recent usage}}{\text{Total inventory book value}}$$

The main problem with this percentage is figuring out which inventory to include in the numerator. Whatever method is chosen should be used in a consistent manner, so that trends in the percentage can be more reliably tracked over time.

EXAMPLE

The warehouse manager of Mole Industries wants to investigate the extent of obsolete inventory in his warehouse, so that he can remove items and consolidate the remaining inventory. He prints a parts usage report from the company's manufacturing resources planning system that only shows the cost of those items that are in stock and which have not been used for at least two years. The total cost listed on this report is $182,000, which is 19% of the total book value of the entire inventory. The warehouse manager brings this high percentage to the attention of the purchasing manager, who immediately contacts suppliers to see if they will take back the obsolete items in exchange for a restocking fee.

Percent of Inventory Greater than XX Days

A variation on the obsolete inventory percentage is to track the amount of any inventory that is older than a certain number of days. If an inventory item exceeds the threshold, it could be targeted for return to the supplier in exchange for a restocking fee. This approach is particularly useful when a company has instituted just-in-time deliveries, but still has excess inventory on hand from before implementation of the new system.

The precise number of days used for the threshold in this measurement can vary, based on several factors. Consider the following:

- *Warehouse-specific.* If tighter inventory controls are being implemented at just one location, set a minimal threshold for that facility, in order to target the largest possible amount of inventory for disposition.
- *SKU-specific.* If a particular stock-keeping unit (SKU) is being targeted for reduction, set a minimal threshold just for that item. This is particularly common for any SKUs for which a company has a large amount of funds tied up in inventory.
- *Class specific.* The measurement can be restricted to just raw materials, in order to focus on tighter purchasing practices. Alternatively, it can be restricted to just finished goods, in order to focus on production scheduling and sales forecasting issues.
- *Early warning.* Analysis of obsolete inventory may have shown that any inventory over a certain number of days old is more likely to eventually be designated as obsolete. Thus, the threshold can be set for a certain number of days prior to when inventory is usually declared obsolete, which gives the company early warning to draw down these stocks.

The steps required to calculate the percent of inventory over a certain number of days are:

1. Set the threshold number of days and the inventory type to be measured.
2. For the block of inventory to be measured, determine the dollar amount of all inventory items exceeding the threshold number of days.
3. Divide the aggregate total from the second step by the total dollar amount of inventory. Note that this should be the ending inventory balance (not an average balance), since the inventory figure derived in the second step is as of the ending inventory date.

The calculation of the percent of inventory greater than XX days is:

$$\frac{\text{Inventory dollars greater than XX days old}}{\text{Total inventory valuation}}$$

This measurement can be misleading in two situations, which are:

- *Seasonal production build.* A company may build inventory levels throughout the year, in anticipation of a short selling season. If so, the amount of all types of inventory may appear inordinately old with this measurement. In this situation, consider only using the measurement immediately after the selling season, to identify the extent to which inventory items did not sell.
- *Production schedule.* Certain raw materials may only be used in specific products, for which production runs are only scheduled at relatively long intervals. If the measurement is generated just prior to such a production run, it could

reveal what may appear to be an inordinate amount of raw materials on hand. This issue can be spotted by comparing the production schedule to any items appearing in an initial version of the measurement.

EXAMPLE

Rapunzel Hair Products sells a hair spray that has been proven to lose much of its hold characteristics after six months in storage; at that time, any remaining stocks cannot be sold, and so are thrown in the dumpster. Accordingly, Rapunzel's sales manager requests that an inventory report be generated that aggregates the percentage of this inventory that is more than 90 days old, so that coupons can be issued in a timely manner that will spur additional sales of the hair spray. For example, as of the end of the last month, the ten products that use the hair spray formulation, and which were more than 90 days old, had an aggregate book value of $80,000. Since the total hair spray inventory value was $1,000,000, the percent of inventory greater than 90 days old was 8%.

Returnable Inventory Valuation

Only a portion of all excess inventory can be returned to suppliers. Other items are too old or damaged to be returned, or suppliers refuse to take them back, even for a restocking fee. Management should be aware of the total dollar amount of returnable inventory, since the amount of cash that can be realized could be of considerable use to the company. This measurement usually takes the form of a report, which itemizes in declining dollar value the amount of inventory that can be returned, based on the expected disposal price, net of any restocking charges.

A key concern with the returnable inventory valuation is not to include in the report any items for which there is a reasonable short-term prospect of usage. Otherwise, the company will incur a restocking charge to return items to a supplier, followed shortly thereafter by the repurchase of the same items at their full retail price.

One concern is whether to include in the valuation report any items for which suppliers only offer a credit, rather than a cash repayment. If the company does not expect to make any further purchases from a supplier that only offers a credit, then the credit is essentially useless. In this case, it is better to exclude such items from the report.

Opportunity Cost of Excess Inventory

Most companies have pockets of excess inventory on hand. This inventory may be obsolete, or there may simply be more on hand than the company can reasonably expect to use or sell in the short term. In these situations, the purchasing department should be working on ways to disposition the goods in exchange for the largest possible amount of cash. The disposition value of inventory almost always declines over time, so there is an opportunity cost associated with not actively pursuing inventory dispositions. To measure the opportunity cost of excess inventory, follow these steps:

1. Compile the units of inventory that must be disposed of.

2. Estimate the disposal price that the company can obtain for these units if it were to do so today.
3. Estimate the rate at which the disposal price will drop on a monthly basis.
4. Estimate the direct cost of holding the inventory on a monthly basis.
5. Multiply the disposal units by their estimated disposal prices, and multiply the result by the monthly rate of price decline. Add the incremental cost of holding the inventory.

The calculation of the opportunity cost of excess inventory is:

$$((\text{Disposal units} \times \text{Disposal price}) \times \text{Price decline \%}) + \text{Inventory holding cost}$$
$$= \text{Opportunity cost}$$

When deriving this opportunity cost, be careful not to include fixed costs in the inventory holding cost, such as the cost of warehouse utilities. The only relevant inventory holding costs are those that will be eliminated if inventory is sold off – thus, only completely variable holding costs should be considered.

An issue that will likely arise when this measurement is presented to management is the amount of loss the company will record on its books as a result of an inventory disposition. The correct response is that the company should be recording an updated obsolete inventory reserve each month, irrespective of whether the inventory is disposed of. Thus, the only decision remaining for management is whether to hold onto old inventory or sell it now and convert it to cash at whatever prices the company can obtain.

While there are a number of estimates involved in this measurement, it is still one of the best ways to get the attention of management regarding the cost of holding onto inventory for longer than is necessary.

EXAMPLE

Green Lawn Care sells battery-powered lawn mowers, for which the selling season is quite short. In the current season, the sales department estimates that the company will have 5,000 excess lawn mowers. The company can expect to sell these units for $200 right now (August), and can expect this price to decline by 5% in each successive month. There is also a holding cost of $2 per unit, per month, since the company is renting storage space for the units from an independent warehouse. Based on this information, the opportunity cost of excess inventory is:

$$((5,000 \text{ Disposal units} \times \$200 \text{ Disposal price}) \times 5\% \text{ Price decline}) + \$10,000 \text{ Holding cost}$$

$$= \$60,000 \text{ Opportunity cost}$$

In short, the company stands to lose $60,000 for each month in which it does not dispose of the excess lawn mower inventory.

Honeycombing Percentage

Honeycombing is the amount of space in a warehouse that is not being properly utilized. It can be triggered by a variety of issues, including the following:

- Assigning a specific rack location to goods, but not having any goods to store in that location.
- Creating a long stacking lane but having insufficient pallets to fill the lane.
- Putting just one pallet in a double-deep storage rack.
- Incorrectly storing cases, so there is not sufficient room to store adjacent cases.

There are two ways to calculate the amount of honeycombing, either as a proportion of storage locations or as a percentage of cubic warehouse storage space. The calculation of the first method is as follows:

Empty storage locations ÷ Total storage locations = Honeycombing percentage

This calculation is imperfect, for it does not account for those storage locations that are partially filled, assumes a single stacking lane is one storage location (despite its considerable size), and also assumes that all storage locations have roughly the same footprint. Nonetheless, it is easily calculated from a warehouse report of storage bin locations, or simply by walking through the warehouse and counting empty storage locations.

The more accurate honeycombing measurement is to track the percentage of unused cubic warehouse storage space. This approach requires that you divide the warehouse into locations of varying sizes, and then estimate the cubic volume of each location size. The cubic volume of empty spaces can then be calculated and compared to the total volume of storage spaces. The calculation is:

Cubic volume of empty storage locations ÷ Cubic volume of total storage locations
= Honeycombing percentage

The second calculation is still not perfect, for it does not account for partially-filled storage locations. This issue can be corrected by conducting a manual walk-through of the warehouse and adjusting the calculation for these partially-filled locations, but doing so is quite labor intensive.

EXAMPLE

Entwhistle Electric operates a warehouse for its battery manufacturing facility, which houses raw materials for battery construction, as well as finished goods for a variety of cell phone battery products. It is becoming increasingly difficult to putaway goods in the warehouse, so the warehouse manager wants to determine the effects of honeycombing to see if additional storage space can be found. He accumulates the following information about the storage locations in the facility:

Location Type	Number of Locations	Cubic Feet per Location	Total Cubic Feet	Empty Locations	Empty Cubic Feet
Pallet storage	600	100	60,000	80	8,000
Case storage	350	50	17,500	50	2,500
Broken case storage	150	40	6,000	20	800
	1,000		83,500	150	11,300

The warehouse manager first calculates honeycombing based just on the number of empty locations, which yields the following result:

150 Empty locations ÷ 1,000 total locations = 15.0% Honeycombing

The warehouse manager then runs the calculation based on cubic feet of storage space, with the following result:

11,300 Empty cubic feet ÷ 83,500 Total cubic feet = 13.5% Honeycombing

Summary

It may appear that all inventory measurements are designed to draw attention to an excessive investment in inventory. This is largely true, but can also represent a problem, for *some* investment in inventory is usually needed. If inventory levels are drawn down to near zero, the logistics and production functions of a business must be precisely tuned to operate correctly at such a minimal level. If not, the business will likely experience continually-stalled processes that interfere with its ability to produce and sell goods to the satisfaction of its customers.

Glossary

A

Advance shipping notice. An electronic message sent from the seller to the buyer, stating which items have just been shipped to the buyer, along with additional information.

B

Backflushing. The concept of recording raw material withdrawals based on the number of units produced.

Batch sizing. A policy that states the standard number of units that will be produced as part of a production run.

Bill of materials. A list of the parts required to build a product.

Bullwhip effect. The enlarged impact of a customer order as the effects of the order move down through successive levels of a supply chain.

C

Consigned inventory. Inventory owned by a business, but stored at the location of a reseller.

Cross docking. Moving goods from the receiving area to the shipping area, with no storage in-between.

Cycle counting. The practice of continually reviewing inventory records for accuracy, and correcting any underlying problems found.

D

Deadheading. When no useful function is performed during one leg of a putaway or picking trip.

Dependent demand. Demand related to the demand for other items.

Distribution requirements planning. Software that tracks inventory in all warehouses, as well as inventory in transit, and which plans restocking transactions.

Drop shipping. When goods are shipped from a supplier to the ultimate customer, with no handling by an intermediary seller.

Dunnage. Materials packed around and between storage containers, to protect inventory from damage.

E

Economic order quantity. A formula used to derive that number of units of inventory to purchase that represents the lowest possible total cost to the buyer.

Engineering change order. A document specifying a change to the composition of an existing product.

Expediting. The practice of accelerating a customer order or production job through the production and shipping processes.

F

Forward picking. The aggregation of many small orders into a single picking document, to minimize picking time.

H

Honeycombing. Empty spaces in storage locations.

I

Independent demand. Demand for goods that comes from unrelated third parties.

Interleaving. The practice of assigning an additional task to a person engaged in a putaway or picking trip, to avoid deadheading.

Inventory. Tangible items held for routine sale, or which are being produced for sale, or which are consumed in the production of goods for sale.

Item master. A record that lists the name, description, unit of measure, weight, dimensions, ordering quantity, and other key information for a component part.

J

Just-in-time. A set of concepts that focus on minimizing waste within the production process by only manufacturing products as needed.

K

Kanban. A notification system for ordering more parts, which may take the form of a container, card, electronic message, or some similar method.

Kitting. The assemblage of parts for inclusion in a production job.

L

Lead time. The time required to complete a process.

M

Material requirements planning. A push-based planning system that orders parts and schedules production based on an estimate of customer demand for goods.

Monument. A machine that is too large and complex to be easily moved, and around which other production activities must be scheduled.

O

Order line system. A reordering method that calls for a replenishment order when the stock level in a bin falls below a marked line.

P

Periodic inventory system. The updating of inventory records only at set intervals, using a physical count.

Perpetual inventory system. The updating of inventory records on a continual basis, based on every inventory-related transaction.

Purchase order. A legal authorization for a supplier to ship goods or deliver services to a buyer, under the terms stated in the purchase order.

R

Reorder point. The inventory unit quantity on hand that triggers the purchase of a predetermined amount of replenishment inventory.

Replenishment. The refilling of warehouse bins from reserve stock locations.

Reslotting. The practice of shifting inventory within the warehouse to minimize replenishment and picking travel times.

Reverse logistics. The receipt of goods sent back by customers.

S

Safety stock. Extra inventory maintained to mitigate the risk of a stockout.

Spend management. The examination of spending patterns to consolidate purchases with a small number of suppliers, as well as the use of controls to ensure that purchases are only made with those suppliers.

Split delivery. A single purchase order under which a number of separate deliveries of goods are made.

Stock keeping unit. A unique product or component.

Supply chain. A network of companies that work together to produce and deliver goods or services.

T

Two bin system. A reordering method that calls for a replenishment order when the first of two storage bins for an item is emptied.

W

Warehouse management system. Software designed to control all warehouse operations and track inventory.

Wave picking. The timed release of orders into the warehouse, with the intent of deriving a consolidated cluster of picked customer orders.

Work-in-process. Unfinished inventory that is either currently in the production process or waiting in queue for additional finishing work to be performed.

Z

Zone picking. The assignment of a picker to a specific warehouse location, with responsibility to only pick goods within that location.

Index

240

Made in the USA
Monee, IL
11 May 2022

96263326R00142